Not Quite Famous

A Life in the Theatre

by **John Harrison**

[signature: John Harrison]

With a Foreword by
NICHOLAS HYTNER

THE
BIRMINGHAM
Stage
COMPANY
Publishing

*for my friends
at the Mamria*

© John Harrison 2004
Not Quite Famous
ISBN 0-9546903-0-3

Published by:
Birmingham Stage Company Publishing
Suite 228
162 Regent Street
London
W1B 5TG

A CIP catalogue record for this book is
available from the British Library.

Design and production co-ordinated by:
The Better Book Company Ltd
Havant
Hampshire
PO9 2XH

Printed in England

Grateful acknowledgements for the provision of illustrations
goes to Helen Hargest of The Shakespeare Birthplace Trust;
Mark Piper, director of the Theatre Royal, Windsor; and
Kathy Webster, archivist of the West Yorkshire Playhouse.
Permissions have been sought wherever possible.
All other illustrations are from
John Harrison's private collection.

CONTENTS

For Gus and Toby
Sarah and Max

FOREWORD

By NICHOLAS HYTNER

All theatre directors tend to think of themselves as pioneers, but almost invariably someone has been there before. John Harrison, however, was there when the job as we now know it was being invented. He was there, a young actor struggling to make his way amongst the dinosaurs of theatrical pre-history when a teenager called Peter Brook arrived, looking for allies. He found one in John, and another in John's best friend, who was doing rather better than John, and whose name was Paul Scofield.

John was part of one of the great theatrical sea-changes, (as well as the director, eventually, of Scofield's own sea-change in an unforgettable 'Tempest'). His story is also the story of the emergence of the modern theatre; and once he'd seen that through, he moved on to be there at another birth - that of television drama.

When I met John, he'd moved again, and was the director of the Leeds Playhouse (to become under his guidance the West Yorkshire Playhouse). There could not have been a better place for a young director to learn the craft. John had created what I still consider to be the most committed and astute audience in the country - and if you missed what the audience was trying to tell you about your work, there was always John. Like many of my colleagues, I had come to directing through a University English course, and I learned only gradually how to talk to actors. I was rehearsing one day a particularly knotty scene, and as my cast struggled through it, I pored over the text. John was standing secretly at the back of the theatre, and when the rehearsal was finished owned up to having been there. "You seemed to spend most of the rehearsal looking at the book," he said. "I don't know what you think you'll find there. Why don't you look at the actors?" A simple lesson, an obvious one, but I made some sort of leap, under John's guidance, from being a smart undergraduate with ideas about a text to being a real director.

John's book tells it how it is - he glosses over none of the disappointments, failures or betrayals; and he tells how hard it is to work in the theatre and to find domestic happiness at the same time. But John is one of the few who found it, and his account of his life with Linda Gardner is as full of joy as she herself was. Most theatrical autobiographies are pretty unbearable, and largely unbelievable. This one is for real.

'Yes, even to be a minor writer must be nice,
when all is said and done...'

CHEKHOV. 'THE SEAGULL' (Sorin)

PROLOGUE

White-maned and majestic in his anorak Paul Scofield strides the concrete deck. 'Full sail, and man the guns,' he roars. A bunch of actors on a disused jetty somewhere on the Sussex coast between Brighton and Seahaven are larking about as eighteenth century seamen before the dangling rod of a microphone. As the rain drizzles down I am sheltered with the production team in the van, listening on headphones and marvelling at their outsize gestures through the dripping glass. A BBC Radio 3 Sunday Night Theatre production of BILLY BUDD is being recorded. No longer do actors stand in a semi-circle round a studio mike trying desperately not to rustle their pages. Nowadays they are in full cry as if making a movie and the seagulls from no desert island disc but calling and dropping for real. And I am here because I have dramatised the Melville story for my old chum. For over five decades now, on and off, sporadically we have worked together, since as young men in the aftermath of war we acted under the even younger Peter Brook in Sir Barry Jackson's Birmingham Repertory Theatre and shared digs in Birmingham's Hagley road where breakfast was often a forlorn and solitary pilchard...

The distinguished director, first maverick then guru of World Theatre in the second half of the twentieth century, has come to the West Yorkshire Playhouse to talk and promote his new book. Peter Brook and I meet with open arms for the first time in many years, quoting at each other from ROMEO AND JULIET as we do so, 'Two households, both alike in dignity...' and the years drop away and I see and hear us energetically putting the theatre to rights in a cheap and greasy restaurant. 'Of course,' he is saying in all earnestness, 'if I were an actor the only part I'd be right for is Hamlet....'

The finally knighted actor, long time farceur of the rich and bulbous tones, Sir Donald Sinden, takes his bow in a West End theatre and I wander uninvited but always welcomed into his dressing room where he is being dressed by his grandson... Can we really have shared a flat in an Elizabethan house in Stratford-on-Avon in 1947 where I cooked and he cleaned and we met our first serious loves...? Did we really win a boat race on the Avon...?

And where (and even who) am I in all this?

Time, high time, to get something down on paper.

CHAPTER ONE

Beginnings and a Twelfth Night

'The Stratford Shakespeare season opened last night with Mr. John Harrison's tranquil and musical speaking of the prologue to "Romeo and Juliet". Moving across a stage darkened in swirling northern mists... Mr. Harrison hung upon the air sweet sorrow's jewelled sounds. It was an auspicious beginning to a production, directed by Mr. Peter Brook, which never lost sight of the fact that fine verse should be finely spoken.'

HAROLD HOBSON. Sunday Times. April 1947.

I grew up in London with a South London accent. If I had kept it there would have been less confusion about my origins which are usually assumed to be middle class and posh. But when I was about ten or eleven I went into a booth rather like a telephone kiosk on a main line railway station and made a voice recording for sixpence. You put your sixpence in the slot, spoke into a built-in microphone, and came away with a shiny metal disc to be played at 78 revolutions per minute with a special fibre needle in your gramophone pick-up.

Apart from being amazed at the sound of my own voice, which in the 1930s was not the common experience it is now, I simply didn't like the sounds which came out. So, using, I suppose, BBC English as a standard, I changed them. This had nothing to do with upward mobility. It was my ear that had been offended. I loved the sound of words. If what I'd heard had been the pure-bred Devonian or Scottish of my not-so-remote ancestry I might have felt no need to change. But the miserable South London sound (now kindly dubbed Estuary English) was never a thing of beauty.

My dad was a baker and for most of the time when I remember him had his own shop. Shops. Finally three. And ultimately none. But I was evacuated to South Devon by then so didn't feel the blast.

My mother had been a milliner when she met him, in a big old

Edwardian draper's shop in Falcon Road Battersea called David Thomas's, where my dad, not yet a baker, was dressing the windows. And I imagine they fell in love and it was all rather early H.G. Wells: KIPPS, MR. POLLY, that sort of thing.

But we were not entirely Londoners. My mum's mum, my maternal grandmother, had left the then mainly fishing village of Sidmouth in Devon as a young girl to seek her living in the Smoke. Leaving behind a family of fishermen and landscape gardeners she went into service with smart folk in Kensington. How she met Mr. Cockram I've no idea, but he was from Bow in North Devon so I imagine being Devonians abroad must have drawn them together. Anyway, she left service - where she had been a lady's maid, none of your scullery girl - and they married and came to live over the bridge in Battersea.

Mr. Cockram was a builder, and they had two children, Harold (known as Fred, and therefore later my Uncle Fred) and Florence Emily. My Mum. Sadly Mr. Cockram died of asthma when Florence Emily was thirteen. Mrs. Cockram was a plucky widow (and by the time I knew her a real old termagant of a Grandma) and set herself up in a little general shop where she worked long hours and kept her children respectable. Not always easy in old Battersea where the local nippers would sneak in and let off stink-bombs in the shop when her back was turned. Fred went to the Battersea Poly where he did well and later qualified as a quantity surveyor and when I knew him was General Manager of Welwyn Builders before drink got the better of him. Florrie left school at fourteen and went into the millinery at David Thomas's. Where she met George Harrison. With the aforementioned consequences.

When I wrote for the TV series "Upstairs, Downstairs" about life in an Edwardian household I drew heavily on Mum's reminiscences of Grandma's girlhood at the big house in Kensington. It left her finicky for life about not mussing up the drawing room on weekdays. She lived with us, you see, which was death to my mother and father's marriage. But more of that anon.

Grandma, when I knew her, was poker-backed, rarely smiling, hair in a bun and with always a band of black velvet at her throat. Never without the band of black velvet. Even, I believe, in bed. I think she had probably been a jolly enough youngster and a happy young wife and mum. She had a Rabelaisian friend from those days who used to visit us called (by me) Grandma Jennings who could never have teamed up with the sobersides that Grandma had become. But widowhood and the enormous premium exacted by respectability in the Battersea of those days, the need to pinch and scrape and be the boss of a family, had hardened her into a pretty formidable figure.

And George Harrison. George Henry John Harrison... Well... I don't know much about what made him tick, because he died when I was twenty-one, except what I can feel from the inside, and from patching together bits of memories. It can never have been the easiest of marriages with his mother-in-law in permanent residence but I imagine, I have to say it, he needed her money. A life-time saver who would never spend two pence if one would do, Grandma had amassed enough to set George up in business. There had probably been a life insurance on careful Mr. Cockram the builder.

I don't want to make George out to be a heartless adventurer. That would be far from true. I'm sure he loved Florrie. Or thought he did. She was a wild enough, shy gypsy-looking girl, with wonderfully lambent eyes. In yellowing photographs taken with her class-mates she is quite clearly 'the pretty one'. I'm sure it was a love match. But I'm sure the fact that Florrie's mum had a bit tucked away crowned his happiness.

George's mum certainly didn't have anything tucked away. They were a vast London family (somewhere around a dozen brothers and sisters) and old Harrison gambled everything away on the dogs. I believe he was, when working, a greengrocer. Anyway, to me he was amiable and whiskery. She, on the other hand, was Scottish and a cut above. Née Henrietta Stevens her father had been a monumental mason and she was herself an amateur sculptress and poet, writing lengthy, rhyming Lives of Joseph and other religious figures. I should have liked to have known more of her but we never saw much of the Harrisons as Grandma didn't approve. Family jealousies were strictly observed in our circles. Grandma Harrison would write me a letter on my birthday every year in a finely flowing and eccentrically curling ornamental hand. 'You take after me for poetry,' she would say. But our relationship was given no room to flower. I don't even remember her death. I'm sure I didn't go to the funeral.

So Florrie and George were married and set up in a little millinery called 'Florence'. In the wedding photographs they look an attractive couple. But not long after his marriage George had what would now be described as a nervous breakdown. I shouldn't be surprised if the reasons were sexual but I should be very surprised if anybody knew that at the time. My mother was very sheltered about such things and once said, feelingly, to my sister's husband apropos a woman's sufferings in labour, 'and all for the sake of your silly five minutes'.

When George had recovered Grandma bought him a bakery. We were living at this time at Wembley, in a house that still exists. In our day it backed on to a field, but now on to other houses. I made a pilgrimage round there when producing a Television series at Wembley studios. I had my nostalgic antennae fully extended but nothing showed up on the screen.

I don't know why Dad decided to be a baker. I do know that we shortly moved to 175 Northcote road Battersea where there was a shop as well as a bakehouse and we lived over the shop. This is where my childhood memories really begin. Battersea in the thirties. And I remember I was shy.

I used to play with Joan Murless whose people lived above an off-licence across the road. I wasn't shy with Joan. She had a rocking horse. And a doll called Fat Annie. And records of Layton and Johnston ('coloured duettists') - although I suppose these were, strictly speaking, her parents'. The Murlesses were thought to be a bit 'posh'. A bit stuck up. Particularly him. Mrs. Murless was quite a cheery soul, but Murless was a bit of a stewed prune. It was a matter for great delight in our family when one day, being shown round our house, he accidentally kicked the po under the bed. Murless pretended not to notice. Our family recounted the incident with delight for years. I liked Joan. I think. And riding the rocking horse and mucking about with Fat Annie. This was pre-school.

My other earliest memory of little girls is being stuck on one in a shiny peachy dress at a party. Mum and Grandma loved giving big children's parties with lots of jellies in cardboard cups and organised games like Postman's Knock. I don't remember her name. I don't remember whether the postman brought us together outside the door. I only remember being gone on her in a way that was quite different from my cheerful relations with Joan. I can remember her blonde aura, her shiny dress, and being speechless in her presence. It was my first, and perhaps only, experience of love at first sight.

I could never understand why the Murlesses were not to be found in the off-licence shop. In those days I believed that if you lived over a shop the shop was yours. I still think so in my heart of hearts. There was the cosy world of the shop-parlour which opened up at the back of the counter. This was where we really had our being. This was the nest. Unless Dad was being very fussy about it we came and went through the shop. On best behaviour however and after shop-closing hours we used the heavy street door beside the shop front. These were rather like the stage-doors of shops. It opened into a hallway complete with monster dark oak hall-stand and a flight of stairs to the upper floors.

Continuing down the hallway you passed the cellar door and thence to the bakehouse at the back. Or if you turned left at the foot of the stairs that was your alternative way into the shop-parlour. At first Mum and Grandma took it in turns to serve in the shop, summoned by the tinkling bell. So we always had lunch, called dinner, in the shop-parlour listening to Christopher Stone's record programme on the wireless. Grandma liked Christopher Stone, cosily avuncular, a sort of precursor of Richard Baker. She dearly loved a ballad and much enjoyed a singer called Tom Burke. She couldn't stand anyone who sang in a foreign language or anything she might term 'dry old muck'.

The bakehouse represented industry in my juvenile life-picture. I don't know what other people's dads did. To me the bakehouse stood for work. The world of men. There was Jack, who was very cheerful and worked days making cakes. And there were more surly men who came on at night and mysteriously worked away beneath me all night, while I slept, making bread. And in the morning there it all was in trays, smelling of new life. And not just rows and rows of standardised tins but the fairy-tale cottage loaf, the coburg, the batch, the flowery bap, the twist, the Danish, the milk loaf and, speciality of the house, Harrison's Golden Crust. Collect six wrappers and you earned a free loaf.

In the bakehouse stood machines - big floor-standing dough mixers - that had for me the charm of guided missiles, or Terminator, or CPO2. There they stood, like robots indeed, with great fat mixing bowl bellies. The smaller cake mixer had a friendlier, more approachable personality. The giant bread mixers were dour like the men who worked them and, unlike Jack, had no time for little boys. I was sufficiently a son of the bakehouse to cut out photographs of these mixers from my father's trade magazines and stick them on to cardboard. I had a boxful, a regular robot army. At the far end of the bakehouse loomed the oven doors. A row of black portals on Hades. Into these went the long flat wooden spades to fish out the sacrifices that had gone in all pallid and pasty and bring them back fire-tanned and edible.

175 Northcote Road, the last time I went down there, is now an Italian restaurant. On a safari down memory lane I ate there with actress Jennifer Hilary. From outside nothing had changed. But once we sat down where the shop had been and were being waited on memory blacked out.

Just now I mentioned the cellar door. This was a terrifying place, requiring every bit of courage if you were perhaps sent down to get a bucket of coal. I can smell it now. Dust, flour, coal and damp. It wasn't too bad if you left the door at the top open and could hear people moving about and talking. But sometimes they shut it in a fit of tidiness, not knowing you were down there, or thinking it mattered anyway. Then you had to shovel breathlessly and get back up those stairs before you went out of your mind. It was a big walk-about cellar. There were rats and mice no doubt, but these were nothing to the nameless horrors of the underground.

As a child I often had the horrors. I must have been very timid. A pain in the neck to my father who was - or seemed to me to be - a very manly man. There was the night when there were unfriendly Red Indians (as small boys then called native Americans) all over my bedroom wall. If only he'd had the wit to say he could see them too and then we might have discussed the phenomenon.

I mustn't sound critical of my father. I admired him tremendously, as all good little boys should. I liked nothing better than to ride round with him in the van with G. HARRISON on the outside. I don't suppose princes get any more of a kick in a coronation coach.

I went to a fee-paying boys preparatory school on the far side of Wandsworth common. It was called, somewhat grandiosely, King's College. The head was the very model of an elderly walrus called Mr.

Tatham. Every day I used to walk to and from school across the common with my friend Colin Wheeler. No one then imagined rape and slaughter to be lurking in the bushes. Colin was, I suppose, a friend from convenience rather than from choice, but like many marriages of convenience our relationship weathered surprisingly well. Certainly until we were into our teens. The thing was we started school the same day and as he lived round the corner in Broomwood Road our mothers took it in turns to take us, finally leaving us to cope together on our own. He was a fat boy and I was a thin one so we must have been rather like a juvenile Laurel and Hardy.

I went to a fee-paying school because, you see, we were Trade and not Workers. Both my parents had themselves left school at fourteen and such education as they had, basically the three Rs (Reading, Riting, and Rithmetic), had been provided by the state. But we had great notions of respectability, if not of advancement, and - like so many English Castes - voted Conservative and described ourselves as middle class. My father's greatest ambition for me was the security that he had been denied: a job in a bank and a pension.

Colin's father was a skin merchant. I don't mean he was in strip-tease. From trundling a barrow with Colin's grandfather collecting rags and bones he had worked up a very profitable business in skins and furs whose proceeds were the envy, I might add the spiteful envy, of our family. Grandma would never let pass an opportunity for reminding us that she remembered them barefoot and shouting 'Rag and bo-o-one.' It was really rather insufferable that they should have done so well. Particularly as George Harrison's business obstinately failed to prosper. Another sore point was that Mrs. Wheeler didn't buy her bread from us but from the big A.B. Hemmings combine on the corner.

I can't remember much about the early days of school. I don't think work made any strong appeal. Mostly I remember walking backwards and forwards across the common spinning yarns to Colin. I seemed able to make him believe the most incredible nonsense. For instance, I convinced him that a character from the penny comic we favoured, a cheerfully grinning black boy named Smiley, came to tea with me regularly. When he in turn told this to his mother she of course scoffed at the story. Which made me dislike Mrs. Wheeler rather. Stuffy old trout. I hated being punctured in this kind of thing - a trait I noticed and re-appraised in my second son when he was about the same age. It created a sort of lurking fear of being 'found out' which persisted for years, and applied much more to being found out in yarn-spinning than in masturbating or smoking in the bushes. (Not that these were preparatory school diversions.)

The biggest adventure of our prep school career was the day Colin and I decided to take the afternoon off. We told Mr. Tatham that my mother was taking us to the pictures. (You will get some idea of the sort of school it was from the ease with which this procured us an early pass.) Off we went, and could think of nothing better or more sensible to do with our free time than swing and play on the railings outside the Hope Tavern at the end of the road about five hundred yards from the school waiting for my mother to come and meet us. Here it was that Mrs. Tatham found us. Then my mother found the three of us, and the story was exploded. (Rather ironically she *did* take us to the pictures and I remember it was the Marx Brothers.) The next day we were caned, on the hand, before the whole school for this offence. Colin said, very loud and clear after the first stroke, 'Didn't hurt.' But I'm sure it did.

Memory has taken very few prints of this period. I was uncomplicatedly living in the moment. I remember the agony of copper-plate handwriting books - mine were always *so* smudgy. And the first poem to impinge - Macaulay's 'Horatius'. Stirring, rhythmic - always give them a strong tune to begin with. There was the very real fascination of French and Latin. And the growing lunacy of Sums. These had started out in a perfectly ordinary way like everything else - I can still add quicker than most people without benefit of calculator - but then became deformed into nightmares like long division of pounds shillings and pence. My sympathies here remain entirely with the White Queen. 'I can do addition' she said 'if you give me time - but I can't do subtraction under *any* circumstances.' One of the reasons for my speedy addition is that I used to play cribbage with my father so, to this day, I add in combinations of single digits that make fifteen. It's a marvellous way of getting rid of awkward looking pairs like 8 and 7 or 9 and 6.

At the age of ten or eleven I moved on, still as one of now a tiny minority of fee-payers, to Sir Walter St. John's School, High Street,

Battersea. 'Sinjuns' was a big boys' grammar with almost five hundred pupils founded, as was proudly proclaimed over the entrance portals, A.D.1700. Motto, 'Rather Deathe Than False Of Faythe.' I went into 'prep' under Dr. Billinghurst who I thought looked like the crooner Dick Powell. Our classroom was a 'cowshed'. The playground was big and hard. But there was the Priory Garden that you could walk round at break. And I did. For years. Round and round. Not for me the rough and tumble of the asphalt, the ball-kicking - and balls kicking - the punch-ups against the walls. Round and round the Priory Garden I went, with my friend of the moment, sedately talking and spinning the later - and more sophisticated 'Smileys'. Actually I don't suppose I had to fabricate much by this time because I was already a fairly sophisticated figure to the Battersea boys, because I now lived on the far side of Wandsworth common and I went to the theatre. This was a pretty unheard of thing in their lifestyle. The pictures on Saturday afternoon, yes. But the theatre was something almost Babylonian.

The reason for my weekly debauch was that my father exhibited posters in his shops for the Streatham Hill Theatre, then a regular post, or prior to, West End touring date. And with each poster (there were two) went two free passes. Two seats for Monday night and two seats for Tuesday night. So if Mum and Dad went Monday I went with a chum on Tuesday, and vice versa. Or sometimes I went with one of them, or even on rare occasions with Grandma. But mostly Grandma begrudged the idea of enjoying herself. On the nights when Mum and. Dad went out - which was never more than this once a week - I have an early memory of her sitting me on the kitchen table roughly washing my knees (baths were for Saturday) and grumbling grim-faced, 'Don't know why they always want to be off, gadding about.' (The knees were washed because of course they *showed*.)

I don't know what the first play I saw was. I can remember crying and having to be taken out of a pantomime at the Lyceum. (Somebody had been put through a mangle and come out pressed flat the other end.) But I can remember enjoying a later one in which hoarse-voiced George Jackley sang 'We all go up, up, up, up, up, up, up the mountain, and we all come down, down, down, down, down, down again', with audience participation and the big thermometer to register the relative vocal strengths of stalls against circle, upper circle against Gods. 'You up there on the shelf!' We up there on the shelf always laughed at this. And always won.

I liked a laugh in the theatre. Or (long after the mangle episode) I liked a fright. I didn't much care for the no-man's-land between. At Bobby Howes and Cicely Courtneidge in HIDE AND SEEK I laughed till I cried, like all the most quotable critics, and really, literally, did roll in the aisle (having to be helped to my feet by my mother) when Bobby Howes, with a pretended hare-lip, had to keep repeating the name Cynthia. We took our humour raw then, with no notion of political correctness. It helps me to understand the casual Elizabethan acceptance of things like bear-baiting.

And I gloried (Jacobean now) in the horrors of Emlyn Williams in NIGHT MUST FALL with all those heads in hat-boxes. I liked horror films too, but it was always far more frightening on the stage. The people were real. It happened before your very eyes. And most of all I liked it when they mixed the two, comedy and thrills - the likeable idiot in the supposedly haunted house. What a marvellously cathartic presence that was! Sometimes I ventured Up West by underground on a Saturday for a matinee of Gordon Harker in Edgar Wallace's THE FROG at the Prince's. Or Leslie Henson, Fred Emney and Richard Hearne, unbeatable comic trio, in a show at the Gaiety - GOING GREEK, RUNNING WILD...

This was a question of going up early on Saturday morning and buying a sixpenny stool for the gallery queue. The little crocodile of stools would grow throughout the morning while you were then free to wander. You came back half an hour before the doors opened and sat on your numbered stool. Bliss.

But nine tenths of my theatre-going was done on the free passes at Streatham Hill. There I would sit in that half-empty great barn at the beginning of the week, totally enraptured at the rise of the curtain. And the next day would recount the more hair-raising details, or the best jokes, as we plodded round the Priory Garden. And so way out did the idea of theatre-going seem to the other lads that this gave me the sort of cachet that I suppose nowadays must cling to the habitual pot-smoker or free-range fornicator.

I mentioned that we now lived on the far side of Wandsworth common. This was a folie de grandeur (or possibly de Grandma). She and Mum aspired to gentility and to leave behind the cosy world of shop-parlour and bakehouse.

However it wasn't long before we were taking in lodgers. Mr. Robilliard and his son Stanley. Mr. Robilliard was a teacher, a dour widower with possibly a heart of gold. Stanley was a couple of years older than me and, once I had got over the shock to my pride of having to share my home at all, a useful opponent at billiards and table tennis of which we played a great deal in the evenings when I should have been doing my homework. Dad had bought a second-hand quarter-size billiard table upon which I became so proficient that I have never been able to transfer my skill to a full-sized table. Nobody played snooker then, with all that endlessly monotonous potting. We enjoyed the variety and sophistication of cannons and in-offs like Gayev in THE CHERRY ORCHARD.

Did I mention homework? What a pain that was! How one longed to leave school behind at the school gates. I didn't mind English. I'd write and over-write for hours on an Essay subject. Essay! The very word has gone to be replaced by the clinical 'assignment'. With Maths though... well, one was just driven to cheat. There was only one Maths master at Sinjuns who managed to teach me anything at all and I think that was because he was still teaching himself. He'd get stuck in the middle of working out a problem on the blackboard and have to get one of his colleagues to help him. At this speed I could still take things in and in my year with him I became quite adept at solving quadratic equations. But the rest were impatient, hard-faced men with apt names like Mr. Stripp who would emphasize your inadequacies with sharp tongue and brutal ruler. Schoolmasters still had absolute rule: there were no liberal-minded parents with banners at the school gates. So I'm afraid my mind shut down and refused to open again on this particular subject. Which means that with Maths Prep I needed a little help, for which again Stanley Robilliard was useful.

In a class of thirty the master didn't really have time to check whether it really was all your own work - until the dread denouement of exams.

Another helper was McNamara. Douglas McNamara. And this brings me at a bound to first love.

'Mac' was a small, sandy-haired, quiet, round-faced, not un-pretty boy with a slight stammer. He sat in front of me in class and I loved him. He was good at the things I was bad at, like Maths, backward at the things I was good at, like English, and boxed in the gym in the evenings. He must have been gnat-weight rather than fly-weight, but he looked pale and vulnerable in his shorts and his singlet and was thought to box rather well. We would walk part of the way home together, up Falcon Road to save a penny on the bus fare, to the parting of our ways at Clapham Junction, where he turned left for a tram up Lavender Hill and I caught a 19 bus for Upper Tooting. On the way we would call in at Dad's Falcon Road branch for a free cake. I've no idea what he thought of me or whether he reciprocated my feelings in any way. Our love, if it was ever mutual, was quite unspoken. I just wanted to be with him. To sit behind or next to him in class, to trudge up Falcon Road while he did my Maths Prep, to inveigle him into joining me on the far side of Wandsworth Common for a rare Saturday afternoon's cinema - an illicit treat, quite outside the still regular outings with Colin (who had gone on to a different secondary school). 'Mac' was not really a cinemagoer. He had to be wooed. And it was with a bounding heart that I climbed out of Clapham South underground to find him waiting outside the Odeon. I told no one about 'Mac'. Looking back I'm pretty sure he felt nothing special for me other than companionship, but he was jolly nice about it. There were others he could have been with when he was with me. For the first time I had recourse to Dear Diary, entering up all those blessed moments together. 'Walked to Junction with Mac' was sufficient entry for an entire day. I don't suppose we ever touched, physically, except by accident. Oh, the innocent agonising ardour of it all!

The thing which brought me finally half out of my shell was the School Play. Sinjuns had a tradition of Gilbert and Sullivan operetta for its annual event which was no outlet for me because I couldn't sing - or more accurately couldn't sing in one key for very long. We'll come to me and music later. But class reading of 'The Merchant of Venice' had been a revelation - to me of Shakespeare and to 'Ernie' Cozens of the way I could read it. So when in 1939 the school retreated from Operetta for once I found myself, at the age of fourteen, cast as Olivia in 'Twelfth Night'. I still, to the frustration of actresses I have directed in the role, know it by heart. I now realise I learned quite a few wrong inflections through ignorance which nobody corrected, no doubt due to the astounding conviction of my utterance. Clearly the dog had seen the rabbit. I just loved saying the words. That to me was the whole of acting and Shakespeare was the whole of drama. I didn't want to say anybody else's words. Just his. I learned whole unrequired chunks of whatever class play we were reading and disgorged them at random for my own pleasure and satisfaction as somebody else might have sat down and played the piano.

Tidman was the star turn as Malvolio. One of nature's fortunates he could sing as well and I'd seen him stunning them in the aisles for several years previously in the G and S. He was a senior boy while I was middle school and to be translated into his company in the freedom of rehearsals was like suddenly being in the company of the late Lord Olivier. I had my first taste of theatrical camaraderie, the breaking down of barriers and pretensions as you all engage in the one big pretence. It was my passport to acceptance. Begone dull shydom, the boy could do something. Something that other people sat and watched and listened to. And even applauded. No more nose-picking on the outfield and bowled middle stump in the first over. No longer silent in the back row of the class. 'Well done, Harrison!' was the amazed comment. The school magazine in which I had figured neither as scholar nor as sporting worthy suddenly proclaimed, in the words of the invited critic Mr. Victor Barnett from the Central School of Speech Training and Drama, 'Perhaps in Shakespeare's own company of actors were such diverse youths as Harvey, Snell and Harrison, around whom the dramatist created his Viola and Olivia, Portia and Nerissa, Rosalind and Celia.' And wrote of my 'dignified and restrained interpretation.' Dignity and restraint were not perhaps the qualities my father would have chosen for his fourteen year old son but they went down big with my female relatives who made much remark about my swan-like neck and my resemblance to my mother when young.

Yes, as the summer term of 1939 drew to its close I really felt I had come of age in the school. I had started learning German this year and it was going in well. Languages now saw me among the first four in the form. And the fact that I was still 31st in Arithmetic was somehow easier to bear. I looked forward to moving into the fifth form, the School Certificate examination year, in the autumn with equanimity.

I don't remember how aware I was of 'the gathering storm' as we set off for our annual summer holiday in Sidmouth in Devon. I do remember happily singing 'South of the Border', no doubt with a Schonbergian indifference to key, in the car on the way down.

CHAPTER TWO

Devon and a Change of Direction

'J. Harrison. A small remembrance and appreciation of his services as lector at Combe Raleigh Church, with every good wish for his future happiness.

G.L. EDWARDS, Rector. Christmas 1943. Inscription in Bible.

So here I am in deepest Devon, with a world war in the offing, and no notion whatsoever that another five years will see me in the theatrical profession. Nothing could have been further from my imagination.

Sidmouth, before my latter day adoption of Yorkshire, was my spiritual home, the one place that always brought a lump to my throat to re-visit. However much, in certain moods, one longed for a little place in the south of France, it was Sidmouth that had 'Welcome' on the mat.

Mostly throughout the thirties it was the long school summer holiday that we spent there, staying cheaply with cousins for the best part of two months. But the long hot glorious summer of 1939 turned out to be the beginning of, for me, a five year residence in south-east Devon, the land of my fathers. Or certainly of my grandmother. Just long enough, at the most impressionable time in my life, for Tam Pearce's old mare, chudleighs and cream, deep-folded hills, proud finicky people, red cliffs, rock pools pebbles and sand to dig deep into the soul.

We stayed with my cousins, the Locks, in a council estate at the top of the town called Arcot park. Auntie Nina Lock, who was blind, was a daughter of Grandma's elder brother (and therefore not my Auntie at all but my first cousin once removed). She was thought to have married beneath her, because the diminutive Harry Lock, who was stone deaf, was only an under gardener at a big house, and was treated as less than the dust by all and sundry, including his own children, my two cousins Frank and Kathleen.

My main anchor in the Lock household was cousin Frank, a couple of years older than me and already out to work as a clerk in the local brewery. Together we bicycled, swam, and walked the sea front at night eating fish and chips. There used to be an evening ritual, rather like the Mediterranean *passeggiata*, when the inmates of the smart hotels strolled the promenade after dinner in full evening dress and with whom we delighted to mingle clutching our vinegar-soaked bundles of newspaper.

We messed about with a cheap microphone plugged into a wireless set to convince ourselves that we were broadcasters and took photographs which we developed and printed ourselves in Auntie Nina's scullery, blacked-out and all culinary activity banished.

And above all we played records.

I don't know how long I should have taken to discover music, real music if it hadn't been for cousin Frank. Apart from Grandma's resistance to all but the most straightforward ballads, my father had a habit of coming home and switching off anything at all classical that I might be experimenting with on the wireless with a peremptory 'We don't want any of that.'

But Frank had an electric radiogram and about a dozen classical records. In Grandma's words 'Frank's dry old muck.' There was nothing recherché about the choice. An orchestral selection from 'Carmen', the overtures to 'Figaro' and 'Seraglio' back to back (this was the day of fragile 78s), Liszt's Hungarian Rhapsody No.2 orchestrated by Stokowski, the Hallelujah Chorus from 'Messiah', a Rossini overture conducted by Toscanini. They were knock-out. These so-called classical people had all the best tunes. And I started my own collection one summer by buying the orchestral selection from 'Carmen' because it was the cheapest, playing it, back home in London, until it wore out and then buying a replacement which wore out in its turn. Climaxes were always the problem on those old shellac discs, particularly towards the ends of sides where climaxes tended to gather. Oh, and long held notes which wavered like an expiring siren. (It was not until the arrival of the LP that Vaughan Williams's 'Thomas Tallis' variations began to sound like anything at all.)

Why had it taken me so long? We'd had music lessons at school. Dr. Hunt used to walk round with a heavy book in his hand banging the head of any boy who sang a wrong note. Might this just have created a trauma? In choral situations I just opened and closed my mouth like a fish and in private gave relieved voice without benefit of ear, so to speak, wandering from key to key unhindered and unaware. Piano lessons had been mooted at one stage, but I'd shied away from them as something seemingly beyond my scope. Music on the page looked only too fearsomely mathematical. Now I know it as the greatest art, uniting beyond frontiers with the purity of sound, satisfying heart and mind equally, absorbed into its own meaning.

When the war broke out in September my father decreed that the whole family, excluding himself (for reasons which at the time seemed heroic but on later investigation turned out to be not un-motivated by self-interest) should remain in the safety of Sidmouth and find somewhere to live for the duration. That was Mum, Grandma, me, and a late arrival on the scene my sister Shirley who was now five years old. She had turned up when I was ten. My mother had been to the hospital to collect her. In my self-absorption I had clearly not noticed anything out of the ordinary in the run up to this event. It was enough that I suddenly had a sister and I was dotty about her, racing home from school daily to improvise the latest instalment in the saga of 'Mrs. Biddykins'. My love-pattern was from now on locked irretrievably into a preference for younger women and a strong Torvald Helmer syndrome developed which has had to be bitterly subdued over the years. 'A Doll's House' is one of only two Ibsen plays I can truly relate to. My empathy with Helmer is painfully complete. Masochistically I have directed both my wives as Nora (Nottingham Playhouse, 1953; Leeds Playhouse 1975) and given them the vicarious satisfaction of slamming the door.

We found an idyllic place to live. A tiny four roomed cottage in Sid lane, a little track which ran down to a footbridge over the modest river Sid. The sanitation was primitive. Baths were taken in a tin tub in the scullery filled with hot water from the copper. The loo was up the back of the garden. One used a potty in the night and Grandma had a commode. It was the best place I had ever lived.

I somehow begged or borrowed a portable wind-up gramophone and began a new collection with some rejects from the Radway Cinema where my cousin Bert was manager. Fred Astaire, Crosby, and a much-used interval filler called 'The Glow-worm'. Oh, and the first movement of the New World symphony on a black label HMV conducted by Sir Landon Ronald with the orchestra sounding like something squeezed through a mincer. There were two cinemas in Sidmouth in those days with a mid-week change of programme, so any one week brought a choice of four feature films. 'Uncle' Bert (so called out of respect for the difference in our ages) had always worked for the cinemas having previously been the senior projectionist at the Grand. One of my early thrills was to be allowed up into the projection box during performance. The smell of hot celluloid, the whirr of the machines drowning out the distant boom of the dialogue, the tropical heat of the carbon arcs in the cramped surroundings made it Arabian Nights for me. Bert would give me off-cuts of damaged film which I lovingly examined frame by frame and then ran off back home in London on a hand-cranked 35mm projector which Dad had found in some bargain store.

Bert also used to take me bill-posting, careering around the twisty lanes in a rackety old van, slapping up information about M.G.M's latest blockbuster in many an owl-haunted glade as far afield as Seaton.

Memory is behaving like a dog off the lead. Let's stay with gramophone records for the moment and make the World War wait.

I have always been a disc fanatic, from shellac through vinyl to CD. The first gramophone of which I had practically sole use was of course my parents'. It was a large floor-standing model, hand wound, with a lid that opened on the turntable, a fretted speaker enclosure behind cabinet doors and a large shelf at the bottom for records. 'Broadcast 12' seemed to be the family's favourite label, and the selection ran from contemporary dance music to salon ballads. Grandma liked 'Maire, my girl' and 'Until'. But gradually I began to acquire my own from the Marks and Spencer's branch at Clapham Junction. They had their own brand then. 'Rex, the King of Records'. And there, before my awakening with the 'Carmen' selection, I would spend a shilling of my two bob pocket money on a new disc by Jay Wilbur and his band. Alas, this little collection, which I took joy in arranging into 'programmes', was left behind in London with all our childhood toys and became the flotsam of war, never to be seen again. There was a Triang 'Minic' car collection that nowadays would fetch hundreds of pounds; a large collection of Meccano given me every Christmas by Uncle Fred, with which I could never achieve anything but the simplest models. This was disappointing to both of us as I think he saw me as a kind of kindred spirit, a fellow intellectual in the suburban wasteland, and a needed counterbalance to his own cheerful dunce of a son, my cousin Kenneth. Well, anyway, Dad gave the whole caboosh away to the boy next door when he closed the house and moved in with his lady friend. Of which more anon.

So the war. I stood in the front garden of 19 Arcot Park in brilliant sunshine with my elder cousin Kathleen and together we speculated that tonight, September 3rd 1939, London would be wiped off the face of the earth. It's hard to remember what I felt. I can see the memory, but I can't feel it. And of course London wasn't wiped out. The 'Phoney War' gave us all time to adjust and life in Sidmouth went on like an extended summer holiday. I bought 'The War Illustrated' weekly, filled with pictures of brave Finns on the Russian front. There was no action anywhere else, although there were plenty of exciting maps and prognostications. History began to come alive with the notion that one was in it.

Sixteen year old cousin Kathleen was stigmatised as a scarlet woman by Grandma, because she went out with boys and came home late. After the war she married and went to Canada where she had a huge family and drowned tragically young in a boating accident. I liked her. She was dark, gypsy-ish and not unfriendly. But she was going through a challenging puberty so we never became close.

News came that 'Sinjuns' was evacuating to Charterhouse, near Godalming, to share premises with the public school. That's as near as I came to claiming a public school education, for my mother couldn't bear to part with me and it was decided that I should continue my education at the King's School, Ottery St. Mary, where places were found in the fifth form for me and another Sidmouth evacuee, a boy called Mummery whose father was a bank manager.

The King's School Ottery was co-educational, which was a violent culture shock to me at that age. I soon discovered that, alas, girls had no use for a steady, studious lad. Their favourites were the class buffoons who excelled on the sports field. The more they admired, the more buffoonish grew the lads, naturally eager to impress them. This was deeply disturbing to me and has left me with a strong suspicion that a woman-led society, far from leading to the peace that the women's movement imagines, would simply encourage men in all their worst antics, up to and including war. I was the only boy to show any inclination to use the library. This and my London accent made me an oddity and I was forced to make friends with Mummery, although we were not tremendously congenial. My exam subjects were a problem. To my dismay there was no German at the school so I had to throw away a growing strong suit after just a year. It meant I was down to English, French, the lunatic Mathematics, History and Geography. There was nowhere else for me to go when other classes were taken so I had to sit through a great deal of Old Testament History (known as 'Divinity') taken by a towering spinster who always seemed to be ranting on about Judas Maccabeus, of whom I had not previously heard, and of whom I can tell you little to this day except what I have learned from Handel. The Old Testament, apart from a few splendid purple passages, has never seemed to me very relevant either to religion or history. I've always been an avid New Testament fan but that never came up in Miss Mills's Divinity lessons. (She may have been getting it all backwards any way. Several years later after I had appeared at Stratford as Benvolio I met her in Sidmouth Fore Street. 'Loved your Benvoluto,' she said.)

Being pubertal and suddenly surrounded by girls I was naturally smitten all over the place. For a time I yearned after a toothsome blonde in the fourth, but she was much given to the sportsmen. There was little possibility of contact outside of class as the playgrounds were strictly segregated. You could linger near the wire fence though, like wary zoo animals. Gradually I became enamoured of another evacuee, also lower down the school. I think she was thirteen. A pale girl, tall for her age, with long auburn hair and a dancer's figure.

'Oh, rare, pale Margaret...'

Our ways to and from Sidmouth station coincided. This was second love and came upon me in a burst of quite awful poetry. I remember much hanging about on stiles together down by the river Sid, and swimming at Jacob's Ladder beach, where she was always, alas, chaperoned by a posse of friends. I remember her winning the flowerpot race at the school sports and me getting racey photos of her bent double in the act. And there happened one wonderful, magical day. I arrived at school and was in the changing room hanging up my things when I remembered I'd left my prep behind at home - five miles away in Sidmouth. I debated whether to go back on the next train to get it. It seemed an agreeable way of passing most of morning school. But I might not have done so had not the Head Boy happened to remark in passing, 'I saw that kid Ball' (Margaret's unmusical surname) 'down at Ottery station Harrison. She's forgotten something too.' So back I went on winged feet down the hill to the station. And back together Margaret and I went to Sidmouth. It was the summer term and the sun shone extravagantly. In Sidmouth her home was reached before mine. I asked her to wait for me. I dillied and dallied. We met again and dallied and dillied back up the hill to Sidmouth station, just in time to see the train going out. 'We'll walk,' I said. Along past Harpford woods and Tipton St.Johns. Hot and tired after about an hour we climbed a gate and lay down in a field of buttercups and tall grasses.

That's all. We just lay there side by side and desultorily talked, her light voice murmuring. I don't remember the rest of the day, getting back to school or any of that. We never touched. We never kissed. The bliss was almost painful.

Many years later she became a professional dancer. While I was an actor at the Birmingham Rep I discovered she was in the chorus of a musical at the London Coliseum and we arranged to meet. She was so nervous she disappeared into a ladies lavatory and never came out. And then after about twenty years and marriages various we met again at the old British Drama League building in Fitroy Square. It was a tale of might-have-been.

Although not a sportsman I was far from weedy in the gym. I earned the respect of the lads, if not the girls who were not there to see it, by setting a record for the High Jump. I was a first rate vaulter of the horse lengthways (pommels removed), a nifty rope climber, decent long jumper, and a good sprinter up to 220 yards. I just couldn't stand team games with their expectations and pressures and boredom. And once again I was in the school play. 'A Midsummer Night's Dream' in the open air. I got Lysander. But this time, most un-Elizabethan, the girls were girls. Which meant I had to play opposite a plumpish sweating lass called Joan and hold her sweating hand. No thrill. Neither did I greatly take to playing in the open air. You lost control of where your voice went. And real earth seemed a weak substitute for 'the boards'. Again, a loss of resonance. So one way and another I don't think I was much of a success as Lysander.

Meanwhile another kind of performance was really getting off the ground. Cousin Frank was a pillar of the church at Woolbrook St. Francis. And in St Francis's church hall were given a series of concert parties as part of Sidmouth's effort to keep the home fires burning. Somebody, inevitably, would sing 'Widdecombe Fair', a member of the local building family had what would now be called a 'drag act', and Frank and I did sketches which I wrote for the two of us.

The apotheosis was the creation of my own act. This was called 'Mixed Doubles' and was based on the not-too-original idea of crossed radio programmes (a common hazard in those pre-digital days).

I became a sort of comic, in demand beyond Woolbrook, 'guesting' as far afield as Sidford and (one unrepeatable night) at the prisoner-of-war camp in Honiton where Frank and I played, not to the prisoners, but the guards. We did our act in which he was on stage trying to give a recitation and I, togged out in very drop-out fashion, interrupted from the audience with prophecy of doom and woe, finally joining him on stage with threat to his very life. Was I an incendiarist? An escaped prisoner? The denouement, you may have guessed, was that I was trying to sell him Life Insurance.

Performance, that keen drug, was becoming a necessary part of my life. The shy lad who didn't dare kiss a girl could get up there in front of two or three hundred people, all inhibition gone, and make them laugh or make them listen. Is it any wonder shy people become actors? Pretty small beer it may have been, but I know in my bones what it feels like to be a variety star.

Exams done without too much distinction (Credits in English and French, bare passes in the others, and failed in Maths) my sojourn in Ottery drew to an end. Pity was taken on evacuees and the inevitable disruption of their thoughts and I was duly awarded my School Certificate. Now what to do? I had vague thoughts of 'Journalism'. Whatever that was it must have something to do with writing. So, armed with testimonial from 'Tommy' Bowman the English master, I wrote off to all the Devon papers. They didn't even want to see me. I'd have been idyllically happy in a public library but in those days you had to pass library exams before you were allowed even to stamp a book. More study was financially out of the question. The family needed me to get a job. Further education was, to the best of my remembrance, hardly discussed. My parents had made the sacrifice. I had been educated to the age of sixteen. They now sat back to reap the reward. In any case I'd have been dead against it. I'd had enough of school. More than enough. I am a lousy pupil. I will beaver away and teach myself all manner of things but I seem to have an inbuilt resistance to being taught.

So what to do? I remember some deadly interviews. One in a solicitor's office, and one with Mummery's father for the bank (my father's ideal for me, you may remember). But it was all happening to a Zombie. I knew I wasn't meant for any of this. I was to be a writer. Wasn't I already half-way through my first novel? 'Until Dawn'. 30,000 words finished in Sidmouth in 1942. I was soaked in Wells and Shaw and Eric Linklater and Tennyson and Swinburne and Verlaine and Joyce and Rimbaud and anything else that took my fancy on the shelves of the Church House free library or the Sidmouth public library. Missing Streatham Hill Theatre I read a lot of plays. I liked reading plays, imagining them vividly in the theatre of my mind. And I was working my way through the Shakespearian canon. I sometimes wish I'd left a few of them to discover in maturity. My copies of Dover Wilson's 'The Essential Shakespeare' and 'The Fortunes of Falstaff' date back to this era, and a tattered Pelican copy of his 'Life in Shakespeare's England'. I know them by their wartime recycled paper on which ghost letters appear faintly in all the vacant spaces. I boned up on the whole Eng. Lit. scene with 'The Outline of Literature' edited by John Drinkwater, whose savoury quotations led me on to many life-enhancing discoveries. I read Charles Morgan and James Agate's diaries for light relief, and topped up with a biography of Verlaine and the poems and stories of Poe. I was wild, undirected, an enchanted magpie.

Generally I was thought to be slacking as I carefully avoided the commitments proposed for me in banking and the law. A pretty humble clerk I should have been, but I think they could detect my indolence and lack of interest, polite and shy as I was at the interviews. More to my taste an interview with Mr. Wheaton of the big Exeter publishers and booksellers (armed with 'Tommy' Bowman's testimonial) impressed him sufficiently to get Mr. Green in the bookshop to take me on as an extra hand over the Christmas rush.

Something a bit out of the rut had happened just before this. An advertisement had appeared in the Exeter evening paper for a master to teach Maths and English at an evacuated Eastbourne boys preparatory school, now ten miles away at Honiton. The Grange School (Eastbourne in brackets). Filled with a spirit of daring I set to and wrote a letter explaining that I couldn't teach Maths to save my life but I would be really hot stuff at English. Either there were no other applicants or my chutzpah took John Booker's fancy. He was young for a headmaster and passing eccentric. I was called to interview with him and his suavely stunning blonde wife Peggy over coffee and biscuits in an up-market Honiton Cafe. I passed sufficient muster to be taken on for a brief trial period, to stop a gap I think. It was possibly no more than a few weeks but at the time it was like a trial run at heaven.

I'd had enough of being a schoolboy but to be translated at one bound to schoolmaster at the age of seventeen was the stuff that dreams are made on. For a start it's the only thing you've ever seen anyone do and had direct experience of on the receiving end so, if you are observant and a bit of an actor, you've a head start.

I dropped with ease into the role and, more to my surprise, the establishment life-style. My knowledge of boarding school had been gained from the Gem and the Magnet, Billy Bunter and Harry Wharton and co. My background had been as totally lower middle class as Noel Coward's, pictured so graphically in what should possibly be considered his best play, 'This Happy Breed'. (It is usually assumed to be condescending by those who only accept the smart Coward of the comedies, but to me it seems deeply felt and experienced and not without affection.) I slipped into middle-class snobbery, as he had, like a cuckoo back with its family.

My main worry was to keep from the boys that I was not really 'one of them'. As they were all at the age when a choice of public school was imperative they naturally wanted to know which one I'd been to. I sensed that 'Sinjuns' would not pass muster so I played mysterious. How odd it must have seemed to them! What a strange thing to be mysterious about! Particularly as I had clearly only just left. Had I been to some Borstal? But I so wanted to be accepted in what seemed my natural element.

I taught English and History to eleven to thirteen year olds, and French to the eleven year olds. The school was housed in what had once been the Monkton Court Hotel on the main road a mile or so toward London. Dumdon, the ancient hill fort, was in direct eyeline from the front gate. Classrooms were in a farmhouse five hundred yards down the road. Little white-washed rooms, a few rows of desks - classes were never more than about eight strong - and me acting my part (in History like a lawyer stuck in his brief: any questions on last week's lesson had to be cunningly turned aside.)

It was a heart-rendingly short interlude. They seemed unable or disinclined to take me on the permanent strength. It was my sour lot to return home and grieve beside the River Sid like a character in a German song cycle.

After a few more months of this disgraceful idleness, dawdling by the river and writing my novel, I kept my appointment with Wheaton's bookshop in Exeter for the Christmas rush. I was paid twenty-five shillings a week, most of which went on my weekly bus ticket (it's about ten miles from Sidmouth to Exeter). After the hearty breakfast of bacon and egg that my mother insisted on I then used to feel very queasy on the bus for the half hour journey. The first thing you did when you arrived was dust the books. This was done by banging them together in pairs and then flicking over with a duster. Mr. Green was in charge. Very old and white and bent and quite severe but kindly. His life was the outside of books. I don't think he ever read them. His pride and joy was the glass case of bibles and prayer books in their tooled leather bindings with golden lettering. The rest of us were not often allowed the chance of touching these. The other staff were a kind elderly lady called Miss Tetts, and an equally kind and not very good looking younger lady called Miss Sprague.

The good thing about working in a bookshop over the Christmas period was that I was able, as an employee, to buy books at the wholesale price. My relatives were quickly alerted that I wanted books for Christmas and I had the choosing and the spending of their money. The new H.G. Wells, 'Babes in the Darkling Wood'; 'The Outline of

Literature'; 'The Oxford Companion to Music' edited by Percy Scholes. Others I've forgotten. I think probably 'Gone With the Wind' which was a hot seller at this time. Grandma read it three times. And possibly A.J. Cronin's 'The Citadel' and 'Hatter's Castle' and Daphne du Maurier's 'Rebecca' in their glaring Gollancz yellow. Grandma devoured these too. She was the other reader in the family. Mum preferred what they both called "the tale" in her Woman's Weekly. 'Have you finished "the tale" yet?' they would ask each other. And I mustn't forget C.S. Lewis's 'Screwtape Letters' and 'The Problem of Pain' from around this time as I struggled with the imponderables of the Christian religion - though these may have been slightly later.

My discipleship of Wells determined me to try and shift a left-over hardback copy of 'The Bulpington of Blup' from an upper shelf. I'd devoured it myself in paperback. Does anybody read it now? I haven't seen a copy for years. I eventually chatted a customer into buying it. He returned in a few days to give himself the pleasure of telling me that he thought it was rubbish.

Theodore Blup-Bulpington appealed to me because I recognised him only too clearly. A sort of earlier Walter Mitty his fantasy life struck a chord in the moonish seventeen year old. I had a ripe fantasy life of my own based on a character named Johnny Maxine, a pop star equally at home in the world of classical music, who had his own orchestra, the South Coast Symphony, paid for by the success of his popular 78s of numbers like 'Boo-hoo, you've got me crying for you'. As I still had difficulty holding a tune you will see the extent of my dream. I suppose this character was a sort of prophecy of what came to be known as 'Crossover', the Previns and Bernsteins and Nigel Kennedys whom we now take for granted. But in those straiter, narrower times even Dr. Malcolm Sargent's red carnation was looked on as a dangerous concession to the plebs.

Christmas over, I bade farewell to Mr. Green, Miss Tetts and Miss Sprague and returned to Sid Lane to read my books. I mooned by the Sid writing terrible poetry and meekly accompanied Mum and Grandma on whist playing evenings with a gentle couple of retired teachers. Being already a settled loner I liked 'Solo' whist best, and favourite of all was to be able to call 'Misere' and lose every trick. This usually riled everybody, because it could only happen when they all had rather good hands, and as I remember it out-called everything except 'Royal Abundance'. There's glory for you, as Humpty Dumpty might say.

Almost immediately after the holiday period there was a thunderbolt and the clouds opened. A telegram arrived. 'Kindly accept permanent position Grange School telephone Honiton 24 between six eight tonight. Booker.' I suppose I remember it word for word because it was one of the rare times in my professional life when I got exactly what I wanted.

Now followed an intensely lived and fulfilling three years. In a sense, I suppose, my university.

John Mackarness Booker was no ordinary headmaster. He had charisma. He must have been in his early thirties, or possibly even younger, exempted from National Service by his reserved occupation. He had been the junior partner in the school with a Captain Herries who had gone off to the war leaving his sister Jessie still teaching the infant class and disapproving strongly of her brother's usurper. Prep Schools in those days, particularly pukkha ones like The Grange which were listed in the I.A.P.S. Guide, nearly always had a conservative naval or military figure at the top, but J.M.B. was a New Statesman reading Old Etonian pinko.

His wife Peggy was sleek and blonde and slightly glamorous and called me by my Christian name. (To the other ladies of the staff I was always, in spite of my callowness, correctly Mr. Harrison. And not just in front of the boys! Looking back I wonder if they were sending me up. But no: they could never have carried it off so consistently or for so long.)

The Bookers had two children under five, Christopher and Joanna, cherished by a diminutive Scots nanny. Christopher was, very much later, to distinguish himself in the media and on the literary scene; but for the present he was an owlish, bespectacled four-year-old, grave beyond his years.

The senior staff member was a very tall man with sleek dark hair, a beaky nose in a reddish face and a pronounced Adam's apple, Mr. Durell (pron. Dew/rell). He and Mr. Booker and I taught everything between us to the upper school (that's eleven to thirteen-year-olds) except for Geography which they all met for once a week with Peggy

Booker. John Booker took Latin and Maths (having signally failed to find relief in this subject). J.B.O. Durell took senior French. Mr. Harrison took English, History (still one jump ahead of the class) and junior French. Miss Alethea Matheson (also A-Ke-La of the Cub pack) instructed the intermediate form in everything except for a weekly star turn from me for History. And Miss Herries sheltered the babies. The Rector of Combe Raleigh came once a week for Scripture. And that was it. For £80 a term including board. My salary was £30 ditto, which seemed riches. Apart from my weekly half-day excursion to Exeter there was nothing to spend it on. All of us staff, minus the Bookers but with the addition of Nanny and Matron, took our evening meal together. This would have been cobbled together from our pooled rations by the school tyrant, the cook, Mrs. Inglefield, of whom we all went in terror, staff and boys alike. Her kitchen abutted the boys' changing room where she held malignant (totally unauthorised) sway like a concentration camp guard. When the nightly gong resounded the hatch between the staff dining room and the kitchen would be flung open and the inmates' evening repast slung down with an uncanny mixture of pride and ill-disguised contempt. When this was done Mr. Durell would hop on his bike and pedal off to the Dolphin Hotel Honiton to join John and Peggy Booker in nightly carouse. I was too young to be drawn into this raw nightlife and preferred to sit in the staff-room reading in the company of Miss Matheson, Miss Herries, Matron, Nanny and their knitting. A regular hen club. We had no wireless.

Miss Matheson was mannish with a dark page-boy cut and sensible shoes. Miss Herries was sweetly cosy and liked you to confide in her. Nanny was friendly but consumed by her charges' latest exploits. And Matron was a different person every term due to a steady changeover of personnel.

Sometimes Peggy Booker took pity on me and allowed me, in their absence, to spend the evening in their gracious living quarters, where I had the use of a gramophone and Heifetz's recording of the Beethoven violin concerto on seven sides of black shellac.

Mr. Durell and I did alternate 'duty' days, which meant supervising the boys' meals, instead of sitting at the staff table, presiding over evening prep and coping with the afternoon's physical activities.

Football, in winter, on a muddy field down by Honiton town, or a supervised walk. In the summer cricket or a walk. J.B. and J.B.O.D. enjoyed the team games, which was fine by me. I got lumbered with the occasional net practice, but mostly mine were the walks, which I cunningly developed into the attack and defence of Dumdon Fort. I could send the advance party on half an hour ahead to take up defensive positions on the bracken-clad slopes. Then, Mrs. Inglefield's lunch the better digested, I would lead the attacking force through them to the top. No violence, you understand. Just a sort of glorified 'tag'.

Sometimes in the summer term when the weather was particularly fine Mr. Booker would peer out of the windows at breakfast and announce, 'Coast today, I think, Harrison.' The timetable would be abandoned and we would all pile on our bikes and pedal the six or seven miles to Seaton.

'...the sexy airs of summer,
The bathing hours and the bare arms...'

Pedalling over Honiton common on my Hercules bicycle trying to sing the trio theme from the scherzo of the New World symphony all was very right with the world. They do say everybody's war was different. Though I did join the Home Guard eventually. But I mustn't anticipate.

I also re-met my father. He turned up out of the blue one day staying at the Angel, the lesser of the two Honiton hostelries, and I joined him for a long evening in the private bar where he drank beer and I consumed small port after small port. I was not a sophisticated drinker at this time. I'd tried beer and noted in my diary, 'First glass of beer. Very vile and no effects.'

It was a meeting to amaze me. The rather distant 'Dad' of my Battersea childhood became an ordinary human being with problems. He told me in detail of the collapse of Harrison's of Battersea. How he had fiddled the books to sell the firm to the big rival, Hemmings, becoming one of their area managers. So far he had obviously not been rumbled. He told me of the long failure of his marriage, down dusty years of Grandma's sniping, and of his bitterness at constantly having to play second fiddle to his boozy and uncongenially snobbish brother-in-law, my uncle Fred. He told me that only thoughts of his little daughter had prevented him many times from jumping off Battersea Bridge.

As he walked me back in the black-out dark towards Combe Raleigh he begged me to use the influence he imagined I had with my mother to get her to release him to marry the woman of his choice with whom he was now living. Because I had sent him some of my immature poems he imagined me to be worldly-wise about the Grand Passion. He couldn't have conceived that it was all inside my head. He said that meeting me again as a comparatively grown-up stranger he found he liked me.

I'm afraid I wanted to know none of this. I could no more have talked to my mother about such things than to the Virgin Mary. I was utterly consumed with my own awakening to life and was in no mood to cope with the wreckage of his. I thought that parents should somehow 'get it right' and not pressurise their off-spring with their own problems. This sudden and unexpected intimacy was not unpleasing, but it was a profound shock.

I felt, like the Robin, the moment had come to do battle with my father for the territory. I answered no more of his letters on the subject and never mentioned the matter to my mother. After his death I naturally wished we had been able to be closer. But this was the wrong moment. I was of my mother's party. I was on the Devonian side.

After I'd been at the school about a year there were big changes. We left the Monkton Court Hotel for Combe Hill House just outside the village of Combe Raleigh. Mr. Durell went off to war and was replaced by Raymond R.U.Kaufmann, who was not entirely British. I think he had a Danish passport, although he was the most un-Danish Dane you have ever seen: dark and sallow with black hair smarmed down and a drooping black moustache. His whole personality drooped rather, but he had a good sense of humour and a passion for aquaeous coleoptera. Water beetles. On which he wrote learned papers. On his free day he would disappear clad in waders with Buzz his black spaniel at heel for an intensive fish through the local bogs and stagnant ponds; from which Buzz would return less than savoury to steam contentedly before the staff-room fire.

Mr. Kaufmann was not quite 'one of us'. The subtle freeze he was given was my first experience of Establishment cut-off. But how was it that I was accepted? Like a jungle animal I must have taken on protective colouring.

In class the pupils were being prepared for the Common Entrance Examination to the Public Schools and sadly, to my way of thinking, the brighter boys were mostly destined for the Royal Naval College at Dartmouth. As a Wellsian pacifist I tried often to subvert their Tory view of British History. But alas the only subjects that really mattered for entrance to the Public Schools in those days were Latin and Maths, with French a fair runner up. English, History and Geography were the stragglers in the field, which is probably why a seventeen year old and the Headmaster's wife could be entrusted with them.

One of my favourite pupils was a good-looking but not very academic eleven year old called John Nott. His ambition was to go into the army and become a General. You could say that, as Minister of Defence during the Falkland invasion, he got within striking distance. But somewhere he seemed to have lost his looks along the way.

I had a variety of eccentric 'digs' before I was eventually awarded a tiny attic room in what had once been the servants' quarters at Combe Hill House. I was lodged for a time in a cottage opposite the school gates which was more than a touch Brothers Grimm. It was inhabited by a very elderly couple and their retarded daughter who was never seen but who made disturbing noises in her room whose door I had to pass each night to reach mine. Do you know James Whale's marvellously Gothic horror film THE OLD DARK HOUSE? The babbling behind the door? I preferred it on film.

Then I spent a happier term at Combe Raleigh Rectory, a wonderfully rambling early Victorian monster without electricity. You picked up an oil lamp from the hall table every night and flickered up to your room, making grotesque shadows and feeling like Jane Eyre in Thornfield Hall. I used to read in bed a lot at this time, after all there were twenty odd centuries of literature to bone up on. Have you ever tried reading by an oil lamp? I was continually turning up the flame and cracking the glass cylinder which brought down on my head the wrath of Mrs. Rector because these cylinders were precious on a rectory stipend.

It was in this room that I had my one and only drug experience. In those days to relieve a congested head you could buy Benzedrine inhalers across the counter in any chemist. They were the latest thing. Benzedrine inhalers. We all had them. One night with a heavy cold I used mine after it had been warming gently under the oil lamp for an hour. I stuffed it up my nostril and inhaled deeply, which produced instant euphoria and total identification with the universe. I didn't make the connection until years later when they had been withdrawn from the market.

The rector was a dear old man called Edwards, a sort of low-church agnostic, kind and cultured with a strong theatrical bent. I regularly read the lesson for him when I accompanied the school party to Sunday matins. This was performance again and I relished it. Particularly when one was rewarded by passages like 'Though I speak with the tongue of men and of angels...' Even the boring ones like St. Paul's reproving letters were a good sight-reading challenge.

My more overtly theatrical activities continued.

I devised an annual school play in the summer term on the lawn at the back of the house which had natural 'wings' of topiary and an ample terrace to accommodate an audience of fifty to a hundred parents and friends. 'This green plot shall be our stage...' The first summer I did an adaptation of Pilgrim's Progress and awarded myself the fruity role of the foul fiend Apollyon. Roaring out of the hawthorn brake this seemed a more positive experience than had Lysander. I think at this stage I had not yet taken Hamlet's advice about moderation. The second year I strung an anthology of poetry and prose together in a 'Wings For Victory' Week extravaganza called 'Is Robin Hood Awake?' Pillaged from all the more jingoistic writers from Shakespeare to Alfred Noyes it called, totally against my own personal grain - for was I not a Wellsian pacifist?- for a reawakening of the national tendency to fire and sword. A piece of rank opportunism, you might say, all principles sacrificed to my rage to write, direct and act.

I said just now I was a pacifist. The question of my 'call-up' for the forces became imminent and had to be addressed. I should have dearly loved to have registered as a conscientious objector. But I knew, with no hint of exaggeration, that to have a 'Conchie' son would have broken my mother's heart. And I wasn't brave enough for that. So I filled in 'Royal Air Force' on the forms and waited stoically for the event. I was duly called to Exeter for medical inspection. At the end of the round of undignified pokings they asked me if I felt all right. I said yes. They said I had a high temperature and suggested I went home to bed. I went off wonderingly to eat a poached egg on toasted cheese at the Kardomah Cafe and visit the pictures before returning, still feeling fine, to Honiton.

A few months later I was sent for again. After the usual weighings and proddings and sample-cooking they shook their heads over me sadly and graded me III. Which meant exemption from military service. I suppose I was relieved at this, though a little taken aback, and felt so well that it never occurred to me, until about four years later at Peter Brook's insistence, to have a private medical check-up.

So there it was. No 'Johnny-head-in-air' for me.

Soon I got a directive to join the local Home Guard at Combe Raleigh as a Private. The school gardener, Roo, (or possibly Rew?) was, as lance-corporal, my immediate superior. I was issued with khaki uniform and army boots and the boys would cheer me off once a week to the meeting in Combe Raleigh village hall under the command of a cockney ex-regular-army corporal. There were about half a dozen of us to defy Hitler's intentions in the area. We shared one rifle which we took it in turns to practise with. I turned out, to the surprised admiration of my mainly farming colleagues, to be quite a good shot. We did elaborate night manoeuvres. 'This exercise,' intoned the corporal, 'is normally executed lying flat on the stomach. But as the grass is a bit damp tonight we'll omit it.' Our manoeuvres always ended well before closing time.

The Luftwaffe used to drone overhead on their way to bomb Exeter and Bristol and Cardiff, and sometimes they would jettison the odd leftover on their return before they crossed the coast. We would gather next day to look morbidly at the gaping crater and the entrails of cows. Back at Sid Lane during the holidays we used to huddle together as instructed in the cupboard under the stairs when the sirens wailed. 'Blimming old Germans', Grandma would complain. After two world wars they were her natural enemy. It wouldn't do for me to talk of Beethoven. Goodness knows how she would have taken the news that her great grandson would eventually marry one.

More school productions occupied the winters in the ballroom which was our assembly hall. Scenes from A MIDSUMMER NIGHT'S

DREAM with Christopher Booker as Mustardseed. And in my final term a pottage of bits and pieces mainly to give myself the opportunity to play the King in Richard the Second's return from Ireland. 'Within the hollow crown...' Surrounded by my twelve year old courtiers I had a splendid time of it, although the Bookers thought I should stick to directing. But by then they were too late.

In the Spring term of 1943 they had told me my services could not be retained beyond the end of the year because the school was being forced to close. Numbers had dwindled to about thirty pupils all told and we were driven to admit day-girls from Honiton into Miss Herries's babies' class. So, once again, what to do? 'Until Dawn' had by now been the round of every publisher in London and the rejection slips, meticulously filed as was all my correspondence at that time, were mounting. Fame and fortune were not coming quickly that way. I had sent it together with a long piqued letter to L.A.G. Strong, broadcaster, novelist, writer on English in schools, who was on the board of one of my rejectors. I had been particularly stung by their reader's recommendation to 'read more widely'. I sent him my current reading list, eclectic beyond the call of reason. He wrote back, kindly and courteously, to say that I did not yet seem to have a style of my own, 'but, and this is a long shot, your novel suggests to me that you may one day write a play.' Being but "a moonish youth" I had settled only too easily and comfortably into my peaceful, un-ambitious life at the school, relishing the long holidays in the Devon countryside, writing long letters and scraps of poetry. I had already, at the age of nineteen, learned to eschew ambition.

"After all, at rock bottom, what more does a man want than food, warmth, a job to do, a roof over the top of him, a bed to sleep on and somebody to share it? Why worry and fret over elusive unattainable ultimate values? Will he never be content?

'There is no greater crime than seeking what men desire;
There is no greater misery than knowing no content;
There is no greater calamity than indulging in greed.
Therefore the contentment of knowing content will ever be contented.'"

UNTIL DAWN, 1942. Complete with quote from the Tao-Te-King.

I wrote something in similar vein to my old Sinjuns English master, 'Ernie' Cozens, he who had opened the door on Shakespeare. He wrote back in horror to say that at my age I shouldn't be thinking about peace and to read Carlyle's 'Sartor Resartus', which I'm ashamed to say I never did.

I did acquire a modicum of ambition from somewhere nevertheless.

My interest in the drama had led me to subscribe to The Stage newspaper, that unique weekly amalgam of amateur and professional gossip and information. From it I had learned that a new drama school was to be opened at Sir Barry Jackson's famous Repertory Theatre in Birmingham. I sent for particulars and discovered that the course was not to be a particularly long one and that the fees were relatively modest. Entry was to be by audition.

Now I knew I could act. I hoped I could write. But I *knew* I could act. There was not much saved from my £30 a term, which was often in arrears, arriving half way through the holidays and then frequently under protest 'I note your somewhat too peremptorily worded request for thirty pounds and enclose my cheque herewith. J.M.B.' Or on another belated occasion: 'Blame Montefiore for me, will you, and one or two others.' I was beginning to learn that noblesse didn't always oblige.

So I needed some money. I sent off to Gabbitas, Thring and Co., the legendary and much mocked scholastic agency, and landed a summer holiday job in Wales, not at Llanaba Castle but at Lapley Grange, Glandyfi near Machynlleth. This was a polite form of crammer run by a retired housemaster from Stowe with his much younger wife who had I think been the matron, Mr. and Mrs. Ivor M. Cross. I arrived after a typical wartime night train journey in the course of which I had slept for a while on a table in the waiting room of Exeter St. David's and for a longer while in a luggage rack on the troop crowded train. Finally in the dawn light I pushed my bicycle (having cycled the last miles from Machynlleth) up the steep drive to Lapley Grange, imposingly situated above the Dovey estuary.

The boys here were a motley but pleasant crew, several of whom had returned from premature evacuation to the U.S.A. with American accents and little of the knowledge that would be necessary to pass their common entrance examinations. I took my usual subjects and was

35

accepted, after some initial surprise at my callow youth, as easily as I had been at The Grange School (Eastbourne in brackets). My experience of both schools has more than doubled my delight in Evelyn Waugh's 'Decline and Fall'. I remember a pool in a mountain stream where the boys bathed naked and I, with the typical prudery of a lower middle class upbringing, was too shy, though longing, to join them. It was to be another thirty years before I could shake this off to plunge and cavort with the rest of the European Economic Community on open French beaches.

And I remember reading aloud to them in the dormitory from Jerome K. Jerome or Edgar Allan Poe. Still going for laughter and frights.

The summer passed and thus agreeably I acquired a little money to stake me out on the grand adventure to Birmingham. My mother, wondrously supportive ever, lent me all she had in the world, £50, and so, between us, the first term's fees and living expenses were assured. After that? Well, it would be a gamble, wouldn't it? Either they would discover that I could act and if my confidence was misplaced... well, there was always Gabbitas, Thring and Co. My father wrote that I was going to live among people who 'lived by their wits' and that his advice was to 'chuck it and settle down and work your way through college.' I don't think he had any more idea than I how this might be accomplished but it was a handy phrase. As for living by one's wits, which to him carried serious overtones of the fairground, to me it seemed literally not a bad idea.

So, some time in the Autumn of 1943, I travelled north to Birmingham for my audition.

CHAPTER THREE

Birmingham Rep

"John Harrison (Arnholm) woos her at 37 with the anaemic hauteur of dyspeptic 60....".   BIRMINGHAM MAIL. November 1945.

It was my first visit to 'Brum', or indeed to any Midland city. I had never previously ventured north of Welwyn Garden City where Uncle Fred had an imposing house and garden. (I realise I have not told nearly enough about Uncle Fred: his addiction to 'Sodi Bic.' as a cure-all for his excesses, his violence when in his cups. I remember a breathless evening at Wandsworth with Dad on the phone to poor beleaguered Auntie Elsie at whom Uncle Fred was throwing the household china... But you can't cram everything in unless it's going to be as long as 'War and Peace'.)

In my innocence I put up at the rather grand station hotel, the Queen's, and crossed the old New Street station bridge for my first visit to the famous Rep in Station Street. It is still just there, for the earnest seeker, almost smothered out of existence by the often rebuilt New Street Station. For many years it was sadly under-used as a theatre school and a platform for the local amateurs. But now Neal Foster (with Paul Scofield and Derek Jacobi as influential Patrons) is trying, and often succeeding, to bring the building back to theatrical life. Logically, it should have been taken over long ago by the New Rep as its second house.

The late J.C. Trewin has called it a brown cigar box. A long, narrow auditorium with a steep rake in both stalls and circle to match the fall from Station Street to Hinckley Street at the back, it seemed to me then, and does still, a near perfect instrument for the actor, without the visual distraction of the glorious Theatre Royal in Bristol which can so often up-stage the player. It was built by Sir Barry Jackson in 1913 with his father's money (Maypole Dairies) and in 1944 he was still presiding over the annual deficit. His founding purpose was starkly simple: 'to serve an art rather than let that art serve a commercial purpose.' The last of the patrons, and indeed the only significant one of the drama since Shakespeare's time, his legacy should have been as secure as Christie's at Glyndebourne. But in the theatre things don't happen so logically and inevitably as that, nor with so much justice. The new Birmingham Rep is a travesty of his ideals on which his bust looks out mournfully from an obscure corner of the foyer.

The night before my audition I sat in the circle and watched the young and lovely Margaret Leighton in 'The Beggar Prince'. It must have been just before Christmas. Another in the cast playing some sort of mandarin and amusing me highly was Peter Streuli. He was to be director of the school. I thought I shouldn't half mind being taught by him. (Decades later he became a revered and successful teacher at Central School.)

For my audition next morning I stood on the same stage, now bare of scenery, and gave them my 'Richard II.'

'Let's talk of graves...

within the hollow crown...'

As I collapsed sobbing to the floor there was a little patter of applause and some approving murmurs from the darkened auditorium, so I thought I had probably done all right. The unusual reaction must have been euphoria at finding, in those war depleted days, a young man who could stand up straight and speak at all. And with exemption from call-up to boot. Not long afterwards I received confirmation that I had indeed been accepted.

Now I had to find somewhere to live in Birmingham. My mother worked at this time (supplementary income being essential) in the shop of a Sidmouth jeweller of the old school called Mr. Mountstephen. (I realise as I go on that some of these names would seem extravagant in a novelist.) He had business connections with Birmingham, then still the workshop for small jewellery, and thus board and lodging, including breakfast and evening meal, were procured for the manageable sum of thirty bob a week (£1.50) with Miss Doris Coleman, 321 Hagley Road, Edgbaston, which my mother's friends assured her was the respectable end.

We were an unexpected and polyglot household, dominated by a group of Austrian Jewish refugees, all women, who had fled the Anschluss. The matriarch was Mrs. Reif, a warm, dignified and charming old lady, who talked to me enthusiastically in her rich deep voice about Mahler and studiously pointed out for me his differences from Bruckner which were seldom clear to us in England then as we had hardly heard either of them. Being Viennese Mrs. Reif missed her Mahler sorely from the Sunday concerts of the C.B.S.O. in the town hall conducted by George Weldon.

Liesel Sternberg, in her early thirties, I suppose, though her black hair in its severe bun was misleadingly ageing, was ready for earnest discussion of drama or music at any hour of the day or night, poised on the landing in her cheap flannel dressing gown with pressing invitation to enter her first floor back to continue the conversation over a cup of hot milk and a home-made cinnamon biscuit.

This is what was new for me about these people. Their seriousness. And wonder of wonder the things they were serious about included art and drama and music and literature as if these were as natural to conversation as football and the weather. They weren't without laughter, but their basic approach to any question was gravely, courteously serious. They conversed together in German, which was the first time I had heard the language in familial use, and to the rest of us in fluently grammatical if charmingly fractured English. The youngest of the ladies was Irene Spanier of whom we saw less because she had a boyfriend, Franz, who visited and whisked her into the great outside. She had a lot of fuzzy dark brown hair and laughed continuously. Whatever she had left behind Franz had replaced. She was happy.

The Britishers who completed the brood were more lugubrious. Miss Slythe (Here we go again!) who was tall and dark and debilitatingly adenoidal and tended to incline graciously from the middle; and her desperately short-sighted admirer, Mr. Turnbull, myopic behind telescopic lenses, creeping carpet-slippered in her wake; Mr. Woodcock, a red-faced commercial traveller out of J.B. Priestley, who came and went and had little influence on events. And me. The only 'Theatrical'.

You will gather it was a large house. Doris Coleman ran it without much fuss or use of the duster, aided by her tiny, frail and elderly mother who could hardly reach up to the wallmounted telephone in the hall. In the kitchen every workspace was covered in cats and piles of newspaper. Breakfast could consist of a solitary pilchard. The evening meal not much more substantial. But this was wartime and we were probably healthier without. Doris was hearty and jolly and red-faced, seldom out of humour, and you loved her. I had a tiny cell-like room where I was completely at home. The one bath was large and cracked and yellow. My mother had made me a dressing gown out of army blanket material for the digs and a thinner one of curtain material for the theatre (these were the days of precious clothing coupons) and I was to post my dirty washing home to her. Parcel post was affordable then, the launderette was yet to be invented and it would never have been contemplated that a boy might do his own smalls.

I was ready for the Birmingham Repertory Theatre School.

My fellow students turned out to be all Brummies so once more I was a foreigner. Girls again. About a dozen of them to only three boys. No wonder they had needed me. Having been a monk for three years I was woefully unprepared for the shoals ahead and nearly capsized on the first day when one of them coolly announced, 'Oh, I'm used to men going about naked. My brother and his friend always do.' This was the world with a vengeance, and with luck and courage flesh and the devil might be just around the corner.

The best thing about the school was that all the classes were taken by the 'pros' in the repertory company and as our classroom was an unused wardrobe at the top of the building we were part of the life of the theatre from the very first.

Each day began with a movement class taken by one of the Rep actresses and went on, basically, to scenes from plays and more scenes from plays. And then in the evening you could find yourself delivering a few lines as a servant in the current production. An apprenticeship in fact, as theatre training should be. Like those Elizabethan boys once again, I found myself apprenticed to a trade.

Being the quite self-consciously famous Birmingham Rep the historical side of our education was never neglected. We boned up on Sir Barry Jackson's modern dress Shakespeare at the Royal Court in the twenties, his creation of the Malvern Festival dedicated to Shaw in the thirties. We rehearsed scenes from his West End successes:

Drinkwater's 'Abraham Lincoln', Philpotts's 'Farmer's Wife', Besier's 'Barretts of Wimpole Street', sometimes under the direction of old hands like magical Maud Gill who had played in the originals and were garrulous with anecdote. We knew we trod boards that had been hallowed by Donat and Richardson and Olivier and Hardwicke and Frangçon-Davies and Edith Evans and others to infinity.

Why had it been so successful in training already two generations of classical actors? Apart from a catholic play choice and a reasonable rehearsal period, I think the answer has to be the building itself. Because of its steeply raked auditorium you presented yourself night after night to a wall of faces. You weren't projecting into or across a void. You found yourself invited, forced even, to inter-act with the audience. It was intimate, 450 seats, but not pint-sized. Not theatre in a room over a pub. There was plenty of depth and resonance if you felt like projecting a 'God for Harry!' to the back of the gallery. But you could equally feel eye-contact with row 'M'. You played 'with', not 'to'. And then again in those days we had the luxury of a permanent ensemble. There was no television to tempt us, few agents to lure, and films were a world apart. If you were lucky enough to get an engagement with the Birmingham Rep you settled down happily for at least a year. Barriers went quickly. We didn't need to prove ourselves each month to our immediate colleagues. Modern actors waste much nervous energy justifying their talents afresh with every fresh engagement. We knew each other. And going out there night after night, in that sweetly reverberating cigar box, we honed our craft. In my acting days there were Scofield, Quilley, Gwen Nelson, Margaret Leighton. Subsequently Finney, Hepton, Pleasance, Neville. The roll call is endless. When I returned as Artistic Director in 1962 there were still Jacobi, Rosemary Leach, Julie Christie, Linda Gardner, Linda Marlowe, Jennifer Hilary, by now bravely fighting off the demands of their agents that they should concentrate on television.

My first servant was in Sir Barry's own version of Griboyedov's TOO CLEVER BY HALF (a title since appropriated for another play altogether). The leading actor was his friend and companion Scott Sunderland whom I'd seen as Colonel Pickering in the Leslie Howard film of PYGMALION. It was amazing to me that I was standing night after night at the foot of a flight of stairs underneath the stage (up which I bounded at intervals to announce a fresh arrival) chatting to a film actor. Pretty outrageous chat, too, from Scott. 'Have you got a Chinese dictionary?' 'No, why?' 'Miss Nelson is playing her part in Chinese tonight.' Scott was a brazen introduction to the tuppence-coloured tradition who used to start his own exit round with a loud hand-clap in the wings.

I fell in love with the girl 'on the book' in the prompt corner. Her name was Charmian and she was a fellow student. Short, with dark hair. Pale face, straight nose, honest grey eyes. A boyishness. Well, I was used to boys. Sir Barry had regular seats in the front row of the circle for the town hall concerts which he hardly ever used and when, through Scott, he discovered I liked music, they often used to come my way. So I'd go with Charmian and then back to her house for tea. They were a quietly prosperous, centred family. Just the three of them. (I think there may have been a brother in the forces.) Father was a doctor and both parents welcomed and encouraged our union. I spent many a happy Sunday evening in the garden, or listening to a play on the radio. We went up to her room and looked at her books and talked. Even read a few poems to each other. It was a nice, warm feeling, this love, but it made no physical showing. I respected her too much and I had no kind of notion what women might want in that direction. And neither, it seemed, had she.

After about six months came our school 'show' on the Rep stage. I was Abraham Lincoln in a scene from Drinkwater's play, Cardinal Wolsey in an excerpt from HENRY VIII, and Mr. Fainall in an act from THE WAY OF THE WORLD. I really had no idea what I was doing or saying in that one but I began to achieve quite a fond and demonstrative relationship with my Mrs. Marwood (whose real name was the musical Hilary Mole). She was the first girl I kissed. Because, you see, I had to in the play. Which was licence to kiss her again outside the play. But regrettably somehow the licence was not transferable to Charmian whom I really cared for and with whom I felt more and more awkward. There was a party at Margaret Leighton's home one night (another Birmingham girl) to celebrate the fact that she had been chosen by Laurence Olivier and Ralph Richardson for their new London Old Vic company, and I'm afraid I got exceedingly drunk, which trebled the licence I took with Miss Mole before witnesses. So the next time I turned up at Charmian's home for a little Sunday spoiling I was received very frostily indeed by her parents and our relationship petered out from then on. She became a very successful business woman and never married. I think perhaps I owe her an apology.

It was now the end of the first term and my money had run out. Time for the great gamble.

They had seen me as various footmen and as Abraham Lincoln. Scott had told me I had come breathlessly close to playing Orlando opposite Margaret Leighton, who was in despair at the sibilant and rather fey war-time reject actor Sir Barry had cast. But it couldn't have been. I was only a student and must be content with playing that second son of old Sir Rowland who bursts on in the last ten minutes to sort out the plot.

'I am the second son of old Sir Rowland,
'That bring these tidings to this fair assembly...'

At least I was getting myself talked about so I thought I'd risk letting it be known that the money was running out. I leaked it in various sympathetic ears and was eventually sent for by Sir Barry.

There he sat in his impressive long book-lined room (one day to be my own) behind his magisterial desk and his elegant cigarette holder, a man whose urbanity masked deep reserve. The fact of his knighthood alone was a matter of awe in that little Station Street cigar box in those far-off days when theatrical knighthoods were not two a penny. 'Sir Barry this', 'Sir Barry that', was whispered up and down the stairs. There was no 'Call me Barry' about it from this benevolent autocrat. He came and went at random hours and to no one's timetable but his own. He had no need to preserve a distance because it was there naturally. But when he did unbend to speak to you on the stairs (everything happened on the stairs at the Rep) it was always with immense kindness, like royalty. On this occasion His Benevolence informed me that I was to be taken out of the school and into the company at a salary of £3 per week. This was rock bottom but it was salvation. Thirty bob for Doris Coleman and thirty bob in the pocket. The gamble had come off.

One of the first small parts I was given was a poet in THE CIRCLE OF CHALK. This was a version by James Laver of a version by the German Klabund of the old Chinese fable that was better treated by

Brecht as THE CAUCASIAN CHALK CIRCLE. But trust Sir Barry to avoid the rebarbative Brecht in this artful manner. A new actor had arrived this Autumn. Very still he was as Prince Po. We all marvelled at his stillness. Then he put on an ill-fitting grey wig and played Reggie in Shaw's GETTING MARRIED with wonderful comic eccentricity. I decided I liked this actor. His name was Paul Scofield. Both of these productions were directed by a woefully irresolute director who had little time for me. 'I don't know, John,' he said to me one day despairing, 'it's something about the way you stand.' But the Shakespeare production, THE WINTER'S TALE, was entrusted to the veteran H.K. Ayliff who, having been cheated of my Orlando, cast me, no doubt this time with B.J.'s full approval, in my first big part, Florizel.

In my short spell as an actor I was lucky to come under the influence of two (and I use the adjective carefully) great directors, the fledgling Peter Brook (not yet on the scene) and this giant of an elder, Henry Kiell Ayliff. 'H.K.'

He was Sir Barry's director of plays on and off since 1921, had been responsible for the controversial modern dress MACBETH and HAMLET in the Jackson Royal Court seasons, and had directed the premieres of all the Shaw plays in Jackson's thirties creation, the Malvern Festival, dedicated to G.B.S. Sir Barry was the ennabler, the Diaghilev, but H.K. was the maker, the craftsman. It often annoys me to read in theatre histories of Barry Jackson's productions of this and that when they were in fact Ayliff's productions. They probably wouldn't have happened, of course, without B.J., but Ayliff was the man who masterminded rehearsals and actually put the pieces together on the stage.

By now well into his seventies, he seemed about seven feet tall, very thin and bald as an egg. He had a deep, sepulchral voice and a countenance not unlike Boris Karloff's. His power over us all was mesmeric. He would sit at rehearsals in a great leather coat with his legs crossed and his head buried in his hands, listening but not looking. Occasionally the dangling foot would start to swing. This news carried through the building like wildfire. 'His foot's swinging.' Because we knew it was the prelude to a withering comment that would reduce some unfortunate actor to the comic scapegrace in a Bateman drawing.

He was a particular terror to winsome young actresses. At a dress rehearsal for THE WINTER'S TALE one of these unfortunates failed to pull her side of the drawstring that would reveal Hermione's statue. 'Fool,' he intoned, in hollow basso profundo from the back row of the stalls (nobody else was ever allowed to sit in the auditorium when he was directing). 'Fool, fool, fool, fool, fool...' And he kept it up like a ground-bass to the end of the scene. On the other hand, to a promising original like Margaret Leighton he would give unstintingly of his time and his knowledge. I knew he had a soft spot for me, either because he thought he spotted talent or because, as he glowered down at me one day and mournfully pronounced, 'I used to look just like you at your age.' Not that this guaranteed me any favours. 'Don't touch her as if she were sticky,' he complained as I daintily handled my not very congenial Perdita. I received extra tuition in the evenings in his little cupboard-sized room half way up the stairs.

'"When you do D..A..N..C..E!"' he would intone, stretching the word out like a chant.

'"When you do dance',"' I repeated, all modern and flip and natural.

'"When you do D..A..N..C..E!"' he insisted, inexorably by the hour.

He never praised. But you knew when he was pleased. He loomed up beside me one day in the prop room next the stage as I came off from a matinee. It was obviously going to be a pronouncement. A confidential one, just for me. 'Watch yourself and listen to yourself and you won't go far wrong.' I remember ever single blessed word he said to me, as if they were the tablets from the mountain. How do you resist an influence like that? Repeated his remarks look trite and unfashionable. It was the tone of voice, the look, his great age and venerability (Only Scott called him Harry. To the rest of us he was 'Mr. Ayliff'. Out of earshot 'H.K.'). What counted most I think was the revelation of an attitude of mind, a caring seriousness, dignifying what we were about as if nothing else mattered in the whole of existence. His were not showy productions. He wasn't interested in self-display. But they had a rightness, an inevitability. You trusted his instinct and went along with it unswervingly. In those days there was never much question anyway of debate between actor and director. 'The Producer' (shades of Reinhardt and Basil Dean) was expected to be authoritarian. But H.K.'s authority was always put to the service of the play.

What I imbibed like mother's milk from both H.K. and Sir Barry was seriousness of purpose. Their theatre was a temple and we were its priests and acolytes. This, combined with the earnest chats at 321 with Liesel and Mrs. Reif, was just the job for a young man newly dedicated to his unexpectedly chosen profession.

At that age you always seem to be in love, and it was not long before I was in again, up to my ears. It was the Christmas run of TOAD OF TOAD HALL. Paul was Toad and I was the Policeman. One day I looked at him in the dock and we both simultaneously realised that we were pulling the same face. Long and down at the corners. Little things like that become the cause of dreaded 'corpsing' (suppressed laughter at private jokes which don't cause the public any mirth at all.) Among the field-mice was a new student with red-gold hair, pale, lightly freckled skin, shy smile and gentle voice. It was hard not to be in love with someone who wore large pointy ears and had a grey painted nose. The Policeman started writing her little notes. 'Dear Jennifer Fieldmouse...' And it wasn't long before he was taking her out for tea and cakes at the Kardomah between our twice daily performances. She lived with her parents in Stourbridge but the late hours were making it necessary for her to look for digs in Birmingham. Naturally I asked Doris and luckily there was another little cupboard going at the other end of the passage from mine. And there in these havens we spent long hours locked in each other's arms or reading poetry aloud. I was an absurdly romantic fellow with a head full of verse. Any love object was immediately idealised and put on a pedestal. And Miss Fieldmouse really was rather enchanting. We had our whole future mapped out - the cottage we were going to live and love in. We neither of us wanted children. We were going to live a poem from then until our dying day.

My lack of practical knowledge of the art of love-making began at last to be genuinely worrying. Miss Fieldmouse and I still never went beyond what the Americans used to call 'heavy petting'. One dark night as we lay cuddling in her cupboard she suddenly removed her nightdress. I was choked with wonder. I wanted to put the light on immediately and feast my eyes on the vision but she wouldn't have it. 'Am I really so different without my nightie?' she wanted to know. I didn't dare remove my pyjamas to display the erection I still had no clear idea how to make use of without causing instant pregnancy. The next day I began urgently buying books on the subject. Dry and clinical they were then. Together we had to leap this hurdle, although I had a faint suspicion that she was already ahead of me - not, certainly, in deed, but in understanding. Yet I felt, foolishly and romantically, that as the man I should be taking the lead. It was all very fraught. You didn't talk about these things then. Not even in the sinful world of the theatre.

Soon after this I had a few weeks off and went home to Sidmouth to see the family who were agog with my bohemian life as retailed in my regular as clockwork weekly letter. Now I wrote to Jennifer every day (Poste Restante Stourbridge, because she didn't want her father to know she was in receipt of a daily billet-doux). On paper my passion knew no limits, ran way ahead of reason. Gradually her replies slacked off to a trickle. Became cooler. Stopped. I went back to Birmingham in dread.

It was over. The Sub-Postmaster in Stourbridge had alerted her father. There had been an almighty scene. At seventeen it was all more than she could cope with.

Her cupboard at Doris's was bare. She was busy rehearsing with her fellow students for Birmingham's summer 'Plays in the Parks'. I called at the rehearsal room. She came out on the steps. White, tense face.

"Red-haired girl in green,
with your innate sense of theatre
you have dress-rehearsed a scene
that will stand you in excellent stead,
time after time,
even to the beautifully stage-managed farewell,
the lips pursed to the warm last kiss,
the touch of pity in sorrow,
the quick turn and disappearance up a flight of steps..."

The hurt yellowing note-books still lie complaining in a bottom drawer. Misery of miseries she even returned my letters.

I was inconsolable. I trudged from pub to cinema to pub with an ache in my throat and tears behind my eyes.

"This is not the time
for open fields
bare heads beneath the sky
neither for the comfort of the single friend..."

Echoes of every poet I had ever read welled up and were regurgitated in my grief. Originality might be a long way off but I hurt as I had never hurt before.

"Something in me
has been killed at the source
heavily bouldered
mightily damned
Call it a thought
a hope, an inspiration
Call it love
Call it the divination
of an eternal somewhat
Call it the voice that shouts above the fox-trot
but in the name of peace
and thunder-weather quiet
call it goodbye..."

"When a gentleman is cudgelling his brains to find any rhyme for sorrow, besides borrow and to-morrow, his woes are nearer at an end than he thinks for," wrote Thackeray in PENDENNIS.

There was a merciful diversion that Autumn. We had a new director. His name was Peter Brook and he was nineteen.

We had a new director because there had been some boardroom bust-up between Sir Barry and H.K. After all his years of valiant service H.K. expected a larger say in play choice and casting than Sir Barry was prepared to give him and so he went, soon to be partnered in West End management with Robert Donat, an old protégé. A pall of gloom hung over the building. It was like the fall of an angel.

Our opening production of Shaw's MAN AND SUPERMAN was to have been directed by another veteran, William Armstrong, but 'Willie' got a West-End engagement and cried off, not before recommending young Master Brook whose E.N.S.A. production of PYGMALION had impressed him. (Entertainments National Service Association, for taking productions to the troops.)

I knew something of Peter, having read a C.A. Lejeune notice in The Observer of an amateur film he had made while up at Oxford of, of all things, Sterne's 'Sentimental Journey.' The breathtaking quirkiness of choice for a home-made movie had stuck in my mind.

Sir Barry, bless him, was always ready to take a chance on youth and Peter's erudition was impressive ('Speaks six languages,' babbled Scott, possibly exaggeratedly.) Even so, on the occasion of our first rehearsal B.J. must have been a little apprehensive because he took up station outside the rehearsal room door, poised to come in and quell riot with a mandarin word or two. (You never had 'observers' at rehearsals in those days. Just the lions and the lion-tamer.)

He needn't have worried. Paul and I in particular rose to the new boy like hooked trout and even the elders were respectful. Actors soon know when they are in the hands of a 'natural'. Orchestral musicians are the same with conductors.

It's a tricky thing to pin down. Natural authority is part of it, but not the whole story. And anyway how do you define natural authority? Something that doesn't require a big stick or special clothes? I suppose an aura of knowing what you're about, together with such a single-minded concentration on the work in hand that nothing short of an earthquake will get between you and it. Something in the eye that leads straight to the mind short-circuiting blah and pretence. Even more simply, I've always remembered what Jack Brymer, the clarinettist, said in a far-off radio memorial tribute to Sir Thomas Beecham. 'It wasn't so much anything he did or said at rehearsal: you just knew you had to play well for him.'

For all one used to enjoy being in awe of H.K. it was suddenly rather heart-warming and privileged to have someone of our own generation to relate to. I was 21, Paul 24. We could even condescend a little to the new boy.

He turned out to be short, shuffly, a cross between a penguin and a teddy bear, with a small, squeaky voice and a beatific smile borrowed from a canvas cherub.

He did three productions that autumn. MAN AND SUPERMAN was fairly straightforward, although he insisted on a lot of intense white light for the Granadan heat. This was unheard of then, when there was usually a preponderance of Strand Electric's No.36 'Surprise Pink' gels in the footlights because its soft violet hue was supposedly flattering to the actor. (Yes, we still had footlights, blinding and protecting us from the groundlings in the first few rows. Fortunately for us, as I said earlier, the steep rake of the Rep helped to lift the rest of the audience into vision. Actors who played in more conventional houses never saw the audience at all and many of them would have been terrified if they had.)

Peter was obviously feeling his way in his dealings with the actor and this enabled us to go our own way a lot in rehearsals which was breath-taking after H.K.'s monitory tutelage. My part of Octavius (Ann's poor 'Ricki-ticki-tavy') was perfection for a young ass emerging from heartbreak and rejection. I had a floppy linen suit for the Spanish scenes which I dubbed my 'sad suit' and indulged myself to the hilt from the safe cover of tongue-in-cheek. This brought my first good reviews and I felt no end important and to hell with field-mice. Paul was a splendid Jack Tanner, rumpled and explosive. Acting with him I was aware for the first time of that extra bond between him and the audience that you were not part of. He didn't deliberately exclude you. It was just as if for the duration of the performance he knew them better than he did you. I came to believe that this is something which marks out the star actor from the rest of us.

Sir Barry immediately offered Peter the next production but he said no thank you and went across to Ireland for a holiday. Genius is a great blessing from the Gods, but so is a private income. Peter's parents were wealthy industrial chemists (remember 'Brook-Lax' anybody?) so worrying about the next penny was never part of his life story.

When he returned he directed us in Shakespeare's KING JOHN. Trewin has written of it frequently. He was the only London critic to catch us and was justifiably proud ever after. I was somewhat unexpectedly cast as Hubert de Burgh, the heavy entrusted with the putting-out of young Arthur's eyes. I might perhaps have expected the

French Dauphin but Peter insisted that to mis-cast was sometimes to cast most well. By which of course he meant the actor would have to dig deeper into his psyche to come up with something acceptable. I elected to give my fascination with Gothic horror movies a run by playing Hubert as a sort of Karloffian grotesque while still making as silken utterance as I could of the verse.

'My lord, they say f-i-v-e m-o-o-n-s were seen tonight...'

I had, you might say at risk of foot-note, a James Whale of a time.

For the first and only time my little Austrian fan club from 321 thought I was better than Paul, who was the Bastard.

He was now also in residence at Doris Coleman's because his wife (Joy Parker, whom we'll introduce later) was having their first baby and living with her parents in Esher. In these months we laid the foundation of a friendship which has been one of my main planks thrown down across the morass. We walked on the Clent hills on a Sunday. Paul striding always a few yards ahead. We brewed Ovaltine night-caps on an ancient gas-ring back at 321 after the show, giggling into the night so uproariously that we brought down the wrath of Doris in her nightgown with her hair unpinned. We were both writing poetry which we showed each other. His was rather good.

I've always believed with Dr. Johnson: 'A man, sir, should keep his friendships in constant repair.' The next three years of working together gave us bags of reference and a useful kit of spare parts for the life-time ahead.

Meanwhile Peter's KING JOHN had brought us all our first review in a national newspaper, J.C. Trewin's in The Observer.

Brook's third and final production in the Autumn on 1945 at the Rep was Ibsen's LADY FROM THE SEA and I thought it a triumph. For the first time I felt he was completely in control, of the design, of the actors, of the play and what he wanted to do with it. In the last act we had one of the longest pauses in the history of the theatre, when Ellida makes her final choice between her husband and the stranger from the sea. Peter had it meticulously stop-watched in the wings and broken after what seemed aeons by the whistle of a steamer in the harbour. It was uneasy. You could feel the pause hold, break, and hold again, before the whistle's blessed release. This was not something that Peter was then prepared to let the actor control with the audience. It was ordained. He was testing his strength, experimenting like a child to see how far he could go in any direction.

I was Arnholm, a tutor, aged 37, in love with the daughter of the house. This obviously called for a character make-up and a stick (I was 21 remember) and earned me the only review I have ever bothered to memorise which now graces the head of this chapter.

CHAPTER FOUR

Stratford-on-Avon
and a Running Brook

*"But oh, 'The Tempest', 'The Tempest'! Nothing whatever
seemed to me here to be capitally done, except Julian Somers's
toad-like Caliban and, some way after, John Harrison's
Ferdinand, which at least had presence and promise."*
                              ALAN DENT. News Chronicle. April 1946.

The other big excitement that Autumn was the news that Sir Barry
Jackson had been appointed Director of the Shakespeare Festival at
nearby Stratford-on-Avon. Banish all notions of a Royal Shakespeare
Company. In those far-off times Elizabeth Scott's unloved brick
building by the river was called the Shakespeare Memorial Theatre,
and it simply housed an annual Festival of Shakespeare's plays from
April to September. Banish, too, all notions of deficit. Commercially it
was a thumpingly going concern. The Festivals of '44 and '45 had been
directed by a somewhat slap-dash though well-loved old Shakespearian
called Robert Atkins. Mad about the Bard I had been across to
matinees and seen his productions of HAMLET and THE TAMING
OF THE SHREW which were all very well in a roustabout fustian way,
but disheartening to a young man who revered Shakespeare above all
things and would have been happy dedicating a lifetime to his plays. I
had reared myself on Poel and Granville-Barker and longed for a return
to something approaching the Elizabethan fluidity of performance.
H.K. hadn't given me this, but his productions had a dignity and
integrity matching his own, which Atkins's lacked. If only a different
style had been prevailing at Stratford that was the place I longed to be.

And now our own Sir Barry had been appointed to be in charge. The
little Station Street theatre was agog with rumour. Of course none of us
would be asked to join the new company. They would all be star actors
from London. But gradually it was buzzed up and down the stairs that

Paul, if no one else, would certainly be going. He and Joy had been dined at the Queens where Sir Barry maintained a suite. Paul didn't let on much. Actors are superstitiously cagey until the contract is signed. But on the stairs HENRY V was whispered. And then of course Peter, the other rising star, would have to be given a production. Peter also had a room at the Queens and Sir Barry's ear. It was all going on over there on the other side of the station while we chafed and bit our nails and wondered.

Scott was an unstoppable source of information, much of it doubtful. No, he wouldn't be going. Sir Barry would need him at home. The opening play would be THE TEMPEST. Paul was being very difficult. Wouldn't go unless Joy was in the company too. Scott was fairly scathing about this. 'Shouldn't have saddled himself with a wife. Great mistake.' Gradually he started to hint that I might be one of the fortunate Stratford pilgrims. He stopped me on the stairs one day. 'They're doing MEASURE FOR MEASURE. You'll be Claudio.' Oh, how I longed to be Claudio!

Eventually, one bright morning, without either asking or being asked, a long envelope appeared in my pigeon-hole at the stage door containing a contract for the 1946 Stratford-on-Avon Shakespeare Festival at £12 a week. This was riches. I had climbed to £7 at the Rep through persistence but had been made to feel rather ungrateful because of it, shades of John Booker. Some parts, too, were specified. THE TEMPEST - Ferdinand. CYMBELINE - Guiderius. LOVE'S LABOURS LOST - Longaville. MEASURE FOR MEASURE - A friar. (This was a blow.) HENRY V - as cast. (I eventually got the Dauphin.)

I was mountains high. But I should have liked to have played Claudio.

First we had to get through the Rep's Christmas production of the satirical revue 1066 AND ALL THAT. This was a regular Jackson Christmas stand-by and earlier West-End triumph. Modest fun for the two 'special guest' actors who went through the show as the Compere and The Common Man (the one before Robert Bolt's), but back-breaking for the rest of us who had to double and treble and quadruple and sing and dance our way through this 'Comic-strip History of England' twice daily. We were for ever charging up and down stairs to and from the dressing rooms changing costumes and wigs and make-ups. I bobbed up as Henry V and Charles II in between historical nonentities various. In long white robes and tonsures that balanced wobbly haloes Paul and I and an actor called Bill Ross were three medieval saints hymning the barbarian Celts:

'Three saints
  From Rome
  Came over the hill,
  If they hadn't
  Left Rome
  They'd be there still.
  They all
  Left home
  To escape their wives:
  (PAUL:) St. Patrick...
     (ME:) St. Pancras...
         (BILL:) And of course St. Ives.'

At the end of which we processed solemnly through the auditorium with collecting boxes in which the audience tradition was to put anything except money. (Yes, there were audience traditions before the ROCKY HORROR SHOW.)

This was poor stuff for the incipient Shakespearians we fancied ourselves to be. In the dressing room to keep our pecker up we sang our own even feebler version of the World War One song from the trenches used in the show, 'When this old war's finee...'

'When this old show's finee,
  Gawd knows when that will be,
  When the larst number is dropped down the dry-een,
  We can get back to some acting agy-een.
  Never no maw-er no maw-er
  There won't be no encaw-er
  This is the last blinking ree-view for me ...e...e
  When this old show's finee...'

So we kept our superior minds anaesthetised throughout the daily grind with always the beckoning light of Stratford at the end of the tunnel.

One day the routine was savagely broken by a phone call. It was my mother. This was so rare it could only be bad news. She had no home telephone. We'd always had one in London, for business, but I had not been brought up to see it as a substitute for the post. Standing by the stage door dressed as a Norman baron from the Bayeux tapestry, with white knuckles I grasped the phone. Dad had died in Hastings. Hastings? 1066 and all this? For a moment it seemed a malicious time-warp, a practical joke. But no indeed. We were required by the police to go and identify the body. Well, I suppose, strictly speaking, Mum alone would have done, but she was going to need support.

Getting leave wasn't easy as there were no understudies at the Rep, but Paul gallantly offered to take on my parts as well as his own so for a brief spell it became 1066 And All Scofield.

Hastings in January. I joined Mum in London and we travelled down from Victoria. We were met at the station by the police and driven to the morgue. They lifted back the sheet and there he was on the slab, blue and pinched and cold. Mum very naturally collapsed in floods. I remained stoic, or more possibly traumatised, in support. In the presence of tragedy I often used to feel out of the body, looking on: a specialist in delayed shock. I suspect because I had yet to meet the Lady smack on face to face. We were then driven by the police to 'an address in Hastings'. There was the unmade bed he had been suffering in. There were his spectacles and some medicines on the bedside table. It all seemed very cheerless and cold, like the worst kind of touring 'digs'. And there too was the lady of his heart. I forget her name but I at once remembered her face. She had been a branch manager at one of the shops. I remembered meeting her when, as I loved to do, I accompanied him on one of his tours of inspection. And I remembered again, with a stab of understanding now, my embarrassment when they had disappeared into the back office for a long time together. Figures silhouetted against frosted glass. Murmuring voices.

The next bit was very dramatic. My mother charged through the house, examining the furniture and exclaiming 'Mine! Mine!' He had certainly ransacked our old home to set up here in Hastings where it seemed they were indeed running a lodging house. The police were sympathetic to the widow, but nothing could be proved and possession turned out to be ten tenths of the law. Some weeks later I received my father's gold wristwatch together with a long letter from his lady explaining how 'those people down in Devon' had ruined his life with their coldness and lack of understanding. How he was always proud of me in spite of my unfortunate choice of profession. How he would have wanted me to have his gold wristwatch which was his most valuable single possession. It was a dignified Omega. I wore it for over forty years until its time-keeping became too eccentric to compensate for its memorial value and I exchanged it for a cheap reliable quartz.

Mum went back to Sidmouth to grow a healing blank over the memory, and I returned to Birmingham. Within twenty-four hours I was back on the stage.

'Three saints from Rome came over the hill...'

'When this old war's finee.'

Oh for Stratford and the Spring!

I had dreams of installing the family there where we would run a lodging house for the actors, but I had no grasp of finances and my capital amounted to £100 from a small legacy which I had come into at 21. (Apparently it would have been more if Dad hadn't borrowed against it.) I even went across and looked at a house, but this was games playing. I hadn't a clue how to make it reality. A mortgage to me was something in the game of Monopoly. It was to be many years before I grasped the fact that you could buy something with money you hadn't got.

Meantime we had to rehearse in London and I needed somewhere to stay. During my melancholy summer in Sidmouth I had been picked up on the Esplanade by a character we shall simply call Tim. I was staring into the sea composing poetry at the time. I soon made it clear to him, in thrall as I then was to Miss Fieldmouse, that my inclinations didn't lie his way. But he was interested in my verse as well as me and we passed many a literate hour in the bar of the Marine Hotel. A correspondence had ensued. He had a one room flat in Hampstead on Parliament Hill and I was invited to share it, no strings attached, for the duration of rehearsals. I don't even remember paying him any rent.

I already loathed my native city with a poet's loathing but the great thing about living on Parliament Hill was that at the end of the day you could stand up there and look back down on The Great Wen as something mercifully escaped from.

Tim was somewhere in his forties. A man of culture and a certain sinister style. He would never confide anything about himself except that the love of his life was an American G.I. who had been killed on the beaches at Salerno. But from a young woman colleague of his at The Soft Drinks Industries (Wartime) Association Ltd. I learned that he was the by-blow of an Earl and had a lordly cousin recently famously prominent at the F.O. I don't think it was a 'con'. He certainly had a patrician profile and accent. He could be intimidating at times and he walked with a slight limp.

His flat was so tiny he confined himself to one row of books. As he read them so he gave them away. The compact little shelf always retained its full complement of twelve. The twin beds filled most of the available space. Mine was under the window. In the daytime they were returned meticulously to divans. He respected my heterosexuality with the utmost propriety and falsely imagined me, from my verse and generally poetical aspect, to be the Byronic hero of countless amours. Here is a letter he sent me later on that year, prior to his visit to Stratford to see me and the plays.

July 26. '46

Dear John,

Re Stratford visit: I do hope you will make no effort to "entertain" me. I like to potter on holiday with no companions save those during opening hours - I hope there's plenty of drink around. Please don't "show me round" I am not making a pilgrimage. Please don't ask me to "go on the river" - it terrifies me. The waves came up and covered Alan when he was shot on Salerno beach. Please don't introduce me to any actors unless it's impossible to avoid doing so. I'm not a sociable person and even with so mild a stage personality as Peter Streuli I feel as ill at ease as an U.N.R.R.A. official distributing soup to Baltic peasants. This sounds like a "don't" list in a boarding house, but I'm so anxious my visit shall not be a burden to either of us. In any case you'll probably be rehearsing and have no time for me anyhow.

My evenings are well occupied so that eating and drinking and sleeping during the day is all that I need. What an unsettling business a holiday is - like waiting in a dentist's anteroom and finding that a tooth hasn't to be drawn after all. Perhaps the annual fortnight is in payment of one's good fortune for having a nice soul-destroying job that keeps the wolf from the door for the remaining fifty weeks. Gratefully one takes up the cross again after the unaccustomed relief. Oh, to drift into sleep one night and never see the morning. How much longer this opening of eyes on an empty day that one's nicest friends cannot cheerfully fill. No visit to a medium can sponge him from my brain or the bodies of others supply his secure warmth and the changing seasons do not touch the grass on which he trod. The tree in the park under which I first saw him sitting disconsolate still stands and if I stare at it he is there again, but not disconsolate. He is telling me instead that he isn't dead, that it was all a mistake and his cap is pushed up from his forehead as it always was in the heat. But in spite of that I have to go home alone and there are the stupid china things and the row of books and nothing else to do but use the toothbrush and go to bed. The Spanish Inquisitor never thought this one up or the writer of Vicious Circle. Of course it won't last forever. I too shall be dust. And nothing on earth will be left to show that two people liked one another a little for such a little while. How disgraceful to love at my age. Love is for the young and it stands to reason for men and women only, in pairs, using their rubber protectives under the crooner's moon. And yet part of me cannot grow old and that part cannot feel the shame it should...

We knew each other on and off for the next couple of years but he faded tactfully out of my life when I got married.

Rehearsals were a see-saw experience. For the first time we were mixing with London 'Star' actors. Robert Harris as Prospero, Valerie Taylor as Imogen... even the small boy playing Ariel, David O'Brien, had starred in a West End success. We rehearsed the first three plays contiguously. Having just been bowled over by Britten's PETER GRIMES at Sadler's Wells in its original production by Eric Crozier I was immensely excited at the thought of being directed by Eric in THE

TEMPEST. Alas, it turned out to be a non-event. He was nice enough and fifteen years later we worked happily together when he was a script editor at the BBC. But he had little grasp of the acting process in 1946, and he couldn't re-create the fluidity of Britten's music in Shakespeare's most static play. And, God save us, there was going to be far too much scenery. Had nobody but me read Granville-Barker?

I didn't enjoy rehearsing Ferdinand. These idealised golden boys from the late plays can be a pain and when you're that age yourself it's difficult to be objective about them. I think I probably looked all right but my handling of the text was far too pedantic. A few embarrassing evening rehearsals were added at Bobby Harris's flat, with Joy along too as Miranda, when they would all look at me pityingly and discuss among themselves what it was I was doing wrong.

One of Sir Barry's innovations for Stratford, as well as decent rehearsal time, was to have a different director for each play.

CYMBELINE was directed by Nugent Monck, O.B.E., a gay old gentleman, sweet, soft-voiced and bald-headed like a little gnome. His fame rested on his creation of the Maddermarket Theatre in Norwich where he directed amateurs on a re-created Elizabethan stage after the manner of William Poel. He at least would be a man after my own persuasion. But no. More disappointment. It seemed that his unexpected translation to the big world had blown his mind. His CYMBELINE was to have as much scenery as THE TEMPEST, including a whole Welsh mountainside for the two lost princes to caper over. I was one of these. A chap called Donald Sinden was the other. We didn't hit it off too well at first. I thought him vocally inflexible and a bit of a pain with his funny stories. He, I am sure, thought me a dull dog and an insufferable prig. But he's not a person you could ever take against for long and before the season was out we were blood brothers off the stage as well.

At the same time there were rehearsals for young Master Brook's LOVE'S LABOURS LOST. The 'West End' actors eyed this infant prodigy with suspicion however staunch Paul and I were in his defence. There was the famous occasion which Peter himself has described in THE EMPTY SPACE. Spliced into his own copy he had a precise choreography of the play, lovingly mapped out with chess pieces on a model stage at home. But the seasoned players were uncooperative.

The blocking had got itself in a twist. The flesh and blood wouldn't go, and more importantly wouldn't stay, where the ivory pieces had. It was a tide in the affairs of men and Peter took it at the flood. He threw his homework away and waded in among the actors. Something more than a traffic jam was broken that day. The whole idea of the director as policeman, the one who keeps the rulebook, went out the window. Peter says openly now that he can only discover what he wants through his actors in the process of rehearsal. In those days the director was always expected to, as Shaw phrased it, 'organise the stage business' in advance. The actor solemnly wrote it down in his book (using pencil only, please. 'Cross DRC. Exit DR.'), went home, learned the lines *and* the moves and came back to the rehearsal room to practise them. A Repetition, as the French have it. You just came in and showed what you could do and the director approved or disapproved. If he disapproved there was not usually much help forthcoming to change things. You went away with a flea in your ear to think again, having possibly (if you were unfortunate enough to work for someone like Basil Dean) been ridiculed before the entire cast. Ayliff had risen majestically above this prevailing attitude with the humility of his utter dedication, so that when he reproved it was more like the Abbot of a monastery. But here was something completely new. The director exposing his human fallibility and admitting that we were on a shared experience, a shared journey.

Peter would be the first to admit, I'm sure, that it didn't all happen in a day. He still retained a measure of the dictatorial, and at that time his frequent changes of mind often seemed more capricious than involving. But it was a toe in the water. Defensive, still with the 'London' actors, he trusted and confided in the tyros from Birmingham. He probably spoiled us rather. For instance he knew that although I was playing Longaville I had an affection for Dumain's poem, 'On a day, Alack the day...' So he switched the poems. We were his mates, as well as his disciples. As he and I were both emotionally unencumbered I seemed to spend a lot of time in his company, either at his family's palatial Hampstead home or in steamy restaurants, talking mostly of the theatre and the job in hand, but sometimes about my poetry of which he was something of a fan. I was managing to get a few pieces published now in specialist magazines like Howard

Sergeant's OUTPOSTS. He also persuaded me to have a medical check-up to find out why I had been graded III. The worst the specialist could find was 'a slight murmur in the heart'. Peter used to wonder why I wanted to be a director. 'Why?' he would say, 'you're a good actor.' As if, had he been a good actor, that would have been enough, would have been the peak experience. And indeed there is a way in which you can interpret his whole directing career as a pursuit of a desire to get closer and closer to living in the actual moment of performance.

His LOVE'S LABOURS LOST took its look from Watteau. We lordlings longed and languished in pale silks and satins in a park in 18th century Navarre where the Princess of France was attended by a sad mute zany. Against this he placed judicious and witty anachronisms. Constable Dull wore a pale blue 'Bobby's' uniform out of a harlequinade and carried a string of sausages. Costard's line about Sir Nathaniel the curate's inability to remember his words in the play within the play was emended from 'Alas, you see how 'tis, a little o'erparted' to 'Alas, you see how 'tis, the part's a bit too much for him.' Peter wanted the public to know what was going on and share the joke. The pedant Holofernes and his friends were viewed at dinner through the eye of a monstrous telescope. These were quiddities indeed and no one, in 1946, had seen their like. Not since Komisarjevsky's pre-war productions had such lèse-majesté been perpetrated against the Bard, and never in recent memory combined with such genuine insight into and reverence for the text. It was the reverence of understanding rather than the fidelity of the scholar's plod.

The production was a delight to be in - though killing on the feet as we never seemed to sit down - and eventually saved the face and sealed the fate of Sir Barry Jackson's first festival.

Unfortunately the first production to be unveiled to the public was THE TEMPEST. 'Oh, The Tempest! The Tempest!' wailed Alan Dent in the old News Chronicle. The designer was Paul Shelving, long time Jackson protegee, but his heyday had been twenty years earlier with Shaw's BACK TO METHUSELAH. He was out of touch now, and Eric Crozier was way out of his depth. In any case I don't imagine there was much he could have done. I'm quite sure Sir Barry saw this one as Shelving's reward for sterling service.

You will recall the play opens with a shipwreck.

For this a vast replica of a Tudor sailing ship had been constructed on rockers so that it would go up and down with the waves on the rocking horse principle. To make an entrance you stood on a high platform in the wings waiting for this monstrosity to rock level with you and then you jumped on. Likewise off. It was an impressive if somewhat dangerous toy and might have been a great success in some future Disneyland - although its motion would probably have seemed a bit monotonous to sophisticated modern tastes. Let me remind you that the opening scene of THE TEMPEST is 65 lines long and plays for about four minutes if you spin it out. So the important thing, for the continuity so vital to any Shakespearian play, is that you should be able to dissolve smartly into the first long scene on the island and Prospero's protracted tale of injustice to Miranda.

Our ship was to sink at the end of the scene. Really sink. (Theatrical spectacle didn't begin with MISS SAIGON either.) The largest trap in the Memorial Theatre stage opened and swallowed it up. At least that was the theory. In practice on the first night it took twenty minutes to go down.

So what have you got? Five minutes shouting in the dark on a monstrous rocking horse, followed by a twenty minute scene change to canned music. (Small consolation that this had been specially composed by Lennox Berkeley as it hiccupped round for the umpteenth time.) Robert Atkins and his last season's colleagues massed in the stalls were the only people having a good time.

Even then something might have been saved if the acting had been up to scratch. But Robert Harris's Prospero was the most boring imaginable. It was like a long Radio 3 poetry reading of the worst kind. He specialised in those and had an iron theory that, in verse, you just said the lines as flatly and with as little inflexion as possible and if, as he had been, you were gifted with a beautiful voice, all things would be added unto you. But the only beautiful thing about Bobby's voice was the timbre, a sort of husky chalumeau. He refused to do anything with it. He didn't appear to think or new-mint the lines. No imagination seemed to be at work. He had, to quote Dent again, 'in his tempers with Caliban... the air of a precentor who has just taken off his surplice and is scolding his choirboys for singing sharp.'

I met Alan Dent the next day over Easter Sunday lunch at Denne Gilkes's. Denne was a retired professional singer who now taught and let off a flat which Paul and Joy (and baby Martin) were inhabiting. After the Birthplace and Holy Trinity Church Denne was one of the essential sights of Stratford, a wonderfully large Madame Arcati-like figure in flowing tweed smocks to be glimpsed bicycling or striding, disappearing round corners like something half seen in Wonderland. Red, cherubic, smiling sometimes quite wickedly like a figure from the prow of a Tudor warship, but with it all a heart of burnished gold. I often used to scrounge Sunday lunch round there, either with Paul and Joy or with Denne in her back kitchen. Her Elizabethan house, up one of those delightful Stratford alley courtyards, then the upper half of a grocer's, is now a restaurant. 'Jock' Dent was an old friend of hers. They used to play piano duets together. Just the three of us assembled for lunch, with Denne hovering over the stove, cigarette drooping from her lips as she talked about Tovey and other great figures she had known, with an inch of ash always threatening to fall into the cooking. Jock was heartily lambasting THE TEMPEST before realising with embarrassment that I had been in it. When Denne thought it expedient to enlighten him he laughed gruffly, said critics and actors should never mingle, but kindly absolved me from the general debacle. I couldn't resist feeling a bit smug when I looked back to those awful evening rehearsals that had so made me smart. But as it had been a disastrous night for the Festival, and therefore for us all, smugness was not really in order. A sombre mood descended on the Stratford Memorial Theatre Company, though mourning would have been premature.

Productions opened hard upon in those days. THE TEMPEST from the Saturday before Easter was repeated twice on Bank Holiday Monday, matinee and evening, two doleful wakes in the light of the reactions, but with a possibly over-lively Ferdinand bouncing on: 'There be some sports are painful...' CYMBELINE was due to open on Tuesday evening, play Wednesday (twice) and Thursday, and then LOVE'S LABOURS LOST opened on the Friday. It seems incredible now but there it is in the scrapbook. And these were productions as complex as anything seen there nowadays, with three totally independent designs making use of all the flying, the traps, and the special rolling stage. It's difficult to escape the conclusion that we just, all of us, worked harder. Dress rehearsals certainly went on all night without a whisper of overtime. I suppose this was immoral. But in a sense we knew we had opted out of the hewing of wood and the drawing of water or nursing inky fingers in the bank. We were privileged, beyond society, doing what we wanted to do. We hadn't made that Sixties leap into assuming that our rewards and conditions should compare with sober necessary citizens.

Nugent Monck's thoroughly old-fashioned CYMBELINE was partly saved by Valerie Taylor's radiant Imogen. 'She has the face, the shape, the voice. She is impulsiveness incarnate. She is, in a word, Shakespeare's Imogen.' Dent again. He wasn't alone. 'An Imogen of April grace... She can fill the stage with light, as we are told Ellen Terry did.' J.C.Trewin in The Observer, who was also shrewd enough to notice how Nugent Monck 'sensibly keeps his production as far forward as possible - an architect should speedily reconsider that Stratford proscenium...' It was to take ten years and Peter Hall before this advice was heeded.

Donald and I enjoyed ourselves larking about our mountainside in monstrous white furs and duetted sensitively enough through the famous dirge 'Fear no more the heat o' th' sun...' Our voices, mine light, his dark, obviously blended to good effect because Peter often used to creep into the back of the auditorium to catch this moment. (Forty years later we were to repeat the performance, two somewhat ageing juveniles, in Argo record studios for a special tape to mark Trewin's 70th birthday.)

So by midweek Sir Barry had had one disaster and one 'will do-quite-nicely-thank you'. Came Friday and LOVE'S LABOURS LOST. After the event even The Times, then still something of a Thunderer, had to admit 'The revival is a feather in the Festival's cap and something of a triumph for Mr. Peter Brook, a producer who has not yet come of age. ' Eric Keown in Punch: 'The originality of Mr. Peter Brook's production is immediately evident in a brief dumbshow prologue showing the tearful women of Navarre confronted by their royal master's ungallant proclamation, and it is sustained with a boldness and judgment made more remarkable by the fact that he is not yet 21.' 'The absurdly young Mr. Peter Brook's production of the absurdly young Shakespeare's LOVE'S LABOURS LOST is an enchanting thing': Alan Dent. You must remember that this was well before to be young in the theatre was a recommendation. The Manchester Guardian took a much more responsible line. '...forget all about Mr. Peter Brook as a possible infant prodigy. Just sit back and look at the play. Even on the first night... one felt that this production was worth going all the way to Stratford to see.'

It was certainly worth going to Stratford to be in, ablaze with style and light and comic crankiness. The Brummagem tyros felt vindicated and proud of their mascot and friend.

Paul's Armado was breathtaking. No boring bombast but an infinitely faded Grandee who reeked word-magic. Almost every performance I would lurk in the stage assembly to hear his soliloquy 'Adieu valour ...rust rapier....be still drum ...for your manager is in love... yea, he loveth...' Not perhaps what the Bard had in mind but such a unique creation that it has stayed with me ever since, quite superceding the original.

I won't make a laborious catalogue of the rest of the productions. HENRY V was a Beta Minus. Never to be Paul's part but what matter? He was winning golden opinions with Armado and his contrastingly lumpen Cloten in CYMBELINE (to which he was yet to add a fantastical Lucio in MEASURE FOR MEASURE).

I was enjoying camping it up as the Dauphin. (As I tried to make sense of his long speech about his horse at the first reading the lady producer - an ex-Shakespearean actress of note - said briskly 'Yes, that's very nice dear, but you'll have to speed it up a lot.' We were given no quarter in those days, let alone the benefit of the doubt.) Hugh Griffith camped it up even more outrageously as my dad, and the Lady Producer placed the only interval between the French and British night scenes thereby striking Shakespeare's precious continuity and contrast a mortal blow through the heart.

Mum and Shirley came up for a week to holiday and see the plays and meet my friends. Shirley who was twelve fell head over ears for Don who played up to her magnificently. My mother, who had also ventured to Birmingham to see me as Florizel, never commented on my performances. I assumed she was just basking in reflected glory. However, after HENRY V she said confidingly, 'I liked you in this one.'

It was not, for me, an amorous season. Perhaps I had subconsciously taken my cue from those lords of Navarre we were impersonating - 'A twelvemonth and a day... LONGAVILLE: I'll stay with patience; but the time is long.' I fancied the boy David O'Brien more than any of the women in the company but I wasn't chasing after that chimera. I suppose part of the problem was that my co-star, in both THE TEMPEST and LOVE'S LABOURS LOST, was Joy. Best friends' wives were quite untouchable and a bit of a mystery in fact. I feel much closer to her now. But then, in those unregenerate times... She was my friend's wife. Like his pipe. Or his bicycle. I had no independent views about her, except that I was privately rather grand about her acting ability as compared to mine. A few years ago the director Andrew Wickes who is a magpie record collector came across an ancient 78 r.p.m. recording of THE TEMPEST on six scratchy sides of black shellac. The label with the usual parsimony of those days just said The Shakespeare Memorial Theatre Company. No cast list. No date. Could I identify it? Indeed, indeed. There we all were, voices from the past, and I just dimly remembered the recording sessions immediately before the disastrous opening. It made sobering listening. The blessedly anonymous Ferdinand was quite awful. Mannered and precious. But Joy was alive and spring-like across the years with a totally unaffected freshness that didn't date at all. I immediately reached for the telephone and told her so. I needed absolution for my far-off sinful pride.

It wasn't all work though. There was a lot of bicycling on the still empty roads and walking the unpolluted countryside and punting on the unsullied Avon. Don and I, with David O'Brien as cox, won a company pair-oar boat race.

I lived at the Rose and Crown, a pub with rooms, in Sheep Street. This was handy for visitors like Mum and Shirley or Tim. The landlord was in the early stages of DTs and cackled maniacally at nothing at all but his wife was buxom and smiled upon me. They used to defy the law after closing time with endless pints for the favoured few over darts sessions in the bar, which was marvellously unwinding for me after the show. Fortunately the local beat Bobby was one of the star players. I drank more beer than ever before or since. One night, very late, Joy and Paul turned up on the doorstep. They had something very serious to impart. They doggedly marched me round the nighted streets of Stratford in a desperate attempt to sober me up. I remember capering foolishly in the road like Charles Laughton in HOBSON'S CHOICE. I finally came to my senses over strong black coffee in their kitchen. Paul had been offered a film test with Universal Pictures in Hollywood. But only on condition that he signed for seven years.

Of course he turned it down and he didn't need me to tell him.

The Rose and Crown had two gay waiters, tiny old men like Tweedledum and Tweedledee. Harry was the comic. He had an astoundingly affected accent. 'What's that?' asked Don, who regularly came to lunch, looking at the dessert on his plate. 'Pah Máhbah,' Harry would announce and flounce back into the kitchen.

Johnny was more sinister. If there was a girl on the scene he would corner me in the Gents and lisp in a nasal Brummie accent, 'Are you going to po-oke her then, John?'

A year went by and John poked nobody.

CHAPTER FIVE

Stratford-on-Avon
Full Stream

"John Harrison (in the quaintest etceteras) is a lyrically intense young Ferdinand to the wide-eyed Miranda of Daphne Slater."
BIRMINGHAM EVENING DESPATCH, April 1947.

During the season I had met a visiting Arts Council luminary. In those days the recently renamed wartime Council for the Encouragment of Music and the Arts (C.E.M.A.) boasted regional directors and Cyril Wood was the one for the South-West. With the idea of giving my career a push I had invited him for a drink at the Falcon Hotel.

"What'll you have, Cyril?"

"A Pimm's."

I nearly fell through the floor. All we ever drank was beer or shandy. Here was sophistication: and a hole in the spending money. But it turned out to be well invested because he invited me to take part in a winter tour of the West Country with something he called his Christmas Merry-Go-Round. Singer, pianist, two actors, a fiddler and Cyril, who read boring stories aloud at the heart of it all like a Dickensian Christmas uncle. I mugged up Edgar Allan Poe's The Raven (my party piece ever since) and with a young actress from Australia dramatised the White Knight's scene from Alice. We were to open in Bridgwater and play Penzance and other places I have forgotten. But I do like to remember that one of them was The Cosy Nook, Newquay. This was a timely break, as I had been re-booked for the 1947 Festival but with a looming gap between the end of September and the beginning of rehearsals in January. The only snag was that the tour overlapped the start of rehearsals. I asked Peter, who had this time been very properly rewarded with the opening production of ROMEO AND JULIET, if this would be O.K. (I was going to be Benvolio.) In a fit of absent-mindedness he said yes.

This still left a blank through October and November so Don and I decided to fill it out with our own show. We cobbled together an amazingly indigestible programme of our favourite bits and pieces and hired halls in our respective home towns of Sidmouth, Devon and Ditchling, Sussex. The posters announced:

JOHN HARRISON AND **DONALD SINDEN**
of the 1946 and 1947 STRATFORD-UPON-AVON
FESTIVAL COMPANY
in

CURTAIN UP!
A NON-STOP DRAMATIC RECITAL.

The programme shows us indulging ourselves indiscriminately. He did great chunks of HAMLET. I riposted with Faustus's descent into hell. He made me feed him through scenes from his favourite drawing-room comedies (on which I am sorry to confess we paid no royalties) and I allowed myself Bottom in the DREAM. It was the most brazen ego-trip imaginable. Our names appeared in the programme fifteen times each. Our final Sidmouth performance was on Friday, December 13th. We were having such a good time I don't think we even noticed the omen. Not even when we counted the takings from the half-empty house.

I was then able to stay on for Christmas with the family. We had been forced to move from the snugness of Sid Lane (for which the owner had other plans) and had been for some time installed with the widow Davey in her semi at 24 Peaslands Road. Shared facilities but we occupied most of the house. Grandma was by now not long for this world, confined to bed and confusing me with Fred, her son. I was in expansive mood, very much the actor on leave, leading the party downstairs in Christmas games and, in a daring access of self-indulgence, the Grand Passion having failed me, I treated myself to a new gramophone.

It was an HMV electric portable, table standing but quite chunky, with auto-change mechanism. For those who don't remember this system you piled six 78 rpm discs on a precarious central spindle contraption which allowed them to drop one at a time on to the turntable giving you something like half-an-hour's barely interrupted music. I intended to console myself with this wonder through another bachelor Stratford summer.

In the Sidmouth record shop there was only one sustained piece of music in automatic couplings in stock. (The sides, you see, had to be coupled 1 and 6, 2 and 5, and so on.) It was Elgar's violin concerto. I had never even heard of this. Elgar to me meant Land of Hope and Glory. Conquering initial feelings of disappointment I bought it anyway to demonstrate my magic machine.

You can't beat an innocent ear. There were no fancy sleeves in those days to tell you anything about the music or the performers. In this case, for some reason, there was not even an album to enclose the records. I expect the shop had lost it. Just six discs in plain brown paper sleeves with red labels on the discs giving the barest information. 'Concerto in B minor Op.61. Yehudi Menuhin (violin), London Symphony Orchestra, Conductor Sir Edward Elgar O.M. Bart.' Only the now legendary performance by the boy Menuhin with Elgar himself conducting!

Oh, the yearning of that main theme in the first movement, the leap-in-the-chest nostalgia of the slow movement - and that extraordinary last movement accompanied cadenza that seems to achieve orgasm and end in post-coital release... 'Herein is enshrined the soul of...' 'Rarely, rarely comest thou, spirit of delight...' And I had stumbled into it by accident!

Now of course I have Zukerman and Kennedy as well. But I still return gratefully to the young Menuhin.

My old prep school chum Colin, on a summer visit a few years back, had turned me on to Beethoven.

"Cor, you should hear the 7th symphony, John. It's like a Scotch reel," he had said with the sort of excitement the young nowadays reserve for Busted.

My next purchases when I arrived in London for rehearsals, at a wonderful bargain browser place that used to exist just off the Tottenham Court Road, were the 'Eroica' and the 7th in the performances by Weingartner.

It was all orchestral music at this stage. Haydn's 'Surprise' symphony and the 'Military.' A few concertos. Mozart's piano concerto in A by Denis Matthews with the C.B.S.O under George Weldon. Haydn's trumpet and Mozart's flute and harp. Beethoven's 4th with Schnabel. Still nothing earlier than Haydn or later than Elgar. It was like a complementary world that I was just venturing into. I knew, the further I got in, I would find the counterpart to every human emotion and experience. There was plenty of time and no hurry. I was visiting opera too when I could - Figaro, Don Pasquale, The Mikado. Ballet I had trouble with but went on persevering for a few years yet.

But where am I rambling? Records again, you see. I become a total anorak.

At Bridgwater, in Cyril's Christmas Merry-Go-Round, I again touched the fringes of romance. There was a nice girl called Anne whose people were big at the Arts Centre there. I was billeted on them in their comfortably moneyed home and Anne drove me out to see their cottage in the Quantock hills. I was alone there with Anne and two dogs. No young man of 22 today could pass up such an opportunity. But I was greener than the grass on the hills. We kissed, and I could feel her puzzlement that I wasn't taking matters further. On our way back in the car she said it was nice not to feel things always had to end in the same old way. I suppose I knew what she was talking about.

I can see now that such paralysing shyness with the opposite sex could easily have edged me into homosexuality.

When I eventually turned up for the ROMEO AND JULIET rehearsals Peter said to me rather petulantly, 'Where have you been?' I reminded him of our agreement but he had clearly forgotten. I had missed a week's rehearsals.

I have just one cache of personal letters that I've kept from the 1940's. Everything earlier went up in a bonfire of all the embarrassments some time in the 1950's. Anything later was quickly consigned to the wastepaper basket. But I'm glad I have these. They work on the little grey cells like a time machine.

Several are from Peter and cover the period between LOVE'S LABOURS LOST and the '47 Festival, when he was working on ROMEO AND JULIET. There's a postcard from Portugal where he went for inspiration. Anybody else would have gone to Verona. Peter went to Portugal.

"Your letter forwarded; thanks poems: adore 'Boat Song': can't promise anything September as own plans in air: have had to postpone doing WHITE DEVIL - however, will do all I can on return, but don't put all yr eggs in 1 basket."

By then I'd put them in Cyril Wood's.

Early in September I'd found, I think it must have been, a facsimile reprint of a Romeo and Juliet Quarto in a Stratford booksellers, bought it on his behalf and sent it to him.

"Many thanks. V. valuable. Enclosed, with gratitude, ten bob. Will owe you 6d. Have meanwhile got hold of Variorum, which includes complete reprint of Q1 and also a translation of Lope de Vega's 'Monteschi e Capolleti' in which J. wakes up when R. enters tomb, so they emerge, make friends with Papa Capulet & live happily ever after. Rather a better end, I feel! Curiously Lope's play has a certain beauty of its own. P.S. Your new poem 1st rate, much to my taste."

One from the 16th November. "Things are hectic. No R and J yet settled, but thousands seen. Saw Paul. Heard that you had been in town without phoning me. Suppose that as a not-replier-to-letters I can hardly grumble... Liked Pome. Interested to hear that Nugent Monck had produced Esme Percy as Romeo in 1904, but would have been much more delighted had you discovered that in 1903 Esme Percy had produced Nugent Monck as Romeo'.

The search was on for two young unknowns. Peter had written to Shaw, by this time the Sage of Ayot St. Lawrence, who advised him to go for really young lovers and realistic fights.

In the end his choice lighted on Daphne Slater, that year's R.A.D.A. Gold Medallist, who had just won a film contract with Herbert Wilcox on the strength of a cameo in THE COURTNEYS OF CURZON STREET, an Anna Neagle epic then still in the can. She was nineteen. Flaxen-haired. Royal Copenhagen porcelain, but with a Dutch look too about the face. Certainly not Veronese.

Laurence Payne got Shakespeare's biggest pill. He was far from a beginner, a twenty-nine year old veteran of Arts Council tours, but he had the Italianate good looks that would make the pair of them look like lovers from different ends of Europe rather than different households in the same city. It was given out that he was twenty-six.

Peter was content. I had put in a strong plea for an actress called Jane

Wenham whom I'd seen as the daughter in Laurence Olivier's production of THE SKIN OF OUR TEETH. If I had been listened to several people's life stories would have been different and some would never even have happened.

I thought I had better show willing with a little background reading to make up for my current indulgence in "The Mysteries of Udolpho". Peter responded on the 29th December. "As for 'Romeo', there are a mass of things I would like you to read, but alas none of them are written yet! I've only read tantalising bits of Udolpho...Happy New Year..."

When I finally turned up to rehearsals I went into a huddle with Paul and Joy. What was she like, the new girl? 'She wears hats,' they said. Indeed she did. Blue ones usually. This was unheard of in our circles.

I didn't see much of her during the London rehearsals. Benvolio and Juliet's paths hardly cross. I had most of my stuff with Larry Payne, and Paul as Mercutio. We all got on well, but we both towered over poor Larry, which wasn't helpful to him, particularly on his first entrance when he has to moan on to Benvolio about the insubstantial Rosaline. Don was Paris, so I didn't see much of him either. He towered over Larry in the second half of the play.

Shakespeare was rarely given uncut then, even by Peter Brook, so he said my long speech to the Prince about the brawl had to come down. At least he allowed me to cut it myself. We had gruelling sword-fight rehearsals with Patrick Crean and Rex Rickman which terrified me. After the Montagu v. Capulet below stairs hassle at the beginning there were long round wooden staves lying discarded all over the ground, always in different places, which Benvolio and Tybalt had to negotiate throughout their own devilishly tricky rapier encounter. A bit like log-rolling if you were unlucky. My heart was in my mouth every performance until the Prince's welcome entrance: 'Rebellious subjects, enemies to peace...'

Peter couldn't make up his mind about the Chorus. I badgered him to let me do it but he fancied the idea of a disembodied voice and had secret dreams of doing it himself. He even had a private go at recording it. Presumably disappointed by his own efforts he let some of the rest of us have a try and eventually my version was chosen. It was planned to boom out mechanically from the expensive new Decca sound installation. At the end of the season I managed to acquire the disc and to my surprise found his version at the end of the side. He ends with a charmingly nervous little upward 'O.K?'

As the rest of the clutch of opening plays were to be revivals from last season the London period was given over entirely to Romeo, and as Benvolio disappears from the play after Mercutio's death I had quite a lot of time off. For some reason I was not staying with Tim this year but with my Auntie Ethel in Balham. She was not kith and kin but in my class we were brought up to call all our parents' friends Aunt and Uncle which caused some initial confusion about the family tree. Auntie Ethel was my mother's age, the daughter of the long ago mentioned 'Grandma Jennings' (Grandma's unexpectedly racy friend: Chap. 1). She was married to Uncle Walter whom she called 'Wo' and they were a couple of childless middle-aged lovebirds with a snug but rigid life-pattern. 'Wo' rose regularly at six to leave the house by eight because he couldn't bear to hurry. In the evenings he sat carpet-slippered by the fire, pipe in mouth, reading thrillers, while Auntie Ethel knitted. Commentators often bewail the loss of the sparkling family hearth before Television. There you had it. In spite of this she was a very jolly soul, loving my tales of rehearsals, and our family believed that she had subdued herself unnecessarily to Wo's undemanding demands. She certainly wanted to hear all about Miss Slater whose fame had reached her Daily Mirror - 'DAPHNE HAS FILM TEST ON STAGE'.

It was a legendarily hard winter. We arrived at Stratford during an Ice Age which was soon followed by The Great Flood. We had to be ferried to the Stage Door in punts. But in spite of the weather there was a better feeling around this year because the senior figures in the company were Beatrix Lehmann and Walter ('Dickie') Hudd, a couple of devoted socialists (It was even whispered that they were C.P.) who practised what they preached. They had no 'side' and were great on company spirit. 'Bea' played Juliet's Nurse, and 'Dickie' her father Capulet. Bobby Harris was still there, somewhat demoted to the Prince of Verona (where he wasn't 'o'erparted' but came on in a blaze of strength). It was only a temporary demotion. He still had Richard II and Faustus (both directed by Hudd) to look forward to.

FAUSTUS was another revival. It had come in at the end of the previous season when we were all totally knackered and was a neat little object lesson for this future director. We had grown used to the cavalier attitude of directors to time, particularly actors' time, so when we read Dickie's precise rehearsal calls we chuckled disbelievingly. I was playing the Good Angel. He and the Bad Angel pop on and off at intervals throughout, wrestling briefly for Faustus's soul, so Leonard White and I anticipated a fair bit of hanging around. We examined the call-board. 'Angels 11.10' it would say, with immaculate precision. Followed by 'Seven Deadly Sins 11.35'. We smiled cynically. But when we turned up at 11.10 he was ready for us and when we looked at our watches on leaving it was 11.35. So all right there's more to rehearsing than the punctuality of a German railway line, but it was tonic, I can tell you, and had a nothing but beneficial effect on our performances. Then again, the dress rehearsals. The preceding production of MACBETH had featured a full-scale shouting match between Macduff on stage and the choleric director in the auditorium. Now the FAUSTUS set was perilously high and precarious. At one point it threatened to fall and engulf the lot of us. 'Don't worry, boys,' came Dickie's silken, gentle, hardly raised tones from the stalls, 'it's all right, boys.' And it was. This certainly taught me that the Captain on the bridge should never lose his cool.

I'm afraid I thought Peter's ROMEO a mess. He was obsessed with his central pair and let many of the rest of us whistle for rehearsal time. I remember Paul and me desperately taking ourselves off to the circle foyer and working out something for the Mercutio conjuring scene after the ball, then literally grabbing Peter by the scruff of the neck and forcing him to watch it. He chuckled a lot and that's how we played it.

One day he asked me to watch Juliet's 'Gallop apace...' soliloquy from the dark at the back of the stalls. It is an incantation to sexual awakening imbued with all the palpitating innocence of a teenager.

'Spread thy close curtain, love-performing night,
That runaways' eyes may wink, and Romeo
Leap to these arms untalked of and unseen.
Lovers can see to do their amorous rites
By their own beauties; or, if love be blind,
It best agrees with night...

Hood my unmanned blood, bating in my cheeks,
With thy black mantle; till strange love, grown bold,
Think true love acted simple modesty...'

Not in this production. Juliet lurched downstage and gobbed it at the audience like a randy old hag on the verge of menopause. I was horrified and had to tell him so. Why deliberately throw away all the advantages of the actress's naturally fluttering youth? Her porcelain fragility? He was deeply offended. Peter, like me, was in thrall to sex-in-the head and would dearly have liked his Romeo and Juliet to make it to sex-in-the-bed, off-stage as well as on.

He became very high-handed with us all towards the end of the rehearsal period in the ball and fight scenes, masterminding through a loud-hailer like a midget Josef Von Sternberg. Only Nancy Burman, our brilliant production manager, pouring copious oil prevented downright mutiny.

A great deal was left to chance inspiration at the dress rehearsals. Mind you, I learned something brave from this too: never be too proud to change or admit mistakes right up to the last practicable moment. But some of Peter's changes were pretty costly in talent and manpower. He's written himself how he and Rolf Gerard, the designer, as each new lovingly crafted piece of scenery was trundled out on to the stage, hysterically called out 'Cut!' 'Gradually,' he writes, 'we came down to an empty orange arena, a few sticks - and the wings were full of elaborate and expensive discarded units. We were very proud of ourselves, but the management was furious.' This was learning in public with a vengeance.

It was not until one of the final dress rehearsals that he decided to cut the reconciliation of the families, thereby removing any ray of hope or promise from the poor children's deaths. Here, no doubt, he was anticipating Theatre of Cruelty before anybody had given it a name. Dickie Hudd's Papa Capulet face was ashen with horror but he still retained his gentle dignity and supported the new young genius with a touching loyalty that brushed off, as it was meant to do, on the rest of us.

Peter was still improvising towards Chorus. To general relief he threw out the canned voice at the last moment and allowed me to do it traversing the stage in semi-darkness in an enveloping black cloak. He even put back, at my request, the second chorus which had been cut, though I think this was to cover a scene change. Finally, to add insult to the senior players' injury, he awarded me the Prince of Verona's final speech as a closing chorus. This time I traversed the stage in the opposite direction...

'A glooming peace this morning with it brings...'

I was very happy about this. It certainly made it worthwhile waiting for the curtain call, although the 'two hours' traffic of the stage' had by now grown to nearer four.

The opening night was stormy, both in the theatre and outside. Not like THE TEMPEST's storm the previous year which had simply swallowed the production in its maw. This was a Lear-like storm as lightning and thunderbolt were hurled at the production's head from wildly dissenting critics which did the box office no harm at all.

Let us hear from age and youth. Ivor Brown magisterial in the OBSERVER.

'Avonian Stratford, blamed of recent years for humdrummery, attempts fanfares and has already been no less blamed for their flourish. I salute this spirit of adventure, but cannot welcome the deed in the case of ROMEO AND JULIET, which has just opened the seasonal fixture list. Peter Brook, the young producer, who started with much achievement on his side, has made a gallant mess of things for once. He claimed (in an interview) to have studied the play exceeding long and hard: in the end he has entirely missed the point. As producer of "Love's Labours Lost" he had received the Bardic warning: "Small have continual plodders ever won." Let him read less next time and trust in common sense the more. This play, one must, at risk of platitude, advise him, is one of the finest helpings of verbal noise in a language and literature notably rich in such aural provender. Here is a lyric love indeed, and, if the poetry is slurred, if the matchless wedding of melody and moonshine be dissolved, then the horrified listener may contemplate a leap into the Avon, now torrential...

Brook's idea is to make the play a simple tale of boy meets girl and cast it for youth and simplicity.

Plot and poetry appear to be trifles to him. His cutting certainly does not simplify, and, despite cutting, he lengthens the "two hours traffic" to three and a half. And what if the chosen young couple can't cope with the glorious stuff? What if one has to mutter in anguish, "It is the sparrow, not the nightingale, that nightly chirps upon the Stratford Stage". The immature Juliet of Daphne Slater may look as young as Tenniel's Alice, but her untutored prattling and sobbing of Verona's passion will not do. Laurence Payne I have known as a good character actor, and the melancholy, Hamlet side of his Romeo is right enough. But with the superb lung-music of enchanted lovers he could not cope. In defence of both I would say that they were wrongly cast, worse directed, and nonsensically enscened. The hapless players are not to be faulted for that.

Consider the muddle. There is to be no glamour - just "two lost children" as Brook calls the lovers. Accept that. Surely children imply homes, walls, parents, backgrounds - in this case the sultry heat of passion-racked Verona. If you want to deromanticise the tragedy, play it as a family matter and house it so, too. That would at least be logical. But at Stratford a vast, cold blue cyclorama, with fragmentary scenery in front, suggests chiefly that the play is happening among a few megaliths and air-raid ruins which have been blown into the stratosphere and have somehow stuck there. I never had the slightest sense of earthy and domestic circumstance or of an Italian city. We seemed to be outside the walls not penned within them. True there was abundant pageantry as well as a spate of brawl. But the costumes were so oddly assorted that the hordes of Chu Chin Chow must have swarmed west and occupied Verona. Amid all this what could "lost children" do - except get lost up to the forehead, especially as they had apparently been cast without relevance to the vocal challenge... The company as a whole jumped to it with vigour and displayed all the alacrity, juvenility and muscularity which Brook could fairly claim for his production. But the foolish scenery and unhappy music, meandering into some of the finest lines, were sorry handicaps. "What if this mixture do not work at all?" asks Juliet, vial in hand - and with tragic aptness to this production. Peter Brook will mix again and mix better. But he must really stop trying to put all previous producers in their place...'

Meanwhile the twenty year old Kenneth Tynan was up at Oxford with severe colon-itis writing reviews which "nobody paid me for the right to print... until I came down... in 1949".

'Torrid', I think, may be the word. Or 'sultry': if, that is, we can free them of their associations with Tahiti or Southern California, and make them mean what they ought to mean: something intemperately dry, tawny and madding. Peter Brook plays out this young tragedy under a throbbing vault of misty indigo: the streets crackle underfoot with aridity: it is very warm indeed. Canopies, loosely pendent from the flies, are a necessary shield against this daze of heat. Mr. Brook's colours are dusty whites, sun-bleached reds and dull greys: and the brown, somnolent crowds in his market-place are all bemused and flyblown. The sets, designed by Rolf Gerard and poised, tenuously erect, on slim flimsy pillars, are thrown open to the bare sky: silhouettes balancing in the naked sun. Everyone sweats. When they are not sprawled in a stark, Mediterranean torpor, when they are moved to seize at their swords, they do so moodily, savagely and à outrance. The beggars, clowns and men-at-arms who people Mr. Brook's Verona shape themselves into groupings of splashed tints and high noon-tide frenzy: witness the Capulet revelry and the deaths of Mercutio and Tybalt. The music (by Roberto Gerhard) is tired: wan reeds, distant timbrels, and the lazy beat of tight-strung drums. The whole work is a miracle of masks, mists, and sudden grotesquerie. We come to wait intelligently for the pure drops of unexpected naturalism which Mr. Brook teaches his actors to wring out of Shakespeare's lines; for the novelty of inflexion which, taken with the rest, tells us that he has acquired a recognisable style. There is an elderly group of critics which insists that Brook is not nearly old enough to appreciate ROMEO: to them I say (and I hope rudely) that they are not nearly young enough. ROMEO is a youthful play about miserable young people who confuse catastrophe with tragedy: it is precious, repetitive, superpathetic, overbold - all the tiresomeness of adolescence is in it. How it languishes in the wastes between Juliet's feigned and Romeo's real death! (Mr. Brook does not help matters by cutting the preceding scene between Juliet and Friar Lawrence.) These lovers are not big enough figures; they are too weak for the true woe of tragedy. 'Alack, alack,' says Juliet, 'that Heaven should practise stratagems upon so soft a subject as myself!' That is the key to the play's lameness: they are both too soft, too easily dead.

All that a bizarre imagination and perfervid scholarship can do for the play Mr. Brook has done. Consider the strange solitary tree (can it be a medlar?) which he plants, spear-shaped, in Romeo's Mantuan exile: touches like this are foreign to our stages, and welcome. His cast is obedient to him... Paul Scofield's Mercutio, not the noisy bragger who usually capsizes the play and then leaves it to founder, but a rapt goblin, ruddy and likeable (his pensive delivery of the Mab speech, with demoniac maskers grouped around him, crowns the scene with authentic faery)...and the un-named figure of Chorus, shrouded in greys and far-off blues. I shall remember him for a long time, speaking the lovers' epitaph (rightly belonging to Escalus) at his decent, graveside pace: it pelted one's ears with magic.

I did not wholly sympathise with Laurence Payne's stocky Romeo. There was not an ounce of spontaneous melancholia in all his downright body. Masterly staging, however, came often to his aid: the first encounter with Juliet was a lovely prelude. The stage is emptied for them - he alone in perfect white, she drawn through the upstage fogs to touch lips with him...

About Daphne Slater I am surer... physically she is dissonant with the hard, thick-lipped charm of Mr. Payne. But her pride is her youth; with some other, less *modern* Romeo, I can imagine no better Juliet. Rightly she is excitable and impetuous; and she communicates this compulsive ardour until it becomes our panic as well as hers.'

('Chorus' remained 'un-named' until the printers had caught up with the change of plan.)

It is clear from these two reactions that Brook had the future on his side. Obviously from inside the production I couldn't see all that Tynan could from the outside - and many of the innovations that he was endorsing I perhaps now took for granted. Yes, there was continuity, albeit ponderous at times, colour, flashes of excitement, and perhaps the older critics were a little obsessive about their 'word-music', as if these were lovers in Wagner or Debussy rather than an Elizabethan play. But some things, the cutting of the Friar's explanation to Juliet of how the potion would work, the cutting of the reconciliation of the families (War and Peace without the Peace), seemed to me just perverse and I don't remember Peter ever trying to justify them.

And then I knew that most of these 'pure drops of unexpected naturalism which Mr. Brook teaches his actors to wring out of Shakespeare's lines', this 'novelty of inflexion', had been arrived at by the majority of us by accident and our own devices. Mind you, a significant part of directing is allowing just this sort of thing to happen.

My favourite moment was one that in the past had always fallen unnoticed to the scissors, the little scene of the Capulet's servant Peter ('Got up as a Darkie. Why?' asked one critic in the language of the day), his little scene with the musicians outside the supposed house of death. Their inconsequential chatter in counterpoint to the mourning within was the most truly affecting moment in the whole production, and the most truly Shakespearian.

'Musicians, O musicians! "Heart's ease", "Heart's ease"; O, an you will have me live, play "Heart's ease".'

Perhaps we should let Philip Hope-Wallace, most liberal and urbane of critics, have the last word.

'...despite all this good detail, it is an oddly remote and untouching ROMEO. However, one well sees why people nowadays find it worth while fighting their way to Stratford, and I want to emphasise that if this kind of performance were to be given in Prague or Moscow, we should never hear the last of it.'

After the notices appeared Miss Slater, who was nothing if not outspoken, was heard to announce that she might as well return to London and resume her film career; which didn't go down too well with the rest of us.

Now we started to dredge THE TEMPEST up again from the bottom of the sea. However waterlogged it might have been you couldn't stop the school parties from coming. It was an 'earner'. A new director had been found, Bobby's friend Norman Wright who was basically a radio man. The ill-fated ship was consigned to the timber yard, to groan it out with the rejected impedimenta from Verona, and was replaced by a lot of unimaginative lurching about by the actors on the forestage. As the run proceeded I got so bored by this disorganised melee that I no longer went down with all hands and used to save my energies for my first appearance on Mr. Shelving's too too solid island,

'Where should this music be? 'I th'air or the earth...'

which gave me an extra half-hour's grace at the start of the show.

Joy was translated to Ariel which she did very balletically, all blue and silver and Kurt Jooss. And Miss Slater was my new Miranda.

It was bound to happen...

I was carrying unfulfilled love around like a ton of explosive. As Shaw's wise Bishop says in GETTING MARRIED, 'Nature abhors a vacuum, Antony. I would not dare go about with an empty heart: why, the first girl I met would fly into it from sheer atmospheric pressure.'

It was spring. She looked lovely in her Miranda dress and we had a lot of giggles in the wings. By now I could no longer take this production seriously, if I ever had, and I used to delight in puncturing her composure as we faced upstage for the masque of Goddesses and heavily galumphing nymphs and reapers. Ferdinand and Miranda, while they don't exactly have steamy love scenes, get to hold hands quite a lot. She turned out to be a very bright girl (I don't know why I'd arrogantly imagined she might have been otherwise). It only took walking her home from the first night party. There was a kiss in the dark downstairs hall of her digs that seemed to go on until dawn...

'If you're staying, you'll have to come in and sit down. My neck's cricked.'

I almost danced home through the gathering light.

And then it was poems. Poems on poems...

> What I see there I suppose
> to be you. The outward form
> of someone worn
> particularly close.
>
> But as redness is not
> necessarily the same
> redness for some,
> I wonder what
>
> our oneness looks like
> to those who only see
> twin poles you and me
> superficially unlike.
>
> With you my eye is near
> as the sleeper cornered
> in yours. An ordered
> symbol, a tear,
>
> a shot of blood or blemish,
> fresh push of lip
> on lip, or tip
> of tongue on teeth wish-
>
> ing oneness, stand for you.
> Not the fair-haired walker
> or extravagant talker

alone, but through

all projections of your sense,
like waves in ether,
I receive either
your age or innocence.

We wade deep in oneness
and when we surface
to set distinct face
on each, or dress

the other in a stranger,
this is so ridiculous
and far from us,
as to represent a danger.

We are that buried breath
in the sea-depth cavern
that rises up to govern
life and death.

(I include this poem in no bid for immortality but because it seems to say how we felt and because Christopher Fry liked it.)

Don and I were sharing a flat this season. He had arranged it all. We were installed at 40 Sheep Street, the Shrieve's House, a Stratford Landmark. Here, in Shakespeare's day, had lived William Rogers, a serjeant at the mace, brother-in-law of Shakespeare's friend Henry Walker. I quote from a forties' guide book. 'The upper storey of this half-timbered building, with its early close-studded timberwork on the ground floor, was largely reconstructed in Shakespeare's lifetime, following extensive damage to property in Sheep Street caused by fire. The lofty nature of the building is impressive... The bay windows, one overhanging the other, are also striking, and inside may be seen a contemporary staircase.'

How two young actors, even on, now, £14 a week, were able to live in such style is beyond remembering. It wasn't like nowadays, when the R.S.C. itself owns properties all over and around Stratford to let out to the company. We were each responsible, like the old touring actors, for our own shelter. But somehow Don had arranged it all as only Don could through a strange twilight character, the owner Mrs. Phillips, who occupied the downstairs. It was even better than the Shakespeare birthplace, because it hadn't been tarted up. The dark wooden floors rolled and shone like the deck of the Victory, the 'contemporary staircase' was solid and chunky with the treads worn into bevelled hollows by three centuries of shoes. Our magnificent beamed and panelled living room boasted one of the 'striking' bay windows where we breakfasted looking out over the Sheep Street bustle like Renaissance merchants. There was a bedroom each (Don took the double because, unlike me, he anticipated company) and a modernish kitchen and bathroom. The arrangement was that he would clean if I would cook. I had never cooked in my life but the flat was too good a chance to miss.

We neither of us had much palate then. It was the aftermath of war still so shopping was simply collecting the rations. Housekeeping was making them last. We still lunched across the road at the Rose and Crown and after the show I would concoct un-nourishing messes of fried Spam and re-constituted potato which we greatly relished.

We met our matches almost simultaneously. Diana Mahoney, a tall, dark, elegant girl with an inspired gift for malapropism, had been at the R.A.D.A. with Daphne and was playing small parts in the company. Don has written delightfully of their romance in his own 'A Touch of the Memoirs' so not for me to trespass there. I will add one tiny snapshot: their surprise when I accepted them over breakfast like an old married couple. They had been anticipating a torrent of nudge-nudge wink-wink and hardly knew how to re-act to my nonchalant 'Can you pass the marmalade?' routine.

When it came to Daphne, and our first live-in weekend, I persuaded Don that she was far too abashed to stay when he was around so he gallantly took himself off elsewhere. In truth it was I who was too shy to play this one before an audience. Particularly an audience of nudge-nudge wink-wink.

Eventually we kept their loving visits to alternate weekends to save everybody's faces and before long they had relieved me of most of the cooking. Don still cleaned though. I remember once hearing a racket around 3 a.m. and on venturing cautiously discovered not burglars but Don cleaning out the larder.

It was a vintage summer. Heady compensation for the record-setting winter. Anybody who's ever tasted a bottle of 1947 claret will know what I'm talking about.

We bicycled and punted and picnicked. Miss Slater still shocked the company from time to time. One mid-day as I waited at the back of the stalls with our packed picnic hamper for Dickie Hudd's TWELFTH NIGHT rehearsals (which I wasn't in) to end she was heard to say, in a loud voice, as Dickie gave out the P.M. calls, 'Doesn't that rather break up the afternoon?'

She had a great success as the first really young and 'sassy' Olivia, and another as Marina in PERICLES opposite Paul, who was never quite sure about her socially but had come to appreciate her skill as an actress. Both he and Joy were touchingly pleased at my emergence from my chrysalis.

I was a virgin no longer.

CHAPTER SIX

London: Fry and Ennui

'The bride wore a white embroidered pale blue dress with a small floral chaplet and white veil and carried a bouquet of lilies of the valley. She was attended by the bridegroom's sister, Miss Shirley Harrison, attractively gowned in deep yellow, with Juliet cap. The bride was given away by her father, best man being Mr. Paul Scofield, the Shakespearian actor.'

BRENTFORD AND CHISWICK TIMES, May 14, 1948.

My mother had been pleased that a love-affair of mine seemed to have reached a satisfactory conclusion at last. When I fluted on in Stratford's MERCHANT OF VENICE as an outrageously queenly Prince of Arragon (Michael Benthall's interpretation, not mine) Mum, accompanying Daphne (her 'play out') turned to her, dabbing her laughing eyes, and said, encouragingly. 'He's just like that at home!'

But she was not really happy for us to Live In Sin, particularly as she still had my thirteen year old sister's morals to worry about. Wedding bells (five pounds extra, I seem to remember) would put everything right. And I must say marriage seemed to be the goal. A certain amount of practice was O.K. but in 1948 you were not expected to maintain the practice state indefinitely.

The bride's father was less keen. He scented a fortune hunter. 'You must be mad!' was his reaction to my asking for his still under-age daughter's hand. But we were cunning. We had enlisted the aid of Daphne's Auntie Bea (her father's sister) by letting her be the first to hear our secret over tea and cakes at Stratford's Cobweb Cafe. Auntie Bea was a lady of a romantic turn of mind and with her telling support resistance was finally worn down.

We were married in the pretty Georgian Church of St. Anne on Kew Green on May 10th, exactly one year from our TEMPEST first night. In a courtship master-minded by the old magician Prospero himself what could go wrong? The best man and the groom took a preliminary stroll in Kew Gardens to allay their nerves and were nearly late for the ceremony. The bride looks lovely in the wedding pictures but the groom seems rather ill at ease in unaccustomed suit, and his woolly tie leaves something to be desired. Also the pen inadvertently placed in his breast pocket after signing the register disqualifies him from The Tatler. Indeed the London Evening News chopped him from the picture altogether and headlined Daphne 'Shrew Was Just An Act' - one play we hadn't done.

Son-in-law is not my best role. But Daphne's lively mother worked hard at the relationship and from time to time I did too. The family felt that I had lured the fledgling from the nest too soon, and with hindsight it is difficult to claim that they were wrong. Not that I'd done much luring, but once the bird was in my hands I suppose I was certainly reluctant to let it go. Had we not been blessed nightly by those overweight Goddesses?

'Honour, riches, marriage blessing
Long continuance and increasing
Hourly joys be still upon you!
Juno sings her blessings on you.'

And I believe our off-spring down to the second generation will firmly maintain that much good has come of it.

So here I was living permanently in London again for the first time since before the war. As I said earlier, I'd long turned against my native heath, but there was no real reason to live anywhere else. London, supposedly, was where the work was to be found, and Daphne's films would certainly be made there. I'm not a town person at all really, unless it's about the size of Sidmouth or Stratford, and two years by the Avon had finally spoilt me for 'the smoke'. Birmingham had been somehow different, strange and full of beginnings.

We moved into what would nowadays be called a 'studio', one large unfurnished room with partitioned kitchen and separate bathroom, on the top floor of 24 Queen's Gate, one of those great tall houses at the Hyde Park end. I don't remember a lift. If there was one it must have been permanently out of order. It took about five minutes and a great deal of puffing to reach us from the street, to be rewarded by a bird's-eye view of the roof of the Albert Hall. This luxury cost us the princely sum of £20 a week; but, what the hell, Miss Slater had a three year film contract, and my mother lent us a choice of such of her furniture as Dad had not removed from the store. The flat was close-carpeted so with a new bed which doubled as a divan by day we really felt quite smart. This was pre-Habitat, remember. Pre-G Plan. We were still in wartime austerity and our expectations were modest.

It was a funny old time.

All the old gang, nurtured on daily contact, were split asunder.

Don had married Diana and was understudying in the West End.

Paul had returned to Stratford to play Hamlet: the only one from the last two Festivals to be invited. This was because Sir Barry was being elbowed out by Major Anthony Quayle, recently returned from a distinguished war, in cahoots with the Chairman of the Governors, Colonel Sir Fordham Flower. The two military gentlemen were determined to be rid of this turbulent aesthete.

Although nominally still the director Sir Barry's tree was cropped root and branch. In came Quayle and Michael Benthall (with Robert Helpmann in tow) wielding a very starry broom indeed. Standing on stage with the assembled mighty after the HAMLET first night poor Sir Barry looked very ill at ease: like a high churchman among the cannibals. He retired at the end of the season. Trewin mourned his passing in a long article in the now defunct John O'London's Weekly:

'We had hoped to see him in office until even the most sentimental and the most cynical would have begun to take pride in Stratford's present achievement... It was not to be; Sir Barry has decided to go; and again the Stratford Legend has conquered... The Festival will have such names as Diana Wynyard, Robert Helpmann, Anthony Quayle, and - later Godfrey Tearle, as well as Paul Scofield, the discovery of the last two years... I am sorry that several of last year's cast were not kept. Stratford, after all, has not seen its young company in full flower; we had expected players of the merit of John Harrison and Paul Stephenson to have had another period of development on the Memorial stage...'

I'm sorry we weren't kept.

Not even Peter Brook survived. He should worry. His London career had taken off and he was directing BORIS GODUNOV at Covent Garden.

Joy - without Paul for a while - appeared as a 'native girl' (What would Equity say now?) in a new J.B.Priestley play, HOME IS TOMORROW at the Piccadilly Theatre.

Having been severed from both Sir Barry Jackson and Stratford, a link forged over four years, I found it tough getting work on the freelance London scene. In March I had kept up my South Western connection with another Arts Council tour, this time devised by me and featuring picked students of the Bristol Old Vic Theatre School and the singer Norman Platt, later founder/creator of Kent Opera. It was called MASQUERADE – No.1 (alas, there were no successors) - OF LOVE AND MARRIAGE. A subject on which I was now an expert. I became friendly with Norman. It was good to have someone to talk with about Mozart. He eventually played and sang Amiens for me in AS YOU LIKE IT at Nottingham Playhouse in 1953. MASQUERADE visited Bridgwater Arts Centre, where I didn't go looking for Anne.

I put in some casual radio days at the BBC in Portland Place. There was a strange Third Programme piece about Theseus and the Minotaur, and MRS. DALE'S DIARY in which I played a rotter called Roger who was chasing after Gwen Dale and was eventually thrown down the stairs and out of the series. (My disappointment when that episode arrived through the post knew no bounds. There was the end of the engagement: scripted.) Used as I was to the no-nonsense factory floor attitudes of stage and dressing room I didn't slip easily into the BBC's smooth and clubby atmosphere. Which was a shame because I would have been a good radio actor.

Daphne was in fair demand and went almost immediately into a live television production of Jane Austen's EMMA. (More about the frontline excitements of live TV later.) She still had some over-hype from Stratford to live down but she landed a part in an unusual new verse play at the Arts Theatre Club, then one of the most lively outlets in London, run by Alec Clunes (father of Martin) whose breadth of programming made it a mini-National Theatre.

This one was by a little-known writer called Christopher Fry and was called THE LADY'S NOT FOR BURNING. Daphne 'created' the part of Alizon.

The critics didn't quite know what to make of it. I never knew quite what to make of it either. I remember sitting in our eyrie poring over the virgin script. 'These characters all talk the same,' I complained. A foolish criticism when I think how much I enjoy Shaw. I can find more fun in the play now but then I fear I was pretty stewed prune about it.

Jock Dent headed his review ELOQUENT RAPSODOOCE – a quotation from MR.POLLY.

'Mr. Fry's play is not of this earth. It is something quite beyond me. It is exactly the kind of play at the first night of which the late James Agate (in the days when I was beginning to venture forth as an independent critic) would make a point of approaching me in the interval, with something between a beam of patronage and a frown of warning. And quizzically, alarmingly, gleefully, unhelpfully, he would say: "Don't go wrong about this, Jock!" and pass on.'

Trewin thought that Fry, 'may be the poet-dramatist for whom the stage has been searching so long.'

We were all obsessed then, in what was shortly to become the new Elizabethan Age, with the need for a new form of dramatic poetry. An alternative to cinéma vérité. A resurgence of the word. It was never to happen. We fell into the kitchen sink instead.

'Daphne Slater showed the excellent effect of a season at Stratford" according to the Daily Telegraph.

I concentrated on gathering my poems together and even found a publisher. The Fortune Press. This was a one-man-band run from a basement in Belgravia. I have a faint memory of a pasty-faced slovenly man in carpet slippers, monosyllabic to the point of speechlessness. But his list was amazing. THE NORTH SHIP by Philip Larkin, CONFESSIONS ABOUT X by Julian Symons, POEMS by Roy Fuller, POEMS AND SONGS by Gavin Ewart, 38 POEMS by Henry Treece, three books by Nicholas Moore and one by Tambimuttu... and... 18 POEMS by Dylan Thomas. Both Larkin's and Thomas's first publications. Of course they weren't then who they are now, if you see what I mean, and the most significant name to me on the list was my own.

Peter came to lunch while I was sweating over the proofs. He picked up a sheet and took amused exception to:

We are such shy
backward
awkward beings

We never do
the right
emotional things.

'You can't call that a poem,' he said.

Nevertheless I did, and my first and only volume of verse A HORSE WITH WINGS was published in 1948. Daphne gave a copy to Christopher Fry who was more generous to me than I had been about him.

'I like particularly The Vagrant, Concolinel, and Identity,' he wrote back. 'The Vagrant catches me in the throat each time I read it: it has a complete life of its own, not at all tugged at by influences as some of the others are, or so it seems to me. Not that I'm against influences, but when a poem submerges them all it has a particular vitality that's wonderful. I got a great deal of pleasure from reading the book... and I only wonder why an ear which could contrive Concolinel didn't listen all the time - lines, here and there a whole poem, seem to have slipped in without getting much attention. For example, there's the very good first verse of Epitaph on p.37, followed by a very bad second verse. But it goes against my grain to carp when so much is a delight.'

I think part of my trouble was that I didn't get enough of this kind of literate criticism. I moved in theatrical circles, where people were easily impressed by the mere notion of putting a few lines down on paper at all. Duncan Ross, though, one of my Stratford dressing-room mates, could be caustic. When I showed him a poem with the line:

'back in the balance with windy humanity'

he asked if I was referring to life with Don.

I think I wasn't objective enough. Writing was a kind of therapy. Some people paint their hassles out. Others dance them. I tried to get them into words.

As I said before, it was a funny old year. With 'Just Married' hanging all over us we should have been in a golden glow. And maybe we were.

I don't remember. It's difficult now even to remember how I passed the time, with Daphne so often in rehearsal. We used to meet for lunch at the Buxton Club, a haunt of theatrical goslings opposite the Haymarket stage door, where we would sometimes see Don and Diana. I walked a lot in Hyde Park, alternately dreaming of fame and trying to battle off feelings of rejection. Certainly I was writing. A play about the weird triangle of Ruskin, Millais and Effie Gray, to be called DENMARK HILL. It was never finished but I recycled the ideas some twenty years later in an episode of UPSTAIRS, DOWNSTAIRS.

Meantime real work, real actual paid work, continued to elude me. Daphne spent most of the summer in an International Theatre Season at the Arts, in company with people like Marius Goring and Charles Lloyd Pack, lovingly knitting for me in the dressing-room, and won most of the bouquets in an otherwise brickbatted CHERRY ORCHARD, when even the gentle Trewin complained, 'At the Arts the Festival Company, I grieve to say, is hewing down THE CHERRY ORCHARD...' A weekly called, rightly in this instance, TRUTH, confirms that 'Daphne Slater, as Anya, is the most authentic member of the Arts Theatre's revival.' And this is a nice one, from the Catholic Herald: '...not all the players were as fitting as Miss Slater and Mr. Goring, but it was good to hear once again of Russia - Holy Russia.'

Her film career hung fire. She did a couple of days on SPRING IN PARK LANE, stupidly mis-cast as a cockney maid, and ended up on the cutting room floor. The Wilcoxes (Herbert and Anna) had not exactly relished all the Juliet hoo-ha, nor her unexpected marriage to Benvolio, and seemed to be losing interest in exploiting their property; although mercifully the cheques kept coming in and paying the rent.

And I continued to dawdle about Hyde Park.

One way and another this native Londoner certainly wasn't in his element. Perhaps it was just because he was now the posh side of the river.

In the autumn I at last landed a job in two plays at the People's Palace in the Mile End Road. This was an extraordinary place. I don't remember what philanthropist had built it or why, but it was a vast white elephant. A director down from the Glasgow Citz, Matthew Forsyth, was bravely planning a season of plays there. He took to me because we shared our adoration of 'H.K.' for whom Forsyth had stage-managed at Malvern. I was to do two plays. A dreadful charade called

THESE MORTALS by H.M. Harwood, starring Nigel Patrick and best forgotten. And William Douglas Home's early claim to be a serious dramatist, NOW BARABBAS... written before he succumbed to the simple crowd-pleasing of THE CHILTERN HUNDREDS and its successors. Trewin called it 'a prison document of dignity.' I landed the plum part of a condemned man. I delved into my South London past and pulled out the accent that I had been at such pains to lose. Mum came and wept buckets. It was a weird culture shock to get into the underground at smart South Ken every night and disembark at Mile End. I don't think anyone from Mile End ever came to see us.

My warder and Prison Chaplain were a couple of very decent blokes called Denis Cannan and Kenneth Mackintosh, both down with Forsyth from Glasgow. Ken went on eventually to a life's work at the National Theatre where, as senior staff director, he became something of a legend. Denis I was immediately drawn to. A lean and lively-minded Old Etonian (the second of the species I had come across) married, then, to a friendly ex-nurse, and with a little daughter whose name he wrote for me in grease-paint on the dressing-room mirror, 'Crecy'. He was also writing plays, none of which had so far been put on. He and Daphne got on well too. They were both enthusiastic talkers. We happily shared the mirror and a passion for the right way to play Shakespeare. He had an idea for a portable touring theatre which excited me tremendously.

Shakespeare in 40's theatre, apart from the Stratford Festival, meant, at best, star productions like the Olivier/Richardson 'Old Vic' seasons at the New Theatre (now the Albery). The emphasis was on the performer's versatility and if that meant an absurd prominence for Justice Shallow, so be it. John Gielgud entertained the faithful every so often with his dignified Hamlet, now embalmed on disc. (I was never a Gielgud fan. Like the Dickens and Thackeray thing, you either went for one or the other and I was an Olivier man. He always gave you something new and surprising, worth laying down ten bob of your own money for.) The major repertory theatres managed one Shakespeare play a year, usually from the examination list, and the style was invariably pictorial. Donald Wolfit toured his ridiculous productions in which he stood centre stage in the light and his supporting cast were ranged round him in a cringing semi-circle in the half-dark. (He once said in all seriousness to a friend of mine who, in some minor role, had put on a make-up to out-Lear Lear, 'Any more of this, Latimer, and I shall put you in the back row!') Forget James Agate. I saw Wolfit. His curtain-calls were the peak of his performances, clinging, panting, to the velvet like an exhausted boxer. He was a coarse actor.

Denis and I wanted to do something for Shakespeare himself. It's all been done since but it was new then.

The plays are about what happens, to whom it happens, and are told in words. Where and when it happens only matters if W.S. decides to tell you so. In the 40's all the main published texts (with the honourable exception of my namesake G.B. Harrison's Penguin edition) were still adorned with the prettifications of the 18th Century editors from Nicholas Rowe onwards - 'A room in the palace', 'Another part of the Forest'. Nowadays everybody probably knows these were never part of Shakespeare's original text. If you read one of his plays in its earliest published format (Folio or Quarto) you simply get a continuous flow of characters entering and exiting ('They have their exits and their entrances...') and if he wants you to know where they are they come straight out with it and say 'So this is the Forest of Arden!'

'What country, friends, is this?'

'This is Illyria, lady.'

I always liken it to children playing. True make believe. With a couple of chairs and a broom handle they can be in outer space or Camelot. And if they want to change the scene they tell each other so as the game proceeds. 'We're going into a really snake-infested bit of jungle now, Sharon...'

It's all there in the opening Chorus of HENRY V.

'On your imaginary forces work...
Think, when we talk of horses, that you see them...'

How ridiculous it is to let Derek Jacobi in the movie say

'...Oh, for pity, we shall much disgrace,
With four or five most ragged foils,
Right ill-dispos'd, in brawl ridiculous,
The name of Agincourt...'

and then give us a slap-up news-reel vision of the battle itself. The absurdity only passes because audiences have given up listening and don't really take in what the man says.

The glory of Shakespeare is in the word.

All this depended on his having an unlocalised platform on which to perform. An acting space that could be anywhere the performer wanted you to imagine it.

Most of the 'Gems from Shakespeare' would never have come into being but for this fact. No point in launching into the magical 'I know a bank whereon the wild thyme blows...' if the audience can actually see the bank. '...Light thickens,/ And the crow makes wing to the rooky wood...' is superfluous if the lighting designer can create the effect.

Everything that seems odd to a modern audience in his plays can be explained by the theatre he wrote them for. Any writer instinctively adapts to his medium. You write differently if you are writing for TV or radio or the theatre. With Shakespeare the one medium was his all and he developed it to the hilt.

'Alas, why gnaw you so your nether lip?' is not the kind of remark you drop naturalistically to your spouse, even if he is a little late to bed. But in the fading afternoon light at the open-air Globe Theatre you are giving the most distant spectator a close-up of Othello. Actresses have great difficulties with a speech like Lady Macbeth's 'Unsex me here...' and going on at length about their nipples. What Shakespeare is doing is reminding you, verbally, that this 14 year old boy in a wig is to be taken for a woman. With lines like that the boy is freed from 'acting the woman' at all.

There are very rare stage directions in the Folio where you can hear his director's hand at work. In CORIOLANUS, 'Enter Volumnia and Virgilia... They set them downe on two lowe stools and sowe.' Immediately we are brought indoors from the market-place. 'Enter Caesar in his nightgowne' does the same. Is it a banquet? 'Enter a Sewer, and divers Servants with Dishes and Service over the Stage. Then enter Macbeth.' The simple procession tells you there's a party going on in the next room.

But I wouldn't argue for an historical reproduction of an Elizabethan performance. I've tried that (JULIUS CAESAR, Nottingham Playhouse 1954). It doesn't work. You can't reproduce the Elizabethan audience. But you need to know *why* he wrote as he did in order to interpret the text correctly. It's no good looking for Freudian explanations of Lady Macbeth's obsession with her nipples. That's not what the lines are there for.

Then there's his amazing sense of dramatic continuity. Of lining up scenes, now short, now long, in just the right order like the skilful editing of a movie. Even placing an interval can be dangerous, with an effect like a cinema projector breaking down. (A frequent occurrence in my childhood at the old Grand Cinema, Clapham Junction: a whirr, a splutter, a jagged edge and a blank white screen. Catcalls and hoots until the picture was restored.)

Shakespeare's actors must have been the best, apprenticed to the trade from boyhood. For a writer to have the courage to award lines like

'The West yet glimmers with some streaks of day.
Now spurs the lated traveller apace
To gain the timely inn...'

to the First Murderer, he has to know the player is not going to fumble and drop the ball from Burbage. The senior members were all sharers in the company, so the thickness of their wallets depended on the success of their teamwork.

Shakespeare knew all about acting. I tell actors that Hamlet's advice to the players contains everything they need to know. Forget Stanislavski, whose methods were evolved for the production of Chekhov's plays two hundred years later (when even Chekhov himself ridiculed them).

Consider this,

'...use all gently; for in the very torrent, tempest, and as I may say the whirlwind of your passion, you must acquire and beget a temperance that may give it smoothness.'

Read that a couple of times and ponder it well. That's technique. That's professional acting. Any fool can go on and 'tear a passion to tatters, to very rags, to split the ears of the groundlings'. Shakespeare obviously loathed uncontrolled bombast.

The Elizabethan actor had to be able to do four things - sometimes singly, sometimes in pairs, and sometimes all together.

He had to be capable of naturalistic acting, just as we know it today, for an exchange such as:

'MACBETH: I have done the deed: Didst thou not hear a noise?
LADY MACBETH: I heard the owl scream and the crickets cry.
　　　　　Did not you speak?
MACBETH: When?
LADY M.: Now.
MACBETH: As I descended?
LADY M.: Ay.
MACBETH: Hark! Who lies i'th' second chamber?
LADY M.: Donalbain.
MACBETH: This is a sorry sight.'

He had to be able to slip from that to intimate and unembarrassed communing with the audience.

'To be or not to be, that is the question...'

'Was ever woman in this humour wooed...?'

He had to be prepared to paint the scenery.

'DUNCAN: This castle hath a pleasant seat.
　　　　　The air nimbly and sweetly recommends itself
　　　　　Unto our gentle senses.
BANQUO: This guest of summer,
　　　　　The temple-haunting martlet, does approve
　　　　　By his loved mansionry, that the Heaven's breath
　　　　　Smells wooingly here: no jutty frieze,
　　　　　Buttress, nor coign of vantage, but this bird
　　　　　Hath made his pendant bed, and procreant cradle.
　　　　　Where they most breed and haunt I have observed
　　　　　The air is delicate.'

The Stanislavski-trained actor will decide from this that Banquo is a bird-watcher. Nothing of the kind. He is setting the scene. A gentle panning crane-shot with bird-song for the almighty contrast with the dreadful night ahead when young Lennox takes over the camera-work and the multi-mix sound-track -

> 'The night has been unruly:
> Where we lay, our chimneys were blown down,
> And, as they say, lamentings heard in the air;
> Strange screams of death,
> And prophesying, with accents terrible,
> Of dire combustion and confused events
> New-hatched to the woeful time.
> The obscure bird clamoured the live-long night.
> Some say the earth was feverous,
> And did shake.'

(More largesse for the bit player.)

And he had to be able to act as commentator, to provide those close-ups - 'Why look you so amazed?' 'Why do you seem to start...?' To make us see 'that whiter skin of hers than snow /And smooth as monumental alabaster...'

And he had to do all this whilst presenting a consistent character who was recognisably Othello or Oberon or Imogen.

If I were allowed one trip in a Time Machine it would have to be to a performance at the Southwark Globe.

Denis and I wanted to do, in 1948, what others have since succeeded in doing at the R.S.C.: on tour, in The Other Place and in The Swan. Ironically we even called our prototype The Swan. Basically it was an easily erectable permanent structure. A platform with a semi-circle of arches carrying a walk-way connecting them above. That and a cyclorama. Shakespeare would do the rest. We also, ahead of Lord Miles and Sam Wanamaker, wanted to start the thing off in the City of London. In answer to a power of questions from me Denis replied:

'I am sending you by the same post a letter full of doodles. A touring version of the Swan could easily be made if advantage were taken of modern constructional techniques - like those used for displays such as 'Britain Can Make It'. A portable Swan would not cost any more than the pre-production costs of one Shakespearian production in the West End. The Cyclorama would be the most difficult part, and I have doodled an idea which seems fantastic, but which has worked well for years in Italy. The dimensions of (a) the permanent Swan and (b) the touring one will regulate what we can do with the arches. I should like the centre arch to be large enough for us to be able to insert a balcony in the arch, thus getting a more intimate upper-stage, and a more oppressive lower one. But we must be able also to use the top of the arch for battlements, Henry V and so on. It can't be less than 16' high if this is to be done: I would suggest this height for the touring Swan, and something nearer 20' for a permanent one... The touring version of the Swan will not 'fit' into village halls, though one could build one therein - if you see the distinction. We would have to use concert halls, assembly rooms etc. Prospecting would find suitable sites in most of the larger towns. Gymnasia would do. Overall dimensions would be about 40' by 30' by 30' high...'

A year later, when I had got a toe-hold in directing, we made earnest approaches to the Arts Council where we were listened to politely by the Drama Director and his Assistant. At the end of our exposition all they could find to say was 'Well, we can see what John will get out of it, but we can't see what's in it for you, Denis.' And that was that. It was very frustrating.

Towards the end of 1948 my agent rang me. How grand that sounds! Gordon Harbord was his name and if he was not exactly top flight he did at least have the imagination to go outside London from time to time scouting for talent. There were fewer agents then. I suppose only about a dozen. They all mushroomed much later when Commercial

Television started. I used to feel a real 'pro' as I climbed the rickety uncarpeted stairs to his Charing Cross Road office. Out of work I might be but defiantly 'of the profession'. Phones would ring, coffee would be set in front of one. Gordon, tall, thin and vaguely seedy with RAF-type handle-bar moustache, rather like the stage notion of a bookmaker, would emerge from his inner office and perch on a desk for five minutes. Or his heavily rouged and hennaed wife Eleanor would condescend for a few moments in passing. Actors place pathetic reliance on agents, although most work comes through their own contacts. Twice in my life only have I obtained work through an agent, and each time I have to say it was rather memorable.

'How would you like to go to Australia? You and Daphne together?'

Australia...

It is almost impossible to convey how remote Australia seemed to us then. You went by boat. It took a month. Diggers? The bush? Waltzing Matilda? That was about the sum of my knowledge. It might almost have been North Borneo or the moon. There had already been an exploratory landing. In 1947 Laurence Olivier and Vivien Leigh had headed an enormously successful Old Vic tour (in the course of which, as you may read in his autobiography, Olivier was sacked by the Old Vic Governors from the safe distance of fourteen thousand miles). The Aussies had swarmed to see the film stars. Attached to the tour as the representative of the British Council was an old soak in a wig whose first name perhaps was Walter. He had come back convinced, possibly erroneously, that any British classical company could clean up. To this end he approached a crony of his, an Irish actor manager called Anew McMaster.

Fast-talking Gordon succeeded in convincing me on the telephone that middle-aged Irish glamour boy Michael Mac Liammoir would be leading the tour. That would be some cachet.

Daphne and I were intrigued and presented ourselves for interview with Mr. McMaster whom we assumed to be the organiser. There seemed to be no limit to the planned repertoire. Othello, Macbeth, Hamlet, Lear, The Merchant were all mentioned. Daphne would play

Desdemona and Ophelia for starters. I was offered Cassio and Laertes. I said I'd rather play Horatio. The Irish gentleman was amazed. 'Usually they think Laertes the better part,' he said. 'However it's much more important to Hamlet to have a good Horatio.' So that seemed to be settled. I did my usual audition piece from Richard II while Mr. McMaster crawled about behind the office sofa to get, as he put it, the audience eye view. He seemed a bit fazed by Daphne. 'If I didn't know you'd played Juliet I should think you were a modern actress.' To lighten the atmosphere I jokingly said, 'She has her ham moments.' McMaster looked wounded. 'We never allow that word in our company, dear.' But clearly the fact that she was last year's Stratford Juliet was our strongest calling card.

Later I rang Gordon. The offer was firm for a twelve-month tour at a joint salary of £50 a week. Good money in 1948.

'And Mac Liammoir is playing Hamlet,' I said.

'McMaster,' said Gordon.

'Who?'

'The man you saw today. Anew McMaster.'

'I thought you said Michael Mac Liammoir was going?'

'No. Where did you get that from? I said McMaster was Mac Liammoir's brother-in-law. They've done a lot of work together in Dublin.'

'But they're not together on this trip?'

'No. I never said they were.'

'Who produces (directs)?'

'McMaster.' Gordon slightly nettled now. 'He's very famous in Ireland. Brilliant Othello. Acknowledged to be the greatest Othello of his generation. Gielgud's not in the same class. Not even Larry Olivier can hold a candle to Mac at his best.'

'I see.'

So we started to dig up what we could about Anew (*not* Agnew) McMaster. John Trewin had become a friend from Stratford first nights when cast and critics used to mingle in the bar, scorning Jock Dent's taboo. Peter had introduced us and taught us how to pronounce his name. Cornishly, with the accent on the second syllable. Also, ever my Mr. Puff, he had been plugging the poems and Trewin had published a couple in a monthly he edited, The West Country Magazine. John was a natural enthusiast, a man to contact if ever you were feeling down, when his brightness would unfailingly lift you to Cloud Nine. 'Oh, I *say!* How absolutely *grand*!' was his habitual response. He was also a mine of theatre history. If anybody knew about McMaster he would. We waited with baited breath, confident of encouragement. Sure enough he had seen McMaster twice, as Coriolanus at Stratford in 1936 and in a pre-war season with his own company at the Chiswick Empire. And he was frankly horrified. We might as well have proposed joining the foreign legion.

Peter, on the other hand, had seen the Chiswick season as a boy and been boyishly impressed. He thought we should go for, as he put it, the fun, the sun and the joy of our own sweet company.

To complicate matters Matthew Forsyth was planning to revive the Malvern Festival the following summer with a new play by the nonagenarian Shaw called BUOYANT BILLIONS and invited me to take part. But this wouldn't start rehearsing until May. McMaster sailed for the Antipodes in December.

There was also talk of a West End transfer of THE LADY'S NOT FOR BURNING and Christopher Fry wanted Daphne for Alizon. But there was no date fixed and the unpredictable Gielgud was directing. He might well over-rule the author's choice.

We were in a quandary. John Trewin shame-facedly recanted and admitted that a trip round the world might be quite a honeymoon. His father had been a Cornish mariner and he could understand the wanderlust.

The thought of us both earning and being in a company together as we had been at Stratford was undeniably attractive. Hadn't I been a bit edgy being Mr. Daphne Slater all summer?

And then... space... the idea of foreign travel (something my father had always dreamed of whilst chained to the bakery and confectionery)... the Southern Cross... tropical nights under the stars...

We chewed it over with all our senior friends. We asked Dickie Hudd if he thought we would be making a bad career move. Dickie said, 'Go and enjoy yourselves. I've just come back from six months in New York and nobody's even noticed I've been away.'

The only discordant note was struck by a rather supercilious lady, then in charge at the Lyric Hammersmith. She said, 'Why Australia, I ask myself?'

So we went.

Leaving good openings for two fortunate unknowns.

Claire Bloom got Alizon in THE LADY'S NOT FOR BURNING and Denholm Elliott was awarded my Malvern contract.

CHAPTER SEVEN

With The Bard to Australia

'I'm very sorry indeed that you won't be playing Alizon. As you know, I couldn't have wanted her played more beautifully, but I do see that an opportunity to go round the world together isn't to be sneezed at.'

CHRISTOPHER FRY in a letter to Daphne. Jan.1949.

Before we sailed we had a reading of OTHELLO in Gordon Harbord's office. The sherry bottle was out and Gordon kept making nervous little pronouncements. 'Australia is the home of opals. You'll all bring back opals. Eleanor adores opals.' Paul Stephenson, a dressing-room colleague from two seasons at Stratford, was playing Iago, which was comforting. Dorothy Wheatley, a respected actress from the Birmingham Rep, was Emilia. An elderly silver-haired Stratfordian, Eric Maxon, who dated back to Sir Frank Benson, was Brabantio. A young actor called John Edmund made up the English contingent as Lodovico. All the other parts were read in at this stage by McMaster in a light Dublin accent.

He was a large untidy man in his fifties, swept back fair hair thinning on top. Eyes that glinted greyly under very bushy, very overhanging brows. Pince-nez balanced in front of them on a thick and prominent nose. Liberal of endearments, his voice in ordinary conversation was piercing. His reading of the part of Othello, even after the thousand performances of which he boasted, was hurried and careless. He was patently "marking" as the opera singers say.

When we reached what he called the Tavern scene, 'Now dear,' he said to me, 'the usual business we have there is that in Cassio's drunkenness his hat falls off. He tries to pick it up - they all encourage him - he falls over - ker-ASH! Now, down on his knees what does he think? He thinks immediately that he's in church, doesn't he? So he says his next line, "God forgive us our sins" - Religious drunk you see, dear. Then they help him up. Of course if you can think of any other business you would rather do you only have to say so. Because business is traditional it is not necessarily right.'

He was clearly anxious to appear open-minded on his return to the theatrical mainstream and kept restoring cuts in his acting edition.

'I've never had this bit in before, but we'll try it,' he would say.

'Yes, put that back in. "The guttered rocks and congregated sands..." That's very good, dear. I don't know why we've never had that. I only hope I shall get used to it in time. It's difficult after a thousand performances.'

Although contrary, he gave us to understand, to his Irish practice, he restored the end of the play with the curtain on Lodovico's lines rather than on Othello's dying gasp.

'"Look," read Lodovico, "On the tragic loading of this bed!"'

'Of course,' said McMaster, 'the only difficulty is that I don't die on the bed. I fall down the steps centre stage.' Then, pensively, 'I suppose I *could* die on the bed?'

Well, we had been warned. But the contracts were signed now.

Leaving England in December I can still vividly remember the excitement of sailing south into the sun, especially after being cooped up for the duration. Not that there had been any real sense of claustrophobia because foreign travel was not the regular part of life that it is now. Before the war smart folk swanned off to the Riviera in the Spring and the Autumn (never the Summer) but ordinary people were on the whole content with Clacton-on-sea. Or Sidmouth. But, like my father, I had always relished the idea of foreign parts. It was the exotic I was after. At that time in my life Europe would have seemed small beer. I was very unsophisticated. I hadn't even clued into Bach yet. It was the idea of Suez, Aden, Colombo that was drawing me, with Australia as a possible anticlimax.

It turned out to be not only our maiden voyage but the ship's. The R.M.S. *Orcades*, an Orient liner of 30,000 tons, was, after bucketing through the Channel and Biscay (when the deck-hands could be heard saying she was top heavy and would never make it) in two days cruising comfortably off the Portuguese coast. Each day a new step sunwards.

But this was no cruise liner. The majority of our fellow passengers were emigrants with assisted passages. Whole families uprooting themselves for a transplant to the other side of the planet. There was an underlying gravity that no amount of deck tennis could disguise.

Mealtimes came and went. There were two signals on board for these. A merry fanfare over distant loudspeakers called the First Class, while a blatant "Come to the cookhouse door" summoned the Tourists. Service was by gentle Goanese stewards, who were ruled over by an uncouth bully of an English head-waiter.

We were, of course, travelling Tourist, a genteelism of Steerage, and confined to the back, or should I say, the stern, or possibly steerage, of the ship. Every time you tried to take a bit of exercise round the deck you came up against these barriers. 'First Class Passengers Only'. At least Daphne and I had been able to insist on a cabin to ourselves, but it was a long way down, below the water line. The others were in dormitory conditions.

I made copious notes of the voyage on which to base my letters home, or even, perhaps, a novel.

'The *Orcades*, it was given out, was expected to put in at Port Said, Egypt, at 7 p.m., and would be due to sail again at midnight. Passengers wishing to go ashore must present themselves with their passports to the Egyptian police in the lounge on B deck at 6 p.m. Passengers were reminded that a state of martial law existed in Egypt and were advised to keep to the main streets.

Night was coming on as the engines chugged at last to a standstill and the vessel was eased into her mooring. Beyond the quay was a dark huddle of buildings and the silhouette of an occasional palm. There was about the place an air of expectancy - something theatrical - something akin to the suspense that leads to the cry "Overture and beginners, please!" The actors, the setting, the drama, were preparing on the far side of a black band of oily water. Only the working lights were on: cold blue daylight arcs, destroying colour and the precious illusion of reality. An orchestra of voices tuned up with sporadic shouts and chatter. Vendors of tourist wares besieged the *Orcades* until she was hemmed in by agile bumboats.

"You buy nice pouffy? I sell you nice pouffy. Two poun' ten. Two poun' ten. Shop three poun': me - two poun' ten. Two poun' ten. All-a right. Thirty shillin'."

And down over the side went the English notes amid the vendor's execration ("MacDougal!") and up over the side came a procession of unwanted articles to prove an embarrassment for the rest of the voyage...'

We bought a 'nice pouffy', and paid duty on it, too, into Australia, lugging it around for the whole length of the tour, and then paid duty on it back again into England. It turned out quite an expensive 'pouffy' and sat around to mock us for many years.

'Suddenly, as if we really had been at a play, the lights went on. With staggering impudence the curtain rose on Port Said. First of all a coloured and moving illuminated sign advertised the redoubtable Johnnie Walker, intrepid Scot in foreign parts. Then shop fronts sprang into being everywhere as if a stage electrician were coping with an extremely difficult cue. Whole side streets opened up vistas of lighted windows and the trumpery of the bazaar. Finally, at the end of the quay, a brilliant touch of bathos invited you to "Spend your holidays in the Swiss Alps". Port Said had opened up for the *Orcades*.

The "B" Deck lounge was stiff with bayonets. Grim faces under fezes moved not a muscle as the passports were examined, stamped and held while a slip of paper was given in exchange. The passports would be returned on receipt of this slip when the passengers re-embarked.'

And so the six thousand souls (the word comes naturally on ship...S.O.S...) went off to wobble about, for the first time in a week, on their land-legs. Maddeningly, after this Bond-type build-up, no notes whatsoever about what we did on shore!

The *Orcades* then carried us goggle-eyed with colour down the Suez canal, between the almost white sands of Arabia Deserta and the bright green fertility of the Nile, and through Red Sea sunsets not even Turner would have dared to mix. Inevitably, the newly-published poet, I struggled to find words in verse, but the English words of English poets were over-reached in the opulence of the Orient. You sensed some of Flecker's plight, and longed for honey laments in Arabic.

The temperature rose steadily as we approached Christmas. The Tourist swimming pool, an uncompromising tank which could hold comfortably about ten people standing upright, was quickly over-populated and then broke down.

Aden was a surprise. Going on deck at dawn I was entranced by craggy hard towers of Volcanic rock, and reminded of nothing so much as a Dürer landscape. Pinnacles etched against the steel plate of the early morning sky. They were like mountains drawn by someone who had never seen a mountain, imagined out of a medieval fairy tale existence. Down their bony limbs and crevices could have come sliding the creations of Hieronymous Bosch...

(I wrote as much to John Trewin who was a great fan of the over-wrought phrase. 'How *grand*!')

We spent Christ's birthday ashore in a landscape Jesus would have recognised more readily than the wintry north. We found a sleazy upstairs restaurant (most places were closed) and ate a scrawny chicken. Looking back, we were amazingly impervious to infection. Nobody had ever insisted we had any jabs. Daphne experienced the dubious thrill of being addressed as 'Memsahib' by the shining eyed Arab children.

'Merry Krismiss, Memsah'b. Backsheesh! Backsheesh! Merry Krismiss!'

I know from the film we took that the Memsah'b was wearing a particularly fetching dress in pink candy stripes that she had worn in a modern dress production of TARTUFFE at the Arts.

One little boy, overwhelmed by the vision, enchantingly presented her with a sweat-damp bunch of tired-looking tropical flowers, murmuring bashfully 'Oh, lady!' before turning and running shyly away, forgetting all about his backsheesh.

I should have mentioned this film before. Dating back to the 35mm off-cuts from Cousin Bert at Sidmouth's Grand Cinema, home movies had become a passion. Before the war I hoarded my pocket money bit by miserly bit. By walking half way home from school and pocketing my bus fare I gradually stashed away the almost unimaginable sum of thirty-seven shillings and sixpence which in 1938 would buy me the cheapest Pathescope 9.5mm projector on the market, the Ace. It was a hand-turned model, but with the addition of a super-attachment it could take 300ft reels which I could crank away for twenty minutes without re-loading. And now I could show real films, with opening trade marks and credit titles, all the way through: not just the torn and tantalising fragments from the floor of the Grand's projection box. The films could be hired from libraries in intoxicating round metal cans and this way I first made my acquaintance on the sitting-room wall with THE CABINET OF DR. CALIGARI (three reels) and METROPOLIS (five reels). It was marvellous what you imbibed about editing and camera-work from hand-cranking your way through these old masterpieces.

In 1948 there was no new equipment to be bought, but Daphne had spotted an ad. for a second-hand Pathe 'H' movie camera and bought it for me just before we sailed. It was my most prized possession and I was able to make a record of our whole trip in chilly black and white, because that was the only stock you could buy at the time. And as I had no editing facilities I had to edit mentally as I went along, a discipline that proved invaluable when I later became a director of live television drama.

McMaster, a bored and impatient sailor, was anxious to start rehearsals. He had negotiated with the Captain for the First Class Ballroom, but the keep-out notices remained firmly in place and he was forced to settle for the Tourist children's nursery in the very stern of the ship, directly above the throbbing screws.

We had met the rest of our Irish colleagues by now. Mrs. Marjorie McMaster was tiny. Sharp as a beady-eyed small bird. She smiled a great deal without, seemingly, registering a word you said to her. She was the costume designer, and many yards of garish silks had come aboard at Port Said. Their son Christopher was to play Roderigo. A small, fair, friendly lad in his early twenties, who turned out to have few gifts as an actor, but later became a television director in England. There was a very pleasant boy called Colum O'Doherty, Omnes and general handyman. Finally our stage manager, Ernie Leitch, a bony individual of no recognisable age with ill-fitting false teeth, in total thrall to his master.

And then, of course, there was Walter, the business manager in his wig, who spent most of the time propping up the bar.

If my notes are to be believed we had our first rehearsal in the evening of Christmas Day...

'when the last tired whimpers had died away and the nursery was heavy with childish odours and the hush of settling dust. There, somnolent with food and drink, our little company of players repaired to what no stretch of the imagination could claim as a marvellous convenient place for their rehearsal. Amid a setting of blackboards and brightly coloured chutes, of rocking horses and the scattered snow of jig-saws, we were to roll with the seas through Shakespeare's tragedy of OTHELLO. We found the Moor's palace quaintly furnished with one foot high stools, gaily painted, on which it was difficult to strike any sort of attitude or even retain a balance...

The nursery was shaped like a horseshoe with windows round the curved sides, prettily curtained, and with deep sills. Little Mrs. McMaster curled up in one of these, half hiding herself with the curtains, and absent-mindedly crooned Desdemona's willow song...'

Paul Stephenson and young McMaster mumbled through their opening dialogue while McMaster strained forward to catch the sound, occasionally stopping to give them a move. There was no arty discussion of character or motive.

'He goes over there, dear.' As if the passage of Iago through the play were fixed and immutable. Never You go there, but always He goes there. And you re-traced his steps, feeling like the Invisible Man.

Remember I'd just spent three years working with Peter Brook. 'What can he know about it, dear, at his age?' asked McMaster, genuinely bewildered. Recollected in tranquillity this can all seem a bit of a laugh and comes in handy at theatrical dinner parties, but living through it was no joke, I can tell you.

Next old Eric Maxon made his entrance as Brabantio, stepping straight into the path of one of the ventilating blowers which destroyed his careful swept-back silver coiffure, and proceeded to raise the roof.

"'Thou, Roderigo..!'" with deliberate rolling of the 'r's. No slow approach for him: his performance had stood the test of time.

Finally Brabantio thundered off to the Senate and we came to Othello's first entrance.

'Now,' said McMaster, 'now comes my 'Love Music', dears. It's a bit out of Verdi's OTELLO.'

'Love Music!' commanded Ernie authoritatively, and he and Mrs. McMaster joined Mac in la-la-ing a swooping theme on the highest note of which the martial Othello entered.

"''Tis yet to know, Iago, I fetch my life and being from men of royal siege" and so on, dears,' said McMaster, cutting severely to cue lines, saving the full surprise of his performance for a more auspicious hour.

The action shifted to the Senate. Ernie left the producer's table to preside, twitching with importance, as the Duke of Venice. Could he possibly be going to play the part? McMaster arranged the opening of the scene.

'Pom-tiddly-om-pom-pom-pom-pom!' he announced on a clarion note. 'That's your entrance, dears.'

He allowed the Duke a few minutes toothy debate of the perils besetting Venice and then, 'Now I come on. Pom-tiddly-om-pom-pom-pom-pom-pom-POM-pom-POM-pom-POM-pom POM-POM-POM!'

He had two words, like charms, to cover his production methods. One was 'Business' the other was 'Picture'. They occurred in this shorthand state in the margin of his prompt copy, over which Ernie kept religious watch to remind him sharply on occasion, 'Business, Mr. Mac.' 'Business' covered anything from a kiss to a drunken brawl, and 'Picture' was any particularly favoured piece of grouping. 'We do it like this, dear, for the Picture.'

Every leading player ('Principal') must enter centre-back and be cheered as they came on.

'Iago! Hooray! Iago!'

'Hurrah! Cassio! Cassio!'

When I met Tyrone Guthrie a year later he said, 'McMaster? He's pre-Macready!'

We came to the hat-dropping episode as outlined in Gordon Harbord's office.

'Whoops! His hat falls off, dear. Now, he tries to pick it up - gently - that's it. They all encourage him: Good old Cassio! Cassio! Cassio!' Mac strode about the nursery interpreting various bibulous characters. 'Now he falls over - ker-ASH! Go on, dear,' (encouragingly) 'ker - ASH! That's right. Now. Down on his knees, what does he think? He thinks immediately that he's in church, so he says his next line, "God forgive us our sins" Religious drunk, you see, dear.' This insight was produced as if he were Dover Wilson or Jan Kott. 'Of course, if you can think of any better business...'

'"I have lost my reputation!"' moaned Cassio with feeling.

Aside from rehearsals the voyage was fine. Our next port of call was Colombo in what was then still an island paradise called Ceylon. We had our first swim in warm tropical waters in the breakers at Mount Lavinia.

The *Orcades* ran into heavy seas in the Indian Ocean which was great fun. By the fourth week of the voyage we were more at home on the tilting deck than on steady land (we were always landsick when we first went ashore: the solid earth swaying beneath our feet.) But now we could relish the whiskey glasses sliding across the bar-room tables to shatter on the floor, which would have been difficult to stomach in the first week.

We first tipped into Australia at Freemantle, the port for Perth, and took a taxi into the city for our first sight of Oz (which nobody called it then). It was midsummer. The light, no other word for it, was golden. And I remember the sky seemed further from the earth.

We then spent a few last shipboard days, crossing the Australian Bight before making our final landfall at Melbourne, where we were to open the tour at the Princess Theatre, an Edwardian barn seating about sixteen hundred.

Coming from darkened and rationed Britain it seemed like Christmas every day. The bright lights (I can't remember, now, when the neon signs were restored to London, but it must have been later than this, because we were like Bisto Kids in fairyland) - the stores crowded with goods - many of them our own exports. Unrationed clothes - and food... I remember we ordered roast chicken every night in our hotel to begin with.

My un-processed film had been confiscated by the Customs for fear it might be pornographic. But I don't think even an encounter between Paul Stephenson and a goat in the rough quarter of Aden could have merited that description. When they returned it I desperately needed something to show it on. With our now regular salary bulging in our wallets I treated myself to the latest Pathescope motorised home movie projector, the Gem, which steaded me for a good twenty years. Until, in fact, 9.5mm film went off the market. This was a great blow to home movie enthusiasts because it was without doubt the most economical and successful gauge. You had superb quality from a picture area almost as large as 16mm at a fraction of the cost. This was achieved by putting the sprocket holes of the film in the centre, between frames, instead of taking up a lot of space down the sides. 8mm was a rotten gauge by comparison. But we nine-fivers lost out in the end to economic pressures. The gauge had originally been developed by Pathé in France who were in a sickly state after Vichy and the German occupation so American Kodak were able to bludgeon their way in and advertise them out of the market. Much the same as happened in the early days of Video when the superior Video 2000 system developed on the continent by Phillips had to give way to the Japanese VHS. Ah, Progress...

Bored with rehearsing OTHELLO, and convinced by now that we all knew our lines, Mac announced one day, about three weeks before the planned opening of our season, that we were going to start on THE TAMING OF THE SHREW. This had never been mentioned in London but Mac was beginning to think we needed contingency planning. 'OTHELLO may run three weeks, it may run six months. But we mustn't be caught napping, dears.' And obviously Petruchio would be a better contrast for him than the other plays that had been mentioned. Daphne was Bianca and I was handed Hortensio, who turned out to be quite a lad. Robert Helpmann's sister Sheila came in as Kate to represent local talent and add to the publicity, which had been initially rather hair-raising. When the posters went up we discovered we were 'The Stratford-on-Avon Players'. The three of us who had just recently been at Stratford thought this was a sleight of hand that might not stand up under a Trades Descriptions Act so, as I had unfortunately been elected Equity Deputy, I was deputed to raise the matter with our employer. He was very miffed. 'If Equity know so much about it, dear, why don't they put on the plays themselves?' It was out of his hands, he said. It had been done by the Australian management without consultation. So, to preserve our own good name back home, the three of us, plus Dorothy Wheatley and John Edmund, put our names to a letter to the Stratford Herald back in England, saying something to the effect that we had signed contracts with the Anew McMaster Company and there had been no intent, on anybody's part, to deceive. How naive we were! In the fullness of time, allowing for postal deliveries, our letter boomeranged back on to the front page of the Melbourne Argus. Mac was furious and didn't speak to us for weeks. 'Stabbed in the back again!' he complained to anyone who would listen.

I've often wondered whether I'd recognise Australia if I went back. It all seemed very clean then. Probably still does. Bright sunlight on wide avenues, some lined with palms. White houses. Trams, trams, trams, helter-skeltering with their grinding complaining whine. Badly driven double-decker buses with noisy exhausts. Milk bars. Shanty pubs open all day until the dreaded 'six o'clock swill' when the entire population seemed to reel drunkenly on to the streets. Greek fruiterers. Greek restaurants.

We eventually came to the opening night, a performance graven on the memory.

The eleven piece live orchestra conducted by M. Henri Penn played 'Dance from Othello' by Coleridge-Taylor and 'Musical Moments' by Bayford (I have these details from the programme) and the curtain rose on a solid conventional set to represent the exterior of Brabantio's house. Not unpleasing, not striking.

Ernie, wigged and bearded as the Duke of Venice, held sway in the prompt corner, trying to keep the loose sleeves of his voluminous robe from tangling in the cue switches.

In a feeble glow of amber light the opening scene between Iago and Roderigo proceeded unilluminated and unillumining. A window high up in Brabantio's house was flung open and Eric Maxon nearly fell out with over-acting. From where I sat waiting in the wings I could see his swaying back as he balanced precariously on a step ladder. He looked like a man working a Punch and Judy show.

Suddenly a spotlight shafted down. The music was transferred from the live orchestra pit to a record from the prompt corner. No carefully cued cassettes then. Just 78s with a big white painted cue blob. Mac's Love Music. The great man was coming. Unfortunately his theme from Verdi on fulsome strings was only the introduction to a soprano aria, and it needed a quick ear and a slick hand to cut out the music in time. But Ernie's movements were greatly restricted by his costume and the lady's voice blazoned from the loudspeakers for a full second before it was rudely cut off. 'Otell- ' she had managed.

Mac took the first speeches fairly quietly and with what was for him, as the audience would later come to recognise, restraint.

"'Tis yet to know, Iago..."

My cue approached.

"'But look,'" said Mac without looking, he invariably faced front which made him look rather like a Thunderbirds puppet, "'what light comes yond?'"

I entered to an unsteady trumpet call from M. Penn's boys in the pit. Not much you could do in these circs but belt out the lines.

First scene done. The action so far had taken about ten minutes. The curtain remained down for almost as long again while there was a complete change of setting. Ernie hopped about tripping over his train supervising the very leisurely local stage-hands and lending a hand with the shifting of the flats. Mr. and Mrs. McMaster in person put the finishing touches to the stage dressing. When all was ready Ernie remained to preside over the Senate looking like a hot and breathless Father Christmas.

Mac spoke of his wooing of the gentle Desdemona with piercing monotony, hitting the first word of every line on a high, shrill and unpleasing note with terrible regularity like a man in a trance.

He used to tell us with pride that an admirer had once taken down his performance in musical notation. If so, this bit was ostinato.

"'Here comes the lady. Let her witness it.'"

The unfortunate Love Music returned, possibly by mistake for Ernie wagged desperately behind the council table.

"'O-'" sang the mystery voice.

More music from M. Penn and the orchestra brought the curtain down for the second time in the first of three acts and there was another full-blown scene-change to the dockside at Cyprus with a wobbly back-projection of rolling seas. This device was Mac's pride and joy and he allowed no one to work it but himself. He now set it in motion by giving it several smart bangs. M. Penn served up some oriental wailings on the oboe and the fourth wall was once again banished to the flies.

This was the scene where the extras came into their own. An apathetic crowd of non-actors with modern brown boots poking beneath their exotic gowns, for all the world like Chu-Chin-Chow in the village hall, shambled aimlessly about getting in the way of the action. As Cassio tried to calm Desdemona's anxiety for her lord, lost on the high seas, a cheer from Mrs. Mac and Ernie, presumably down on the beach, announced that her fears were groundless.

'Othello! Othello!'

Mac entered in an enormous helmet like an inverted ice cream cone. He searched out the most becoming light, shuffled into it, spoke, and his helmet fell off.

"'O my fair warrior!'" He crushed her passionately to his bare and blackened bosom, facing front and arranging the folds of his skirt.

After their intimate exchange Othello hurried his bride off to the castle to make the most of his wedding night leaving Cassio to maintain law and order over the unpredictable Cypriots. This was the occasion for a lively and high-spirited dance by six Cypriot maidens (one of them lately of the Ballet Rambert) arranged, unbelievably, and unbelievably badly, by Walter Gore. Then came my painful hat-dropping episode which I had not been canny enough to avoid, and then, mercifully, another interval. Change of costume and an easier shift in the next act. This, as Mac was never too tactful to remind us, was where the play began. The action steadied down. The scene-shifters could knock off for a pint and Ernie, free of his costume but still incongruously bearded, could put his feet up in the prompt corner. The curtain would only be lowered once more to enable Mac to change into yet another of his wife's colourful garments. It would be wrong to call anything so leisurely a quick change as he invariably had time for a glass of whiskey and a sandwich with Mrs. Mac. When the curtain was down it was for him as if the audience were no longer there.

However, let me do justice, it was now that he had his best scene. In the long duologue with Iago where the poison of jealousy is first administered to his mind and where doubts crowd on incredulity thick and fast, there were visible the bare bones of a kind of performance probably not seen since the days of Macready - or more possibly Kean. As the passion grew on him he was like a gathering whirlwind. His great voice soared up and down. His large features worked like a silent film star's. It was Othello splashed in primary colours on an enormous canvas. He forced his way through the texture of the play and came out the other side, leaving his supporting company twittering round him like inconsequential mice. He systematically committed every breach of Hamlet's advice to the players. Paul Stephenson's subtle Iago was swamped. He was fanatical, semi-operatic. He stood facing the audience and stormed them with sound. As loud pedal music it was magnificent.

'............Like to the Pontic sea,
Whose icy current and compulsive course
Ne'er feels retiring ebb, but keeps due on
To the Propontic and the Hellespont...'

It crackled with hard 'c's' and spat with 'p's' and 's's'.

'Even so my bloody thoughts, with violent pace,
Shall ne'er look back, ne'er ebb to humble love...'

A swooping, rising inflection dwelt repetitively, pitifully, on those 'ne'er's.'

''Till that a capable and wide revenge...'

The briefest pause, and then it was resolved as emphatically as a whirlwind could suck it under -

'Swallow them up...
                    Now, by yond marble heaven...'

And it was the brass section of a full orchestra now.

It is in my mind's ear still. Unforgettable. Time had side-tracked and given all that Mac had to give, intact, to the wrong generation. He was not necessarily a stupid man, or even a wrong-headed. He was an anachronism.

But he had given them a memorable quarter of an hour. He had become a medium for the titanic life-force in the soul of man. One brief glimpse and then it was whipped away, covered in scambled verbiage, killed with ugly movement, and buried in the banality of his semi-operatic style. His representation of Othello's fit was a severe test for the audience. With his trunk bent forward as though spewing into the footlights, the sharp voice came harshly in machine-gun repetition. 'Handkerchief - confession - handkerchief - confession - handkerchief...' Then, jumping up and down, up and down, like a marionette on wire, he fell awkwardly to the ground.

'This stops the show in Ireland,' said Ernie in the wings, licking his lips in anticipation. 'Mr. Mac usually has to take a call after this. They won't let him go. You see.'

But they did let him go, and very quietly. The curtain was lowered in uneasy silence. Mac called consolingly to Ernie from a sitting-up position on the stage.

'They're just too bloody respectful, dear, that's what it is.'

To his wife he had reached an acceptable explanation which he clung to loudly and nervously, piercing his dressing-room door.   -

'They don't understand it, you see. They're too uneducated. But they respect us. We're earning their respect.'

The opening of the third act was Daphne's. She was first seen at her rosary while M. Penn's orchestra played The Dream of Olwen. (It's in the programme.) Then with Dorothy Wheatley preparing her for bed came the sad little willow-song scene. Both of them could have made it work by nature as much as by art. By feeling right and speaking no more than was set down for them. But in their necessary effort to make themselves heard over a record of howling wind the sense of it was lost. Over the dressing-room Tannoy it sounded like a Gothic nightmare. The relay system distorted Daphne's tender treble into a mad neigh. 'Ah, weelow, weelow, weelow...' And the wind howled. It was Otranto at least.

She was finally tucked in, soft flaxen hair falling over a tiny hump of white sheet, and Emilia left. She slept. A light grew at the top of a curved stairway, flickered, went out, and grew again. McMaster descended the stairs looking murderous, a lantern in one hand and a scimitar in the other. Strings moaned from the loudspeakers. 'Otello' shrieked a soprano voice without warning.

'Blast!' said Othello under his breath.

Her message faithfully delivered at last the unseen singer was quietened with an atmospheric splutter, symbolic of Desdemona's tragic end to come.

"'It is the cause, it is the cause, my soul,'" declaimed McMaster.

"'Let me not name it to you, you chaste stars.'"

Beauty shone through again briefly, hanging a silver chain of words above the sleeping form.

When she awoke it was to plead with a madman. She staked her all on perhaps the finest line in the play,

"'Kill me tomorrow: let me live tonight.'"

But it was no use. He throttled her without even looking at her, arranging the fall of his skirt the while.

You don't believe me? Then I will quote you a letter in the Melbourne press.

'This Othello constantly drew attention to his black body. While emoting at his wife's bedside he made a conscious change of position to allow much more black leg to be visible through the slit in his satin costume. And oh, those armbands, which were eventually slipped to the floor! In another scene he quickly placed a sword in readiness for a stabbing which was to come later in the dialogue. The Melbourne public knows instinctively these insincerities of acting and tells friends to stay away...'

I'm afraid they did and they did.

The contempt grew on both sides. Mac began to take a little too much liquid comfort. He moved tearfully towards me in the last scene, emending the text with a few private asides.

"'Will you, I pray,'" (Pearls before swine, dear, pearls before swine) "'demand that demi-devil'" (Don't try, dear, they're not worth it) "'why he hath thus abused my soul and body?'"

Othello staggered to the bed and imprinted a last, transferable black kiss on Desdemona's pale cheek. There never died more disappointed man. I remembered that first reading. 'I suppose I *could* die on the bed...' and felt my aching throat pronounce:

'"For he was great of heart..."'

Afterwards we could hear his voice coming brokenly from his dressing-room, 'But where were the cheers...where was the applause...?'

Mac was a generous man. No Wolfit. He said to me in rehearsal for the Ghost in Hamlet (He in his fifties was Hamlet, I, aged 24, was the ghost of his father. Horatio had gone to the elderly Maxon.) 'This is your scene, dear. I'm just down here lying on the ground.'

True enough I had a large rostrum centre back to myself while he lay on the ground and arranged his costume. But if he thought I was losing the audience he would come to my aid. Lifting his head sombrely he would exclaim 'Mother!' Then, sobbing, sink back down again.

The Melbourne season was curtailed after about six weeks, which had included performances of THE SHREW, and we moved on to Adelaide, where the whole sorry business was repeated, except that we had now added a true fourteen carat gem to the repertoire, George Du Maurier's TRILBY. Here Mac was totally in his element as Svengali. Loud, vulgar, funny and frightening He had apparently studied it in detail with 'my great master, Oscar Asche' and for once his style was totally right. I was in my Lugosian vein again as Gecko, Svengali's pathetic violin-playing side-kick. The tour was made worthwhile by the fact that in the scene where Trilby sang 'Ben Bolt' I got to conduct the orchestra in the orchestra pit. This was an adolescent, dream come true with a vengeance.

Alas, by the time we reached Perth, the last date on our severely truncated tour, I was conducting two loudspeakers and an arrangement of potted palms.

CHAPTER EIGHT

In which I become a Director

'Scorning the use of a drop curtain or any suggestion of scenery, John Harrison produced the play (PERICLES, PRINCE OF TYRE) without a single interval. It ran for two hours, one scene following the next in quick rotation, without so much as a suggestion of a hold-up.'

THE STAGE, July 1950.

And so we found ourselves unexpectedly back in England in September after another healthy month at sea. This time on the S.S. *Strathaird*, with no rehearsals, no McMasters who had stayed behind, and with Bombay added to the other ports of call. Paul Stephenson was the only other returnee from our little band. Everybody else was still looking to strike gold in Australia. We embarked at Fremantle on the 1st of August, the ticket foil tells me. Total No. of Souls - Two. In berths 713/714. Again way below the waterline, but what matter? This voyage was total holiday as we shed the traumas of the preceding months.

The peak Australian experience had been crossing the Nullarbor (literally 'no tree') plain for two days by train from Adelaide to Perth. Flatness, like the bottom of a dusty cardboard box, in all directions. 'Why aren't you flying?' asked our Aussie friends, 'there's nothing to see.' 'But,' we explained, 'there's nowhere in Europe where you *can* go for two days and see nothing.' We stopped and wandered about in the gold rush town of Kalgoorlie, feeling like prospectors out of the Old West, before finally rolling down to the lushness of Perth.

There we had the time-jump experience of acting by old-fashioned limelight. There was a strike and a power cut, but the theatre still had its Victorian gas limes, hissing and burning on us like blow-torches. They had a cold mystery, but little charm. Perhaps they needed to penetrate the fog of a thousand pipe-smokers to give the real period essence.

Good correspondents had kept us posted with events on the London theatre scene.

Peter, from Covent Garden Opera House, where he was now the youngest ever Director of Productions:

'...I'm managing to write, because we're in the middle of a Wagner performance. We're doing the "Ring": it's the wild success of London: everyone has been fighting for the last six weeks for the privilege of paying a couple of guineas per seat: meanwhile I'm labouring under a great Guilt-Complex - I <u>have</u> a seat, I <u>have</u> to attend, I'm <u>paid</u> to attend, but, alas, I cant <u>bear</u> Wagner. So amongst the ecstatic orgasmatic crowd I wander lonely as a cloud. But to-night it's Gotterdammerung - the curtain rose at 5 p.m. and wont be down till 11.45!!! - even McThing in all his horror can't equal that - so I've given my seat to Larry Payne and am enjoying myself far more writing to you.

My sweets, my heart broke for you when I read your first letter. And now... what goes on?...how does one cross Australia on the Trans-Siberian railway? ...it sounds a bit eccentric...

What's the news here? I don't really know where to start. For my own part, I'm desperately busy. Especially with the opera, preparing next season, finding singers and so on. We open with a brand new opera written by Arthur Bliss and (of all people!) J.B. Priestley. It's called 'The Olympians', is a charming romantic story set in 19th century France of the Gods returning to earth disguised as a group of strolling players (a la Anew McMaster who may well be Jupiter in disguise, don't you think?) and to everyone's surprise - in view of J.B.P's connection - will have nothing to do with Social Significance. I'm going to produce it, and am working now on the designs. Then I'm doing 'Salome' with an extraordinary diva called Welitsch and, very likely, decor by Salvador Dali! Then maybe a play. Maybe 'Measure for Measure' for Stratford. Maybe a quite marvellous modern opera 'Wozzeck' for the 1950 Edinburgh Festival.

Anyway, a lot in the air, all liable to fall through at a moment's notice!...

The rest of the theatre. Well, as you know, there's Paul in 'Adventure Story'. When I saw it on the first night, he gave a quite wonderful performance. Unfortunately, although the evening seemed a triumph, he hasn't quite made the total success and hasn't really <u>arrived</u> in London. The reasons seem to be (1) that the play isn't good and isn't drawing the town, and (2) that apparently Paul's performance is very variable. So you meet people who think Paul wonderful, and people who are disappointed - and the answer is just that they've been on different nights. I've got a play I want to do with a lovely part for him - we're going to decide about it in the next few days.

Otherwise - you're missing 'Daphne Laureola' not only Edith Evans' fantastic performance, but also - in my (solitary) opinion - the best play in the language since 'Heartbreak House'. Then there's the new 'Lady's Not for Burning'. At the Arts, I hated the play; this time I was enchanted. It's a ravishing production, exquisitely acted and spoken. In every way, magical: Pamela Brown heaven, only Claire Bloom (sincerely!) not terribly good. Then, a few good foreign films. Two incredible picture exhibitions - from Munich and from Vienna. Otherwise, nothing. You're well away. Clothes rationing may have ended, but there are enormous queues for sweets, the bottom has fallen out of the show business, the cinema crisis is worse than ever, all actors are out of work. My 'Dark of the Moon' which you may have heard was a really tremendous hit comes off in three weeks. So be well pleased to have a good job, Shakespeare, your own mutual sweet company, and free sunshine...'

A good period touch that in 1949 he still had to explain to us that WOZZECK was 'a quite marvellous modern opera.' Dali *did* do the decor for the Welitsch SALOME. And as for 'maybe 'Measure for Measure' at Stratford'! This became the production with Gielgud as Angelo for which Peter also designed the sets and wrote the music. A seven league stride towards the simplicity of his mature style. "Adventure Story" was Terence Rattigan's dull piece about Alexander the Great. Paul's first starring role in the West End. I think the play with the 'lovely part for him' might have been RING ROUND THE MOON, Christopher Fry's version of Anouilh's L'INVITATION AU CHATEAU, yet to come.

Next out of the post-bag was dilletante actor, outsize in every sense personality and joker, Peter Bull, who later wrote a lively series of autobiographies including I KNOW THE FACE BUT... He wrote, to Daphne, as the only survivor of the Arts production in the West End's LADY'S NOT FOR BURNING.

'...I hardly know where to start with my news because I don't think you will want to hear very much about the lady. I can truthfully say that I don't think there is any comparison between you and Miss Bloom and a lot of people have confirmed this view. She's a nice girl though and I will say no more. We are a very happy company and the play is an immense success to our great astonishment. We had a very peculiar tour and a lot of people stayed away. I thought during rehearsals I wouldn't be able to stand the pace and Mr. G but I survived by a hair's breadth and now like him very much indeed. David Evans and I share a room and it is very cosy and as I adore Miss Brown and have for years it makes for peace. The slump is here in full swing and only about four plays are surviving. "The Heiress", "Harvey", and "Daphne Laureola" are O.K. but some of the others are having a murderous time. I think in a way you are well out of England as everyone is very depressed and we are in the middle of a heat wave which makes Esme Percy a bit high at matinees and me high all the time. Paul and Joy are in Cornwall I mean Devon. The play petered out a fortnight ago. I didn't care for it at all and thought Paul badly produced. I so wanted him to have the full success on his first big show but I hope next time he'll pull it off. Bobby Harris has made a big personal success in "Ann Veronica" but I fear the play won't run. Gielgud goes to Stratford next season with it is whispered P. Ashcroft. His prod of "Much Ado" is quite enchanting. The film world is moribund and Miss Slater is well out of "Maytime in Mayfair" known to the trade as maytime up the creek. I had a wonderful holiday at Christmas in Portugal and will have to wait until I get back there. Bathing on Christmas day and all and it was heaven. I have lost a stone in weight and rightly and am trying to get more off still. Christopher Fry is going to be very rich and is writing a play for the Oliviers and one for Hermione Gingold. Go and see Bob Morley if you are still in Australia and ask him to send me some more soap. I am still trying to get my war book published but very wisely nothing ever happens. John Gielgud has flown to Aberdeen to-day to get his degree so we are hoping he'll be back in time to give us some notes (we still change our moves most perfs)...'

Gielgud was famous as a director for keeping everyone on their toes by suddenly announcing 'I'm coming on "down left" tonight instead of "up right".' And for sacking a fair number of the cast through the rehearsal period if they didn't match up to his exacting standards.

We missed ADVENTURE STORY but got back in time for James Bridie's DAPHNE LAUREOLA and I certainly endorsed Master Brook's view of it at the time. I don't know how it would stand up now. (John Trewin dubbed him Master Brook.) It's fascinating to see how deeply into text Peter was still.

Paul was in a production of Chekhov's THE SEAGULL billed opposite Mai Zetterling. It was the first time I'd read his name in such large letters. I went backstage to see him, really quite shy, because I'd seen little to nothing of him in the year in which he had become that distanced heavenly object, a 'star'. Almost the first thing he said as I tentatively poked my head round the dressing-room door was, 'Look, nothing's changed. One's friends are one's friends, and I feel no more at home in London than you do.'

I decided the time had come to make a clean break with acting. Gecko in TRILBY in Western Australia under limelight seemed the perfect valediction. I let it be known to all and sundry that I was now a director and stood back to await events.

I'd have got nowhere without my friends.

It has to be admitted that I became a director by default. The acting had been a sort of stop-gap while I had hoped to become established as a writer. But this was not happening. I completed about forty thousand words of a novel about a theatrical company on tour in Australia before finally admitting to myself that it told no story. Also the truth of the experience was far too eccentric for fiction. John Trewin had been encouraging as always ('Grand!') and shown the fragment to Daniel George of Jonathan Cape. He thought 'your young friend should finish his novel' but said it didn't shape like one that would be acceptable to Cape. He put his finger on the spot. 'Is anything going to happen?' Well, no, actually...

And yet to go on with acting...

I could never knuckle under for a lifetime as a cog in the machine. I always wanted to be on the outside cranking the handle. The frustration of being in misconceived productions was intolerable to me. So many directors seemed simply to miss the point. Or wilfully to distort it. I had only ever been happy with Brook or Ayliff. Ayliff was retired or dead and there was no way Peter was going to keep me employed consistently. He wasn't running his own company then. We used to talk about it but he said he wasn't ready.

Another thing. I was very sensitive to the personality risks involved in being an actor: the appeals to vanity, role-playing and dressing up - just plain poncing about. I was perfectly capable of indulging them to the hilt, and didn't like myself when I caught myself doing so. I used to say, arrogantly, it was not a job for a grown man.

My closest friends were exempt from this Puritan stricture. Paul had never wanted to be anything but an actor and had gone about it with dedication and humility. We had once, long ago in Lightwoods Park Birmingham, discussed our ambitions. His was, quite simply, 'to be a good actor'. Not to run the National Theatre, make a million, become 'Sir Paul' or a star. Just 'to be a good actor.' Don was exempt because he had somehow sprung from the womb with:

a high silk hat and a walking cane
a diamond watch on a golden chain...

and was totally in character as an actor-laddie from the age of 24.

But I was a prickly dressing-room companion.

Neither did I have that essential love-affair with the audience. I didn't love them particularly and I never cared whether they loved me. I wanted their attention. I wanted to hold them in the palm of my hand. I wanted to share with them this delight and that. I enjoyed their admiration but I didn't need their love. And yet this is fundamental to the actor/audience relationship. I remember being told whilst still a student at Birmingham, 'all the women in the audience should want to go to bed with you.' I don't think they ever did. (There was a famous actor who did after seeing me as Benvolio, but that was another matter.

I escaped from his house at midnight like Cinderella fleeing the ball.)

Anyway I decided to sit it out for a bit.

We went down to Sidmouth to visit Mum and Shirley and it was whilst there that I received a phone call from Harry Bristow, ex-General Manager of the Birmingham Rep who once used to hand me my Friday pay packet, now gone down-market to the same position in weekly rep at the David Garrick Theatre, Lichfield.

'John?' came the bluff, fruity voice, 'I hear you're a director now?' (I certainly didn't undeceive him.) 'Do you know David Garrick's version of the Shrew, "Katherine and Petruchio"? (Knew of it.) 'And I expect you know Dr. Johnson was born here? We're having a Johnson Week Celebration and the theatre's putting on the Garrick version because he and Johnson were such great friends. Not to beat about the bush, if you were asked to direct it, what period would you set it in?'

Garrick's version? At a theatre called the David Garrick? For Dr. Johnson Week Celebrations? Only one answer seemed possible.

'Presumably around seventeen-seventy-something.'

'How soon can you come?'

Two things transpired. Diana Mahoney (Mrs. Sinden) had been in the company earlier in the summer and she and Don had been cracking me up to the proprietor, a Mrs. Joan Cowlishaw, as a brilliant up-coming director.

The other was that the current incumbent had been about to launch into rehearsals for KATHERINE AND PETRUCHIO when Mrs. Cowlishaw noticed black actors arriving. Nothing racist but she was curious. She made a few enquiries and discovered that her director was planning to set the action during the American Civil War. Without more ado she sacked him. His name was Kenneth Tynan. That same Kenneth Tynan who later became Dramatic Critic Extraordinary and literary manager of the National Theatre and was the first to utter the rudest word of all on live television.

Exit Tynan left, enter Harrison right.

Rather a nice idea, actually, a Scarlet O'Hara/Rhett Butler relationship for Katherine and Petruchio, but eccentric in the circumstance of choosing Garrick's version. I met Ken then for the first time and liked him. His middle name may have been Peacock but he had a quixotic sincerity. He was quite without bitterness at the turn of events. His sights were set further afield than Lichfield and he was just having fun and drawing attention to himself. He had already earned a double page spread in Illustrated Magazine by dressing every member of the cast in a different period in a previous production. This was well before it became a Stratford cliché.

The moment I became a director, oddly enough, my relationship with everybody seemed to come right: with the actors, the technicians, the audience. I became more acceptable to my fellows: an unexpected bonus.

KATHERINE AND PETRUCHIO, in a double bill if you please (Ken's idea again) with Henry Fielding's TOM THUMB THE GREAT, was successful enough for me to be invited to stay on as resident director. I wouldn't have touched weekly rep with a barge pole as an actor, but for a fledgling director it provided me with the one thing I desperately needed - to cover the most gaping hole in my armour - a fresh technical exercise every week. In those days the director did his own lighting. It was part of the job, and an invaluable tool in the hands of someone like Brook. Lighting Designers hadn't been invented. Unfortunately, like most actors, I had been grandly uninterested in how all this was achieved. For the first show I stood nervously on stage with the Chief Electrician (There *was* only one).

'What do you fancy, John?'

'Well... what have you got rigged this week?'

He showed me.

'Wonderful. That'll do perfectly. Don't touch it.'

And I rushed off and bought the only book then available on the subject, Pitman's Stage Lighting.

"Sparks" thought he'd met an easy touch.

'Same again, John?' he asked me a week later.

'No...o...I don't think so,' I said. 'We'll have alternate 52, 54 and 17 in the front bar, 51, 17 and Open White in the floats, and 52 in the front of house. And I think we might try a couple of Perch positions. Here's a plan of the rig and tomorrow we'll go through the cues.'

There was absolutely no way in which you could direct a play in a week, but you could learn about lighting and staging and how to get on with a company. It was an agreeable madness. I even talked Mrs. Cowlishaw into letting me do THE SEAGULL. In weekly rep it must have been a first.

I stuck it for three months. It wasn't all Garrick and Chekhov. There were Coward and Priestley and Dodie Smith and all sorts in a dream-like jumble. Lichfield was a pleasant place to be and I lived comfortably with a chiropodist and his family, very into music, with a huge horn gramophone and fibre needles which you had to sharpen before playing each side. It was here that I heard for the first time Brahms's Liebeslieder Waltzes in the magical Viennese recording by Irmgard Seefried, Hans Hotter and others. I have never heard a later performance capture their ease, that Biedermeier atmosphere of lamplit rooms and a group of friends enjoying themselves around the piano. Fortunately it has now been transferred to CD.

After I'd left Lichfield we spent Christmas in very diggy digs in Birmingham. Daphne had joined the Rep for their Christmas production, DOCTOR'S DELIGHT, Sir Barry's adaptation of Moliere's MALADE IMAGINAIRE which had first been aired in my time there back in 1945. Michael Langham dusted it down and gave it a lively Christmas-cardy production with bags of movement. Her colleagues included John Neville, Donald Pleasance, Eric Porter, and her romantic lead was Peter Vaughan. The Rep was keeping true to tradition.

I was beating on all doors to get work as a director. One that opened to me was the old Guildford Rep in the High Street (which preceded, indeed paved the way for, the Yvonne Arnaud) run by two half-brothers, Roger Winton and Patrick Henderson, who I don't think have ever had their due. I salute them now. Roger ('Roy'), the elder, who acted and directed, was tall, willowy, vague in the extreme, but he had a certain flair. Pat, even taller, upstanding and good-looking, was totally on the ball, a bright administrator who would have had much to give the post-war theatre had he not died tragically young. My first production for them was an adaptation of THE VICAR OF WAKEFIELD about which I remember nothing except that it introduced me to Claud Whatham, then a very young designer, later a film director. (SWALLOWS AND AMAZONS amongst others, in 1974.)

I badgered everybody I could think of with projects.

The Sindens had done their bit. Now it was Paul's turn.

I sat in his dressing-room at the Globe (now The Gielgud) one day sharing ice-cream between performances of RING ROUND THE

MOON which was a colossal hit.

'How can I help?' he asked.

'Play in something on a Sunday.'

He didn't hesitate.

'What shall we do?'

'Pericles.'

PERICLES, PRINCE OF TYRE had been a pet project of mine for years. Hardly anybody knew it when I first used to talk about it to Paul in Birmingham. It had only been seen twice professionally since the turn of the century. At Stratford in 1900 and in Regents Park in 1939. Then Nugent Monck at Stratford in our 1947 season had cavalierly lopped the first act entirely. 'Not by Shakespeare,' he said primly. And apart from a wonderfully affecting recognition scene between Paul and Daphne as his daughter Marina (and an excellent wide-boy Boult from John Blatchley - later a successful opera director) the production had been thin.

Ancient Gower, the sententious Chorus with his doggerel couplets, is the bugbear. Otherwise the piece is an off-beat fairy tale with dark resonances, and the unexpectedly cruel juxtaposition of the lurid brothel scenes gives it a special tang. It also reeks of the sea. Whoever might have had a hand in doctoring the script, Shakespeare's unmistakeable voice sounds early .

'.........the blind mole casts

Copt hills towards heaven, to tell the earth is thronged

By man's oppression, and the poor worm doth die for't.'

That's in Act One.

'Yet cease your ire you angry stars of heaven,

Wind, rain, and thunder, remember earthly man

Is but a substance that must yield to you.'

Act Two. Shades of Lear. And then by Act Three,

'Thou God of this great Vast, rebuke these surges,

Which wash both heaven and hell, and thou that hast

Upon the winds command, bind them in brass,

Having called them from the deep. O still
Thy deaf'ning dreadful thunders, gently quench
Thy nimble sulphurous flashes. O how Lychorida?
How does my queen? Then storm venomously,
Wilt thou spit all thyself? The sea-man's whistle
Is as a whisper in the ears of death,
Unheard.'

Prospero and Lear mixed.

Certainly none of his contemporaries doubted for a moment that the play was his. Ben Jonson even jibed enviously at its success, 'Some mouldy tale like PERICLES... framed to please.'

We needed some auspices under which to present it and approached the lively Under Thirty Theatre Group. One of its founder directors was Hazel Vincent Wallace who later devoted a lifetime to managing the Thorndyke Theatre, Leatherhead. It didn't cost them a bob. Paul and I went halves on all the expenses. But they provided the organisation. I didn't want to do it in a theatre on a standing set, the usual Sunday show practice. I needed to find a hall that would accommodate the sort of simplified design I had in mind. We trekked about all over the place and finally lighted on the Rudolf Steiner Hall in Baker Street.

I asked Claud Whatham to design it. He said he knew somebody much better and introduced me to Voytek. Roman Voytek Szenzikowski had landed up in England with the Free Polish forces, and somehow got himself to the Old Vic School run by Michel St. Denis, George Devine and Glen Byam Shaw. This was the first theatre school to think about training for other than actors, and had a very productive design and technical course.

Voytek was a natural, in the romantic Polish graphic tradition. He could produce you a water-colour idea of a design in five minutes. In those days we worked mostly from visuals. The architectural, model-making designers didn't begin until John Bury in the late fifties. Voytek's models were messy, compared to his drawings which were works of art. Many still adorn my walls. And his ground-plans rarely fitted the stage. But his colour-sense was ravishing. Even the paint splashes on his costume designs were unerringly right. He loved to talk, like most Poles, and was only unhappy when we had finalised the design in our minds and he had to go away and work on it.

'Oh...' he would say, crestfallen, 'no more discarssion?'

Through Norman Platt I had met a composer friend of his called Diccon Shaw, son of folk-song guru Martin Shaw, who had already written a setting of 'When lovely woman stoops to folly...' for my VICAR OF WAKEFIELD at Guildford. Explosive and bearded, school-mastering (or rather 'cramming') for a living, Diccon became a good friend and later agnostic-father (his word) to our firstborn. He wrote a complete score which was played live by a nervous girl harpist, some winds and percussion.

Andrée Howard, a notable Rambert choreographer, was somehow cajoled into arranging a dance. Among the students Claud and Voytek had laid on, making jewellery was Eileen Diss, later a successful stage and television designer.

All our friends were pressed into service. Peter Bull doubled the Pandar with Anthiocus. Don played a fisherman and press-ganged his brother Leon. Beatrix Lehmann was gloriously wicked as the Bawd. Daphne doubled Thaisa and Marina, mother and daughter. Paul asked me to find a part for his Ring Round The Moon understudy, David Phethean, who made a sensitive Lysimachus. Boult was played by a friend we had made in Australia, Peter O'Shaughnessy, over in what Aussies still called 'Home' to seek his fortune. A colleague of Paul's in RING... suggested her friend John Lindsay who brought a wondrous mesmerism to that very Alternative practitioner Cerimon. Ewen Solon (later to be Rupert Davies's side-kick in the first MAIGRET TV series) had acted for me at Guildford and was the Macbeth-like Cleon. Somebody pressed on us an enthusiastic Shakespearian, deaf but game, Reginald Jarman, who made a rumbustious Simonides, though his squawking deaf-aid was a hazard. We chose four all-purpose 'walk-ons' in their last term at R.A.D.A. who included Tenniel Evans and Gerald Harper. And Simonides's incestuous daughter was a statuesque model girl called Dagmar Wynter who later changed her christian name to Dana and became a minor Hollywood film star. Voytek spent more time on her fittings than on anyone else's.

All in all it would have cost a small fortune to assemble this array of talent - except that everybody was working for nothing.

Claud organised the technical arrangements for the simple rostra we needed and brought in a gang of enthusiastic lighting and wardrobe people from the Old Vic School.

I knew how I wanted to tackle Ancient Gower. Daphne was in a play at the Lyric, Hammersmith, called IF THIS BE ERROR, which it was, but among the stars was Mary Morris. I had a vision of her as a seductively modern Scheherezade. Mary said she would do it so long as Audrey Cruddas, her current girl-friend, could design her costume, because, as she sensibly said, 'it would be nice to have something one could wear to Covent Garden afterwards.' I had a brief word with Voytek and agreed. After all she would be outside the action. Mary was the most ravishing looker when young. Paul and I were hopelessly infatuated with her. Jet black page-boy hair, lustrous eyes under firm dark brows, clear lines of nose and jaw ...if you ever see a re-issue of the Leslie Howard film PIMPERNEL SMITH - just look at her. She had a glorious, deep yet ringing, androgynous voice, wore slacks, tweed jackets and a man's pork pie hat with a feather.

When she modelled for us the garment Audrey had designed for her to 'wear to Covent Garden afterwards' we held our breath in wonder and shock. The top half was nakedly transparent black gauze. (This was 1950 remember. Nearly half a century before Elizabeth Hurley could attend a premiere in 'That Dress'.) Mary had no need of artificial support to trammel its purity. They were as firm as grapefruit. Ancient Gower was certainly going to rivet attention.

The period Voytek and I chose for the main play was vaguely Cretan and he designed a ravishing set of costumes - all of which were specially made by Claude's enthusiastic team. Peter Bull is very funny about them in his rare autobiography I KNOW THE FACE BUT... They were hand-died calico for cheapness and the die came off on everyone in the most intimate places.

Daphne and I were living now in a first floor flat at No.3 Shouldham Street, W.1. (in the heady days when the telephone number prefix was still AMBASSADOR), a pleasant row of Georgian artisan cottages just off George Street, a stone's throw from the Edgware Road and Baker street. We were on the end of the row, next door to a pub where we could pop in with a big jug for a fill-up of mild and bitter. For rehearsal we managed to hire a church hall just down the road behind the Marylebone Public Library, and there we worked hard for three weeks.

Mornings only because Paul needed to conserve his energy for Hugo and Frederick, the Fry/Anouilh twins. That suited me fine. I much prefer a long morning session. If I haven't achieved something creative by lunchtime my day is wasted. An awful lot of rehearsal time is spent in unproductive faffing about simply because people don't know how to use the time, or sometimes because they just want to prolong what, for them, is a pleasurable experience. But for me it's always been hard work. The degree of concentration I require of myself is unsparing. At the end of three or four hours I'm knackered. And actors always forget the director has a hundred and one other claims on his time from technicians in every area. So I was happy to work three weeks of mornings. After the weekly rep I'd been doing it seemed an expansive luxury. We didn't waste time with warm-ups in those days. As Wendy Hiller once said to me, in her best Lady Bracknell voice, 'Warm-ups? What ever for? I *arrive* warmed up.' And that was true. We brought our best concentration and full attention to the job from moment one. We didn't have to be wooed reluctantly to attention. Apart from anything else it was a bread-and-butter matter. There was no rehearsal payment then. In a commercial play you wanted to get the work done and open to the public so that you could start receiving your pay packet. And you needed to work hard because unless the play was a success there would *be* no pay packet. I'm not pretending this was entirely a good thing. Rehearsal is the toughest work of all and it's only right that it should be paid for, and possibly paid double. But the old system did concentrate the mind wonderfully and didn't favour time-wasters.

So PERICLES.

The reviews were good. First-string critics didn't usually attend Sunday night performances but we managed to intrigue a few aficionados.

Alan Dent in the News Chronicle, under the heading PERICLES - A RARE TREAT:

> Opportunities to see one of Shakespeare's least familiar plays - Swinburne called it "ill-fated and ill-famed" - are rare indeed... Paul Scofield's Pericles begins as something breath-taking in its youthful power and grace, and grows old and mellow with tragical dignity. Scholars question the amount Shakespeare

contributed to this play. Mr. Scofield makes the whole of his part seem to be written by no lesser hand. There are a dozen other qualities about this presentation not to be missed by any Shakespeare lover. But missed they will be unless the reader ...somehow or other ensures that he sees the only other performance which happens next Sunday at 8 o'clock. The programme expressly says that "tickets may not be purchased at the door."

Philip Hope-Wallace in the weekly TIME AND TIDE:

Putting on PERICLES for two Sunday performances is no task to envy. There were some painfully reach-me-down effects in John Harrison's production, yet all the right ideas are there, including playing the whole piece (narrative, not to be interrupted) in a single "take" of about two hours and of entrusting the chorus part of "Gower" to Mary Morris, dressed for some reason like one of the naughty ladies in an Eric Von Stroheim film. Miss Morris however did the job so blazingly well - with such voice, eye and hand - that everything was forgiven... Daphne Slater made a moving thing of the scene where she buys herself out of shame and where she encounters her lost father. This at any rate was unmistakeably "like Shakespeare" and I have found my whole week since strangely penetrated by the play's absurd dreamlike beauty.

J.C. Trewin in JOHN O'LONDON'S WEEKLY:

Once the piece had begun - I cannot say once the curtain had gone up, for there was no curtain - we were taken straight into the Levantine adventure, and so forward across the years to the last reunion at Ephesus, in Diana's temple. No sign here of that grim medial break when the house-lights disperse every shred of atmosphere and the people next to you assault your toes. Mr. Harrison is clearly fond of PERICLES: we can always tell when a producer is in love with his play. Not a glint of poetry, not a stab of drama, escaped him... Those of us who collected this PERICLES during its two Sunday nights, should not be allowed to keep the splendour of the Shipboard and Recognition scenes to ourselves. I implore an enlightened management to get in touch with John Harrison, through the Under Thirty Group which sponsored the play.

Enlightened managements clearly didn't read John O'London's Weekly. Jack Hylton showed a flicker of interest, without having seen the performance, but once having established that it could only go ahead without Paul, who was tied to the long-running RING ROUND THE MOON, the interest evaporated. There was a mild buzz around the profession but I had not really (to use Peter's earlier phrase about Paul) "arrived" as a director. There were no headline-getting eccentricities like dressing every character in a different period so I was generally assumed to be a mature director who had suddenly materialised from the backwoods, rather than the just-turned twenty-six-year-old that I actually was.

Both performances were jam-packed and the balance sheets make fun reading. 'Expenditure £167.19.10$\frac{1}{2}$d. Income £235.7.2d. In hand £67.7.3$\frac{1}{2}$d.' Better than Micawber's recipe for happiness, and Paul and I gratefully splashed our winnings on a party for the company. (Costume materials cost £53. Hire of drum - like the Mad-Hatter's headgear - 10/6.)

More touching than any reviews were the personal letters. I had a card from Esme Percy at the Savile Club, who keeps appearing unexplained in these pages. But the one I enjoyed most (apart from his sniffiness about the acting which was not generally shared) was Denis Cannan's.

> 2nd July 1950
>
> Dear John, I'm left wondering why there is such a fuss about Pericles being a 'Difficult' play; on Sunday night it all seemed so simple and moving and straightforward. This, to my mind, is the sign of a really good production. Frankly I expected the (Exactly) two hours traffic to be a bit of a strain. It was much less of a strain than one act of Fry. It seemed to take about an hour. Something moved and excited me extremely. It wasn't the acting, because I thought no one except Daphne outstanding. It wasn't decor or spectacle because there wasn't any. I can only think it was Shakespeare, revealed by you, plus the nearness and continuity that Shakespeare wrote for. I really felt as though I were seeing the

Globe company on tour, directed by Will himself, with Kemp and Burbage unavoidably absent, but with his best boy actor as the draw. If I were a critic, I would make a fuss about it, and I hope at least one of them does. The fairy tale atmosphere was exactly right; it had something of Russian Ballet, and something of Lady Precious Stream... If the Arts Council doesn't here and now give you a long contract, Landstone and Moody should be burned in St. James's Square...

It was a blissful moment. I'd finally been able to slough off all the frustrations I had felt at Stratford and in Australia and put into practice what Denis and I had dreamed of in front of the dressing room mirror.

Later, better publicised, directors were to repeat all these tactics in more fashionable places. But for 1950 it was new: the absence of a curtain, the swift continuity, the minimal decor. Alas, 'revealing the play' doesn't usually make your name, but as a director I had no other impulse. 'H.K.'s influence was life-long.

Denis was now about to have a big event of his own.

CHAPTER NINE

To Goldsmith Street

'Daphne Slater, on her day the best ingénue in the country...'
KEN TYNAN. The Observer. October 1955.

In 1989 Denis Cannan's play CAPTAIN CARVALLO was revived at the Greenwich theatre. It didn't create much of a stir. But in the far-off fifties he, along with Christopher Fry and John Whiting, made a trio of names to conjure with, the hopefuls of the post-war theatre. Fry is sure of a place, and Whiting of a footnote, in the history books. But time seems to have forgotten Denis so I shall remember him now.

His first play, MAX, had been done at the Malvern Festival that I missed, and CARVALLO, his second, was seen by Laurence Olivier at the Bristol Old Vic and bought for the season he was running at the beautiful, long demolished, St. James's Theatre. Olivier directed it himself with a top-notch cast including Diana Wynyard, James Donald, Peter Finch, Richard Goolden and Jill Bennett.

In 'Dramatists of Today' (Pub.1953) Trewin encapsulates it as a 'neo-Ruritanian frolic' and in style and setting it did make several graceful nods in the direction of ARMS AND THE MAN.

Somewhere in the Balkans in its usual state of insurrection the personable Captain Carvallo (James Donald, but Olivier should have played it himself) finds himself billeted on a household of partisans who have orders to rub him out. But he chats up his hostess, makes friends with her entomologist house-guest (Peter Finch in a rare and successful character performance) and excites the missionary zeal of her evangelical husband. None of the plotters can bring themselves to kill him. So it is arranged that Smilja should lure him to her bedroom where they sedately read Victor Hugo together while the two men blow up his empty billet in the stables. I was never much good at recounting a plot. It was more fun than I've made it sound and done in a beautifully fluent and fanciful prose.

It was a great novelty to have a West End playwright for a friend so

Daphne and I naturally supported the first night, feeling like the sort of people you read about in theatrical memoirs. Denis was

> ...sorry you came to the first night, because it has gone so much better since. It does demand above all things a carefree relaxation, and everyone was in such a state of near hysteria on Wednesday that I thought it fell as flat as a pancake.
>
> What is one to think? 'Pure gold' says the Times, 'Dish of scraps' says Dent. You like Act II best; Bridie hated Act II, and wrote that III was 'Masterly'. ... Anyway, one just has to go on, knowing that one can't write a good play without writing several bad ones on the way and taking a critical battering each time and being squashed for one's presumption by the playwrights manqué like Baxter and Darlington. The only people who really make me cross are the catalogue boys who want to know what it is, and think you mustn't mix comedy, sentiment, emotion and farce. Good heavens, haven't they seen a French or Italian film, or read Maupassant? I dare say I haven't done it skilfully enough, but it's a purely English idea that it mustn't be done.
>
> But all I ask at present is to become self-supporting as a dramatist, and if I can do that I may give them something a little better one day. So let us pray for a wet August.

No cushioning previews then. The first night was just exactly that - the first time in front of an audience.

Denis kept hard at it over the next few years. George Cole starred in MISERY ME! directed by Alastair Sim. I forget what that was about but the management, if not Denis, should surely have known that the English public won't buy misery unless it's well disguised as something else. This and a likeable extravaganza called YOU AND YOUR WIFE, badly directed at Bristol, just failed to ignite. I was aching to have a go at one of them myself but with luminaries like Sim and Olivier anxious to serve he had no need to suggest it. In any case he probably thought my skills were better adapted to the Elizabethans. I had no reputation yet for stylish comedy. I revived YOU AND YOUR WIFE in 1955 at Nottingham with a lively young cast that included

Joan Plowright, John Turner and Bernard Horsfall, and really wanted him to come and see it. But I think he was already beginning to get badly singed and was for consigning failures to the can.

Sadly I had to accept that our paths had already separated. He had emigrated into films. I north of Watford.

The springtime promise of CARVALLO, of a new kind of Shavian fantasist, was never fulfilled. A little nurturing and the plant might have blossomed. Denis the playwright reappeared at the Royal Court with the shrill and bitter-tasting ONE AT NIGHT in the 1970s, and had a modest success later with the cynical and civilised DEAR DADDY.

But he has not, as yet, reappeared in my life.

I can't help being a bit sad about that.

There was to be not much longer of this curious marking time. I landed a production of HAMLET at the New Bolton's Theatre Club in Kensington, then run by Peter Cotes. Cotes was a Boulting half-brother, famous for a pioneering book called NO STAR NONSENSE and for being married to the actress Joan Miller who starred with no nonsense in most of his productions. They were doing CANDIDA and he had hooked David Markham, who would be a matchless Eugene Marchbanks, with the bait of a Hamlet later in the season. David had swallowed the bait but Cotes was beginning to renege. 'Joan will be too tired after Candida to take on Gertrude.' David bustled around off his own bat and interested Rosalinde Fuller, John Barrymore's 1922 Ophelia who had now matured into a prospectively exciting 'wretched queen'. This must have phased Cotes who next regretted that he would be too harassed with running the theatre to direct a Shakespeare. Determined not to lose his Hamlet David, through Gordon Harbord whose client he was, approached me. I was introduced to Cotes, who introduced me to everybody else as his Dear Friend John Harrison, and started work on the production for a fee of ten pounds. When Gordon had said 'Ten all right?' I'd assumed he meant ten pounds a week which was the going rate at Guildford. Not so. Ten pounds for the production which was blessed with four weeks rehearsal.

Still, here it was. HAMLET. Not a play I had thought deeply about until then but I would put into force everything I had learned and proved with PERICLES. A fairly full text, a composite set and I supposed there would have to be one interval. We'd still get it down in three hours if we went at an Elizabethan lick. I knew that David was very much a prose actor. But a fair old proportion of Hamlet is prose. The advice to the players. The scene with Ophelia. The stuff with the gravediggers. The great 'quintessence of dust' speech. It's easy to forget how much wonderful prose there is in the plays. And not just Falstaff and Bottom and Iago. Almost the whole of Rosalind in Arden for example. So I thought a good prose actor would be more than half way there. In any case I wanted to be done with the then fashionable lengthening-out of a speech like 'To be or not to be' which to me always feels as if it should go like a machine-gun. After all there's nothing very novel about the thoughts. It's the thud-thud of the beating mind that counts.

I had an unbeatable pair as Claudius and Polonius - Andrew Cruickshank and Ernest Jay. And future Doctor Who Patrick Troughton was a splendidly rugged Horatio.

I enjoyed working with David, a child of Aquarius ahead of time, very much into Reich's Orgone Box which he sat in for a while every day at home in Sussex where he and his wife ran a smallholding and hatched their clever brood of actress daughters. Rehearsals proceeded in happy innocence of the storm ahead. Cotes sending his Dear Friend John Harrison friendly little notes about cutting down on the expensive use of the larger rehearsal room and giving the company more time to spend money in the coffee bar.

He had his first sight of the production at the final dress rehearsal. At the end he rose appalled, white-faced, and addressed the company over my head. It just wouldn't do. All too gabbled. They would get the most dreadful notices. It was a disaster they would all live to regret. None of this was directed at me, the true culprit. All at the poor benighted actors. He turned on his heel, cliché incarnate, and left.

What I was supposed to do about it at this eleventh hour, apart from bow out in disgrace, I'd no idea. I was shaken, but Cruickshank and Jay and Fuller were firmly supportive so the rest rallied round. David tried hard not to be stunned and the first performance was given more or less as rehearsed.

Cotes spent the first night in the bar with the critics absolving himself from responsibility and possibly putting ideas into some of the emptier heads.

M-----------W-----------in the Daily Mail:

'"Words without thoughts never to heaven go," says the King. This speech might have been written specially for John Harrison's production last night. Shakespeare's words went up in a confused gabble, the thought behind them falling far short of heaven and almost always short of the audience.'

The Telegraph, on the other hand, who hadn't been in the bar, thought the production 'a small miracle of ingenuity', although he thought David "threw away" the soliloquies too much, so embalmed in custom was their treatment as self-indulgent cadenzas. Come Sunday John Trewin was as loyal as ever in the Observer.

'Shakespearians who are ready for a provocative Hamlet should speed to the New Bolton's... Whenever Mr. Harrison is about there are bound to be ideas. The Boltons now bristles with them...'

The posh Sundays were almost as influential as the New York Times in those days. Immediately there was a healthy queue at the box office. The theatre was packed to the gunnels. But backstage all was gloom. David woefully told me that Peter was cancelling the rest of the run. I searched him out and asked him if that wasn't rather a pity with all this money starting to come in. His eyes glistened with crocodile tears. 'Paper,' he said. 'All paper.' (Which is theatrical parlance for complimentary tickets.) Our Dear Friendship was at an end. The production he had never wanted was consigned to the bin.

Maybe it was awful. Blissfully I can't remember. But the whole company was very committed to it and heartbroken at its sudden dismissal.

I have never returned to HAMLET. Nothing to do with Cotes and the New Boltons. It's always been far from a favourite of mine. I sometimes say I'd give away the whole text provided I could keep the advice to the Players. That's a bit extreme. There are wonderful things. I love the opening on the battlements, one of the most exciting in all drama. I begin to bog down with 'Though yet of Hamlet our dear brother's death the memory be green...' and have little patience with anybody in the story from then on. I find Claudius sonorous and Gertrude a bore,

Laertes a wimp and Osric a pain in the neck. Hamlet says some good things along the way and Ophelia's mad scene is brilliantly clinical, showing that Shakespeare understood long before the doctors that the insane have a - to them perfectly logical - train of thought. It's all a quantum leap from the old text he was revising. But then there's the problem of which of his texts to use. I'm sure the Folio (omitting the whole of the soliloquy 'How all occasions do inform against me...' amongst other goodies) was the company's final acting version. In the long run I'd rather have TROILUS AND CRESSIDA for our times.

Daphne in the meantime continued busy. She was in a very curious piece at the Garrick. You'll remember perhaps that she had spent the previous Christmas in Birmingham in Barry Jackson's version of 'Le Malade Imaginaire, DOCTOR'S DELIGHT. This had been bought for West End presentation by Peter Daubeny and, metamorphosed into THE GAY INVALID (a title that would mislead nowadays), had become a vehicle for Elizabeth Bergner and A.E. Matthews. Bergner was a German sex-kitten who had found international fame with a film directed by her husband Paul Czinner called DREAMING LIPS ('Die Traumende Mund'). She had been an androgynously erotic figure on the London stage of the thirties in ESCAPE ME NEVER (also a film) and it was for her that the besotted J.M. Barrie wrote his ill-fated last play THE BOY DAVID. For a time, as she appeared in films like CATHERINE THE GREAT, it was quite natural to couple her name with Garbo's as continental exotica. This was to be Bergner's risky return to the London stage after an equivocal and unpopular war in which she had scooted off to Canada to appear in the film 49th PARALLEL and then ducked out of the movie and down to Hollywood.

Only Daphne had been retained from the Birmingham production, along with the director Michael Langham and the designer Paul Shelving.

'Matty', darling of comedies like THE CHILTERN HUNDREDS, was eighty-one years old and found Langham's meticulous direction befuddling. 'Pick up the medicine glass on this line - tap- it with your spoon to emphasize this word - sneeze half way through this sentence...' That kind of thing. At the opening in Manchester he remembered very few of his lines and was ignominiously replaced by his understudy for the rest of the tour. From the safety of the train back to London he wrote Daphne a pathetic little note with red ink in a shaking hand.

For Sheila. (Sic)

4 o/c on train

My dear Daughter,

I have never played with anyone that I loved playing with you. (Sic). We will play together again. You helped me so much. I think Crank a great part but they never let me play it on my lines and am happy to go. I meant to do it in New York with you.

Love
Matty

You always told me <u>when</u> to go to the privy.

(The invalid's regular trips to his outside privy were the production's running gag.)

But the show's backers were reluctant to open in London without the popular Matthews. Particularly as it was even feared there might be an anti-Bergner demonstration which his loved presence would defuse. So he was duly reinstated at the Garrick where Tynan, now a fully-fledged drama critic writing in the Spectator, found 'his charm ...considerable, even when ad-libbing ....a cleverly fumbled performance, bemused and floridly childish.' The fifty-year-old Bergner, he said, 'lamely miscast and unexploited as she is, burrowed into my heart in the guise of a young woman in her middle twenties... I do not want to be ungallant but I do not think she can be a day under twenty-five.'

In rehearsals she had offered a few surprises. One day she said to Daphne as they waited to come on, 'You listen for my cues, dolling. I am not used to listening for cues.'

'Daphne Slater' said Tynan, 'gives her wan little apple cheeks a happy outing.' Since Juliet he was always a fan.

Her new suitor was Peter Cushing who was perfectly upstanding and gave no hint of Horrors to come. The play was given complete with Harlequinade, choreographed and led by Walter Gore, which was the most Molière thing about it.

All in all it was an extravagant mish-mash lacking all the charm of the Birmingham version as the star talents tore it apart. Its curiosity value kept it alive for a couple of months.

Daphne was never out of work for long. She appeared, with Virginia McKenna, in a rather special television play (live from Alexandra Palace of course) about the Salvation Army, called SHOUT ALOUD SALVATION. Television plays were real events those days for the few thousand affluent owners of sets. They gathered round for the Sunday Play as if for a Royal Wedding. I shall get round to writing about the amazing feat of live TV Drama when in a few years I start to do it myself. Meanwhile this one was directed by the BBC's Head of Drama, Michael Barry, and led to Daphne being chosen as the first TV Elizabeth Bennett in PRIDE AND PREJUDICE and the first BBC JANE EYRE, both serials in six weekly parts. For her it was onwards and upwards while I seemed to be travelling in no direction at all and still living off my successful wife.

Herbert Wilcox had decided, while we were in Australia, that he had been wrong about Daphne's film career and wanted to abrogate her contract. Her agent had negotiated a very substantial settlement and with the money we decided to buy a cottage in the country.

We had no car, or thought of car. In London we walked everywhere. If we wanted a weekend out we went by train. Cars for All were not yet obligatory. Even at Stratford only Bea Lehmann had one. I never even imagined myself as a potential driver, fearful that I would nervously jam on the brakes for every passing hedgehog.

So we wanted somewhere we could get to from Marylebone Station, just around the corner from our flat.

We were unbelievably lucky. Marylebone to Princes Risborough: just over an hour and several daily trains. Then across the platform and into a one-coach chuffer straight out of Thomas the Tank Engine. A rackety puff over single track line through farmland to Wainhill Halt and down go the steps for us to alight in the middle of nowhere. A hundred paces more and here we are: The Thatched Cottage, Wainhill, Nr. Chinnor, Oxon, one of a mere handful of dwellings in a tiny hamlet at the foot of Bledlow Cross in the Chilterns, just down from the Icknield Way. With a total of about ten minutes walking, public transport has landed us in the heart of unspoilt country. Little did we know we lived in a Golden Age.

The property was actually two 18th century one-up one-down labourers' cottages crudely joined together by the expedient of an intercommunicating door downstairs and a sort of pixies' half-door between the two bedrooms upstairs. It turned its deeply thatched back on the lane and fronted on to a third of an acre of garden with greengage trees and a well.

We thought we'd better be grown-up about it and had a surveyor out from High Wycombe. He jumped up and down on the upstairs boards, stuck his penknife into a few exposed beams, and said, 'Well, it's a question of what it's worth to you. It won't fall down.'

We paid nineteen-fifty cash down for it in nineteen-fifty. I still didn't understand about mortgages or not using your capital or any of that. We'd been assured we shouldn't be taxed on Daphne's settlement. (There had just been a test case of a similar situation involving somebody famous.)

It was a loveable spot. We had plumbing put in and an inglenook fireplace revealed. Otherwise we did the whole place up ourselves. Scrubbing the thick cream 1930s paint off beams with sugar soap and treating them with Cuprinol. Snow-Cementing the outside and painting the inside with what our weekly lady from the village called 'emotion paint'. Filled with Crusoe-like notions of self-support I dug up and tried to make a vegetable garden. (It was no success. I gave up gardening for life after that apart from mowing the lawn.)

It would have been an idyllic life, between W.I and Oxfordshire, if only I had been able to settle for it and accept the fact that I wasn't making the living. I suppose I should have buckled to and become Daphne's manager or something. But I had no gifts for that.

I had one last go at pushing the boat out. We had been enchanted by a French film at the Academy Cinema called SYLVIE ET LE FANTOME. (The 'fantome' was played, in an early appearance, by Jacques Tati.) The credits told me this was from a stage play by one Alfred Adam. I got hold of a copy, translated it as SYLVIE AND THE GHOST and offered it to Roy Winton and Pat Henderson at Guildford with the carrot of Daphne as Sylvie whose baronial father gives her a haunted castle for her sixteenth birthday. They didn't need much persuasion to offer the popular Miss Slater to their audiences, whatever secret reservations they may have harboured about the play, merely insisting on anglicising the name to Sylvia as being more readily understood by the denizens of Surrey. A yellowing cutting from The Stage tells me that as translator/director I 'had a personal triumph.' The great Tyrone Guthrie, whom I had been chatting up as part of the strategy, came to see it. 'I see you have a choreography,' he said with approval. It was very important in those days to 'have a choreography'. Productions by Guthrie and Langham and Michael Benthall often consisted of little else. To me it was a tool of the trade I was later very happy to discard.

There was a good cast. The young Gerald Harper was very funny as a mock ghost, and Voytek did the set.

Alas once again the road led nowhere. In spite of warm reviews in the Times and (inevitably) the Observer, no management could be persuaded to take an interest. This effort too washed up on the tide.

There was no 'Fringe' in those days. The place to fledge your wings was undoubtedly provincial rep, moving up from weekly to fortnightly to monthly and then, if your luck held, London. Well, that's what had happened to Michael Langham. But that would mean giving up W.I. and the cottage. Turning my back on the loving idyll. Daphne had no need for rep. Her next offer was Cordelia at the Old Vic.

Why did I need to compete? What had happened to the youth who had eschewed ambition at eighteen? How triumphant my old English master would have been! Still without having read a word of Carlyle I was feeling I must make myself noticed, stake my own claim. The girl was so bloody clever and successful.

I applied to be Director of Productions at the Nottingham Playhouse, one of the burgeoning Arts Council's pet projects. The director for the first two years had been, successfully, Andre Van Gyseghem. Then there had been an unfortunate appointment and a rocky interregnum of six months. Now, in the Autumn of 1951, they were advertising again.

I applied with stunning referees: Peter Brook and Paul Scofield.

The interviews were held in the Nottingham offices of Hunt, Dickens and Willatt, solicitors. A sticking point seemed to be whether I would act in the company from time to time as well, as Van Gyseghem had. I held out and said no. They even rang me at home later to double check on this point. I still said no. You can find exceptions to prove the rule but I have never believed you could give your mind to the over-all view if you were personally involved with a part of it. And how on earth do you direct yourself? The exceptions I knew of, Olivier and Gielgud, were both stars and knew they were. Directing then becomes about putting your own jewel in the right setting. Besides I had been glad to turn my back on acting and wasn't missing it.

The committee chewed this over for a suspenseful week or two and then offered me the job on a trial basis. 'Subject to your maintaining the standards we so confidently anticipate from you' the position would be confirmed in three months, when the salary would go up from seventeen to twenty pounds per week. Still about half Daphne's lowest, but regular.

My reply is scribbled on the back of the offer. 'Shall be pleased,' I wired, 'accept position on terms suggested and meet board Tuesday.'

So it was to be goodbye after all to the pleasant life between W.I. and the cottage. The end of the idyll. There would be no time for love. I moved into digs in Nottingham. Daphne set off on tour with KING LEAR prior to the Old Vic.

The moving spirit of the original Nottingham Playhouse was Hugh Willatt of the aforementioned Hunt, Dickens and... Much later *Sir* Hugh Willatt and the last truly creative Secretary General of the Arts Council of Great Britain.

Hugh had been impressed by my testimonial from Brook and knew my PERICLES and HAMLET reviews. Knew I was married to the up and coming Daphne Slater. Knew more than any Nottingham solicitor needed to know about the theatre. Just turned forty, Shrewsbury, Oxford and the War had absorbed most of his youth and now he had inherited Hunt, Dickens and... as senior partner. A lovely man with keen blue eyes under shaggy brows and a constant spillage of cigarette ash on his frontage (brushing it away his most characteristic gesture), he had been all his life a keen enough amateur director to know that for him amateur status would never satisfy. But he had missed the bus for any active involvement at a professional level. There was also in his nature a strong vein of caution which probably relished the safety-net of Hunt, Dickens and Willatt. Helping to create a front-rank theatre in Nottingham would be the next best thing. As a committed supporter of the Labour Party he was politically well-placed, in those expansionist times, to achieve it. Those were the days when there seemed to be an agreed attitude in the country towards the good things of life. The list, made up by the exhausted armies returning from all over, didn't include holidays on the Costa Chips or surrounding yourself with electronic gew-gaws. Ordinary men and women who had fought and suffered wanted to make sense of their life's experience. They were finding that theatre and music and art and literature were the things that helped you to do that. The great post-war government did its best to prime the pump and everybody settled down to a life that had been worth fighting for. Well, that's what it seemed like.

Hugh was married to a gifted painter, Evelyn Gibbs. They lived in Georgian splendour on the heights of Nottingham in Park Terrace, where they played host to an impressive collection of cognoscenti and litterati. Evelyn founded the Midlands Art Gallery and Hugh lived, at less than half a remove, the Nottingham Playhouse.

This wasn't the present mis-conceived building, of which more in the fullness of time.

It was a converted cinema standing, aptly, in Goldsmith Street. You always know, when you walk into a place, whether you can 'do it' there. Purpose built like the original Birmingham Rep or converted like the old Nottingham Playhouse, it's all one. There's something in the air. Something about the stage/audience relationship. You get that 'feel', like Peter Quince: 'Here's a marvellous convenient place for our rehearsal.' You stand on the stage and flex your voice. You prowl the auditorium. It's nothing to do with whether you have showers backstage or a state-of-the-art lighting board. The place vibrates. It can have every apparent disadvantage. At Nottingham there was precious little wing space and that only on one side. On the other side, from the street you cautiously opened the soi-disant Stage Door, almost fell down two deep steps and, if you weren't careful, into full sight of the audience. Dressing-rooms, like battery-chicken runs, had been created immediately under the stage. The only lavatories for the cast were up a flight of stone steps on Prompt Side and couldn't be flushed when the curtain was up for fear of creating inappropriate sound effects. No fly tower. No stage machinery.

But it worked, by God. It vibrated. By a happy coincidence with its small circle it seated 464 like the dear old Birmingham Rep.

The change of programme was fortnightly and I got stuck in straight away enthusiastically with the already-chosen MACBETH, almost certainly my favourite among the Big Four tragedies.

'..................Light thickens,
And the Crow makes Wing to th' Rookie Wood...'

Darkness palpable.

Although (or perhaps because) I was defiantly un-superstitious the notorious curse struck. I had been faithful to Patrick Crean as a fight director since he had put me through it for ROMEO AND JULIET. He was a sound actor into the bargain so it was useful to have him around to arrange the fights for HAMLET whilst playing Laertes and he was now, as Macduff, doing the same office for MACBETH. But Paddy's fights were always dangerous. At the dress rehearsal our Macbeth made a false move out of excitement, slipped and broke his ankle. Banquo ambitiously offered to move up one (in a neat reversal of the play's fortunes) and Don's brother Leon was sent for post-haste to take over Banquo, learning the part in the train. In the teeth of this set-back the production limped home and did much to confirm Hugh's faith in me. He was to support me through thick and thin for the next five and a half years with a loyalty so absolute that I came to take it for granted. We shared a vision of where our theatre was going. After board meetings we would relax comfortably in a timbered Nottingham pub, sinking the good old half-pints of warm Mild and setting the world to rights.

Board meetings... The only appropriate comment seems a groan. Those terminally tedious gatherings of a city's amateur Great and Good to lord it over the poor bloody professionals. I've tangled with them now in Nottingham, Birmingham and Leeds, always vowing never again.

The chairman was the upstanding and good-looking B.L. Hallward, Vice-Chancellor of Nottingham University and a mountain-climbing classicist. (Daphne thought him sexy when she met him later. They enjoyed washing up together when he and his wife came to dinner.) He had the charisma of a good politician but little feeling for the drama. When I did my Elizabethan production of JULIUS CAESAR in 1954 he was both puzzled and furious and I was sent for and given a good old-fashioned wigging. Normally urbane the classics scholar was stuttering with rage. 'But Harrison, you even brought Caesar on in something which looked like a - a - nightgown!' (Perhaps the most charming - after 'Exit, pursued by a Beare' - of all genuine Elizabethan stage directions: 'Thunder & Lightning. Enter Julius Caesar in his Night-gowne.' Not flannelette, of course. More of a dressing gown.)

Then there was a little round man, like one of those dolls with weights in the bottom, called A.J. Statham who ran a rather seedy communist bookshop. He became my resident opposition in unholy alliance with Tory Councillor W.A. Rook: as Alan Rook a poet published by Routledge; by inheritance the owner/proprietor of Skinner and Rook, an imposing grocery business, Nottingham's version of Fortnum and Mason's. Statham's alliance with Rook, like Stalin's with Hitler, was an alliance of convenience, in this case for the good riddance of John Harrison. They were not exactly book-ends. Statham's florid rotundity contrasted quaintly with Rook's tall dark Satanic mien: Alan would have made wonderful casting for Milton's fallen angel. I suppose they were more like the comic villains in a pantomime, though I couldn't quite see it like that at the time.

I shall never know why I got up Statham's nose but Rook's antagonism is easily explained. He was almost overpoweringly friendly to begin with and before long was hopefully showing me a verse play which he had written. Alas, with the best will in the world I didn't find it up to scratch. He became suavely menacing (George Sanders in THE PICTURE OF DORIAN GRAY). 'You know, John, you should take care. I personally have got rid of the last two directors.'

Alan was gay and soon found a boyfriend in the company which was very trying. The poor fellow became Rook's Mole (if I may be so Naturally Historical), grubbing up dirt that could be thrown at me in board meetings.

Together for five years Rook and Statham tried to rid Nottingham of this froward and opinionated director, no matter what his public triumphs, and were totally flummoxed when he finally left of his own accord.

If they, to me, represented the Axis powers, Hugh and his little bunch, naturally, were the Allies. (It was not so long since the war. The terminology was at hand.)

These Allies included the University's Professor of Education, Michael Lewis, a bright-eyed bright-minded little man married to the historical novelist Hilda Lewis; Harry Davies, the tall, willowy, forward-looking Headmaster of Nottingham Grammar School; and sometimes affable Ken Baird, the assistant Director of Education. The amiably vague Vivian de Sola Pinto, Professor of English, could also usually be counted on, although he was too innocent a man to be aware of the various cross-currents. (He generously made me an Honorary Lecturer in Drama at the University; though, as he kindly explained, there could be in these straitened times no honorarium.)

The problem with the Allies, as in the larger conflict, was that they didn't always proceed naturally in concert and took a bit of orchestrating. But Hugh was good at this backstairs work. Even enjoyed it.

There was a genuine maverick on the sidelines, our one true representative of Nottingham Man, wiry red-faced builder Sturt Piggin, whose vote was nobody's for the buying. A nice businessman called John Bailey was almost permanently absent through illness. He outlasted the lot of them and was still on the board, in vigorous health in his eighties, when my play SCENES FROM A VOYAGE TO THE INDIES was premiered there in 1983.

Fortnightly rep is the most punishing of all. You can't, as in weekly, absolve yourself from standards. Nor did I want to: hadn't I come to Nottingham to make my reputation? But you haven't quite enough time to achieve them without breaking everybody's back as well as your own. And that's what I did. I became absolutely tyrannical. Pounding on to the stage with notes the moment the curtain was down. Equity had few teeth then and somehow everyone seemed to expect this sort of treatment. Like me, it's what they were there for. Derek Godfrey (never satisfied with his exquisitely varied performances), Graham Crowden (often angry with me but enjoying it too), Joan Plowright, Hazel Hughes, Denis Quilley, Bernard Horsfall... no, I really must resist list-making.

After a year of making sure we could handle him I asked Voytek to join me as resident designer. At the end of every season from then on my Stage Director would say threateningly 'It's him or me.' But it would never be him. The miracles of colour and ingenuity he achieved fortnight after fortnight took your breath away, painting all the sets himself with the help of one assistant and when we did our annual Shakespeare designing all the costumes as well. Which a few youngsters in the wardrobe then made, numbers bumped up by local seamstresses. How we sweated. We felt we were in the front line. We were all young. This wouldn't come again.

The scenery was set up from the moment the curtain came down on the final Saturday of a play and on through the night. Sunday we lit the show and had our first dress rehearsal. Second dress Monday afternoon and open Monday night. First reading of the next play on Tuesday. This gave us all one day off in fourteen for a fixed salary and no overtime. I was my own casting director, fee negotiator, Dramaturg, Lighting Designer. I had to choose a programme that would pass muster with the board and at the box office as well as occasionally satisfying my own secret longings. I gave talks around the town and in schools, wrote the programme notes and the leaflets, looked after the publicity, and dressed in a dinner jacket to dignify first nights. (This wasn't swank. It was a show of solidarity. If the actors were 'dressing up', so would I.) When, after a few years, I persuaded the governors to let me have an assistant director who would take on one production in four an otherwise charming member of the board was heard to say, 'What I can't understand is what Harrison is doing if he is not directing the play.'

It would be as exhausting to chronicle those years in detail as it was to live through them. My first season included THE SEAGULL, SIX CHARACTERS IN SEARCH OF AN AUTHOR and MURDER IN THE CATHEDRAL as well as MACBETH. For light relief there was Maugham's THE CIRCLE and the Fry/Anouilh RING ROUND THE MOON. Hugh in particular was always happier with a meaty play choice and to skip the dessert. He could never be entirely sympathetic about my running Ben Travers farces and the like for three whole weeks so that we might have more time to prepare a world premiere or 'TIS PITY SHE'S A WHORE.

And that's more or less how it went on. Classics and new plays and the occasional oddity. With switchback ups and downs. For five and a half years. Until I had paid off bit by bit the whacking income tax bill that Daphne's film settlement unexpectedly earned us. Until a London critic could write 'We have come to expect a lot from the Nottingham Playhouse.' Until I was ready to drop.

Right at the beginning, after only six months, once my position was well and truly confirmed, Daphne turned her back on London and joined me.

She had decided, with no persuasion from me, that there was little point in carrying on a marriage from opposite ends of the country. So she came and graced Nottingham with a series of performances that would have been a feather in the cap of any theatre in the land: Barrie's BOY DAVID in a resuscitation of genius, Anouilh's COLOMBE, Ibsen's Nora and Hilda Wangel, Strindberg's MISS JULIE. A Rosalind. A Viola. A Hermione. Not to mention a JACK AND THE BEANSTALK. All of them true to the core. Nottingham was privileged beyond compare.

It was high time she came because I was floundering in my first extra-marital affair.

I had engaged a gravely beguiling Rank starlet for my first company. She was to be my Nina in THE SEAGULL: my Isabelle in RING ROUND THE MOON. After about ten days of rehearsing as Boy Macduff she presented herself in my office in tears and asked to leave. At first she would give no reason. Pressed, she said she was in love with me. Now I didn't want to lose her. She was going to be an asset to the company. Here was a facer. The first in a long line of what Nancy Burman and I later at Birmingham Rep came to call our 'White Coat Days'.

I persuaded her to stay. I remember saying she couldn't possibly love me because she didn't know me. Unfortunately, as I found her very attractive, we soon began to repair this omission in what severely rationed time there was outside the job. She gravely asked if I couldn't just love her 'temporarily'. Well of course I could. I wasn't a monk or a saint. And I was lonely too. But I was racked with guilt. Daphne had done nothing to deserve this.

Of course when I finally confessed I found I was wrong and that was much more difficult to come to terms with. My reaction was as pathetic as Angel Clare's in TESS. But we decided that our marriage was still the most important thing in our lives and we'd better start a family. By such inconsequential and ill-thought-out emotional responses does our race propagate itself. Stephen John Harrison was born in Nottingham on the 26th November 1954. He weighed eight pounds and some ounces which I telegraphed to my mother as eight stone and some pounds.

My mathematical grasp was as uncertain as ever.

Grandma Harrison (nee Henrietta Stevens).
"You take after me for poetry."

My 'live-in' Grandma. Anna Cockram
(nee Taylor).

My father, George Harrison, 1937.
"A very manly man."

My mother on the beach at Sidmouth, 1938.

Me baptising cousin Frank (Frank Lock – much later the last mayor of Sidmouth) perhaps for introducing me to real music ("Frank's dry old muck"). 1936.

With sister Shirley, ten years my junior. Sidmouth 1936.

'Twelfth Night' at Sir Walter St John's School, Battersea. 1939. Me seated centre as Olivia.

H.K. Ayliff ("Seven foot tall and bald as an egg") as the Director in Pirandello's 'Six Characters in Search of an Author,' Birmingham Rep, 1944.

Hubert dismisses the executioners in Peter Brook's 'King John,' Birmingham Rep 1945. Stanley Baker, all manly torso, left. Me as "a sort of Karloffian grotesque," right.

159

With Paul in Peter Brook's 'Romeo and Juliet,' Stratford-on-Avon 1947. (Benvolio supports the dying Mercutio). Photo: Angus McBean. ©ROYAL SHAKESPEARE COMPANY

The Shrieve's House, Stratford-on-Avon. 'How two young actors ... were able to live in such style is beyond remembering.'

Alex Clunes (father of Martin). Derek Blomfield and Daphne in the first production of Christopher Fry's "The Lady's Not For Burning,' Arts Theatre Club, 1948.

Arrival in Australia. With Anew McMaster on deck. 1949.

'Mac' in full spate. Othello before the senate. Princess Theatre, Melbourne, 1949.

My first production. Garrick's "Katherine and Petruchio" at the David Garrick Theatre, Lichfield. (Toke Townley 2nd from L. as Grumio). 1949.

"Enter the powers from either side." An Elizabethan production of 'Julius Caesar,' Nottingham Playhouse, 1954.

Daphne as Barrie's 'The Boy David.' "a resuscitation of genius." (With Graham Crowden as Samuel.) Nottingham Playhouse. 1953.

'Volpone' (Ben Jonson) Directed at Bristol Old Vic by J.H. with Peter O'Toole (Corvino) and Moira Shearer (Celia) 1955.

This
EVERYMAN'S LIBRARY
volume
contains the complete
Jane
Austen
story
5s.
net

Daphne Slater, who appears
as Elizabeth Bennet

Peter Cushing, who appears
as Darcy

Pride and Prejudice
Broadcast as a serial on the
B.B.C. Television Service
commencing 2nd February 1952

Daphne the TV Star.

Billie Whitelaw in
'You're A Long Time
Dead' by Elaine Morgan.
My first TV production.
Live. 1958.

Paul Scofield in Pirandello's
'Henry IV,' his TV debut under
my direction, BBC, 1959.

When TV directors still wore suits. Me on location in Paris directing Rupert Davies and A.N. Other in Simenon's 'Maigret'. 1960's.

Daphne and the boys (Stephen and William) at Wainhill, 1962.

Linda in 'Walker, London', a musical. Book and lyrics by me from J. M. Barrie. Music by Christopher Whelen. 'Would you like me to do the splits?' (With Richard Taylor) Birmingham Rep, 1962.

Linda in 'Fiddler on the Roof' at Her Majesty's Theatre, 1967. PHOTO: ZOE DOMINIC.

Linda Gardner being helped into her costume by Sheila Gish for Anouilh's 'Colombe,'
Birmingham Rep, 1963. PHOTOGRAPHED IN NO. 1 DRESSING ROOM BY JULIE CHRISTIE.

*Paul with Margaret Johnston in 'Windmill Near A Frontier,'
written and directed by John Harrison, BBC TV. Live. 1959.*

*Wendy Hiller (with Hayward Morse and Liza Ross) in 'Unaccompanied Cello' by John
Harrison. Directed by Richard Digby-Day. Theatre Royal, Windsor, 1970.* PHOTO: RICHARD TROREY.

Linda and Kenneth Colley in 'Scenes from A Voyage to the Indies' by John Harrison. Directed by Andrew McKinnon. Nottingham Playhouse, 1983. Photo: Alec Russell.

Morag Hood in 'Holidays' by John Harrison. Directed by John Harrison with Jude Kelly, West Yorkshire Playhouse, 1995. Photo: Simon Warner.'

171

Donald Sinden (not yet a knight) turns the first sod for the new West Yorkshire Playhouse, November 1987.

Linda, Don and me at the sod-turning party.

172

'We got into wine on French holidays' Provence, 1980's.

With Canon Christopher and Pat Pilkington, co-founders of The Bristol Cancer Help Centre, outside Wells Cathedral. July 1989.

Brecht's 'The Caucasian Chalk Circle.' Leeds Playhouse, 1972.

"not his but Shakespeare's 'Twelfth Night'." The final production at the original Leeds Playhouse, January 1990. Paul Spence as Orsino. Photo by Simon Warner

Paul as Prospero in 'The Tempest,' Wyndham's Theatre, 1974, (with Nicky Guadagni as Miranda). Photo: Zoe Dominic.

The Maple Tree Game' by Paval Kohout, with which I opened the Courtyard Theatre of The West Yorkshire Playhouse, 1990. (Bob Cartland, centre, Ian Barritt to his right). Photo: Simon Warner.

Full circle. Sophie Bold and Neal Foster in David Mamet's 'Oleanna,' directed by John Harrison for the Birmingham Stage Company at the Old Rep Theatre, Birmingham. 1999.

50 years on. Me, Paul and Joy, Diana and Don, at the Sinden's place in Kent

CHAPTER TEN

Live Telly and a Return to Brum

*"...Did enjoy your play on Sunday. Thought it sensitive,
fascinating and beautifully written. It's such a change to get away
from slice-of-life grumblings and mumblings, and to hear dialogue
with style. And it was beautifully directed. Do write more."*

PETER HALL, on a PC from the Shakespeare
Memorial Theatre, Stratford-on-Avon. Nov. 5th 1959.

I was allowed out of the cage occasionally. I did two guest
productions at the Bristol Old Vic. Ben Jonson's VOLPONE (1955)
with a cast I just *have* to list: Eric Porter (Volpone, the Fox), Alan
Dobie (Mosca, the Fly), Derek Godfrey (Voltore, the Vulture), Antony
Tuckey (Corbaccio, the Raven), Peter O'Toole (Corvino, the Crow),
Moira Shearer (Celia), Edward Hardwicke (Bonario). With that
menagerie I was able to do a very bird and beast-oriented production.
Cunning Old Fox rather than Cunning Little Vixen. And in 1957 a
PYGMALION in which the very young O'Toole gave his Wilfrid
Lawson impersonation as Doolittle.

Moira Shearer had just given up competing with Fonteyn and was
trying to become a straight actress. Her greatest difficulty, she said,
was that for a ballet dancer going on stage meant instinctively and by
training to tense up, whereas for an actor it must be the opposite,
complete relaxation.

O'Toole was a really exciting classical actor in the making: that most
unusual thing a young actor with *heart*. Everything seemed to go
wrong from the moment he got LAWRENCE OF ARABIA and had to
have his nose altered. It had been a wonderful nose, travelling on and
down and across his face with a sardonic emphasis that could wring
your heart at the tip. With that nose he could have been a definitive
Cyrano, sardonic Richard III, pathetic Uncle Vanya. But once his
features were fixed as:

Faultily faultless, icily regular...

a weird dichotomy was set up between those chocolate box looks and the pulsating Leeds/Irish heart and the throbbing plangent voice. Somehow I think all his later excesses must have been in compensation for The Nose.

He was fresh out of RADA when he played Corvino and more than held his own in the heavyweight line-up. I was surprised one day to find him in the third row watching rehearsals. Until then I had maintained Ayliff's fetish about the auditorium being the director's sanctuary. I've been fairly blasé about it ever since. Although there are dangers. One is that you end up with as many directors as there are members of the cast. Even worse you start directing for the onlookers, giving a performance of being a director.

The Theatre Royal in Bristol is a magical time-capsule, basically unaltered since 1766. Its wooden auditorium flatters the human voice like the sounding board of a good Strad. I always liked to put in time before rehearsal just sitting there gazing up at the decorated ceiling, soaking up the history.

It was assumed that in the fullness of time I should take over the Bristol Old Vic as my next step up the ladder. That's to say it was assumed by everybody but me. Paul even congratulated me in his dressing-room at the Phoenix where he was playing HAMLET. (The one that went to Moscow.)

But no approach was ever made. The job wasn't advertised and the incumbent stayed on.

My other leave of absence was to what was then Tito's communist Jugoslavia. The International Theatre Institute was keen to arrange an exchange of directors with the Dramsko (Dramatic) Theatre in Zagreb and they chose Nottingham as a town of similar size. I went for six weeks to direct, through an interpreter, THE WINTER'S TALE in Serbo-Croatian (ZIMSKA PRICA), while in the same space of time my opposite number, Kosta Spaic, who of course spoke fluent English, was expected to knock off two productions in Nottingham. A culture shock for both of us.

Time was not much object to the comfortably subsidised Jugoslav actors. Kosta came over for a meeting and I asked him how things were done at the Dramsko. In his charmingly precise English:

"Oh, we rehearse for two or three months. Until it is ready. Then I go to the director of the theatre, Mr. Pero Budak, and I tell him THE WINTER'S TALE is ready. So he looks in his schedule and finds an opening date..."

And rehearsal hours?

"We start at ten in the morning. If it is a good day we go on to maybe three, four o'clock in the afternoon." Then, with a grin, "if it is a bad day I send them all home."

I realised that the luxury of six weeks for me was going to be like weekly rep for them.

I went out by train in March 1956. First time I had set eyes on continental Europe. I remember waking up in my wagon-lit just as we were approaching Stuttgart and relishing a foreignness that didn't take circumnavigating the globe to find. It was a true Orient Express type train (the Tauern express actually, because it went under the Alps through the Tauern tunnel) destination Constantinople. Alone in my sleeping compartment I shouted with excitement as we wound through the Swiss Alps. Mealtimes were a Looking-Glass experience. Every time you went to the restaurant car it was a different one, hooked up in the various countries we crossed, until the last dinner, beyond the Jugoslav border, was served in exotically Slavonic surroundings of heavy brass and thick velvet curtains, the sort of train the Prozorov sisters never caught to Moscow.

I arrived at Zagreb station a little late for 23.30 to find the entire Dramsko company lined up on the platform to greet me. I couldn't see this happening for Kosta back in Nottingham. They escorted me in noisy triumph back to my hotel where, for the first of many times, the local plum brandy (Slivovic) was uncorked. The tiny pocket diary I kept of the visit overflows with slivovic.

'After to Ritz Bar till 2 a.m.'

'After to Writers' Club till 1 a.m.'

'To the Press Club until 3 a.m.'

'Evening rehearsal and after to Writers' Club until 2 a.m.'

Eventually

'Two peaceful evenings - feeling much better for it - also for the frequent "Casu Mlekno".' (glass of milk)

Morning coffee break was plum brandy break for the Serbo-Croats as they pored over their chess games but I had at last tumbled to the fact that for me it was better to counter the acid.

Three days after I arrived (still no rush, you notice) they read me THE WINTER'S TALE in Serbo-Croatian. (It is extraordinary, in the light of future events, how linked the two nationalities seemed then, in language and culture.) I would never be able to judge the quality of the translation which was a new one, prepared especially, but at least I knew where I was in the script having just directed it at Nottingham the previous Autumn. This had governed the choice. I felt that, to be comfortable working through an interpreter, I must know the play and, in this instance, the production backwards. To 'have a choreography' for once was going to be vital. At least it could look well, however many finer points might be missed. But outrageously enough as the weeks went by I even found myself venturing line notes and stresses. (Something I would never do at home. The actor should ideally seem to arrive at the right emphasis off his own bat or his performance will never belong to him.) But it was all a sort of dream. I even became an unexpectedly physical, illustrative director. Robbed of language I took refuge in pantomime.I used Voytek's designs that he had done for Nottingham, but nobody was going to pay for him to come out as well. People were not yet flown about Europe like parcels. So on my fifth day we had something called a 'Technical Proof'. Scorning the careful ground plans I had bullied poor Voytek into preparing and working only from a model and photographs the technicians manhandled flats and approximate lumps of scenery about the stage.

'Here?'

'A little more to the right.'

'Here?'

'Downstage a little. More ...more...'

And so we arrived at a ground plan by example. The next day we had our first 'mise en scène' (stand-up rehearsal). Diary says 'Tiring but reasonably satisfactory.'

My interpreter, Ivo Jurisa, was not really at home at the Dramsko. He was a good-looking light comedian from the rival Komedya Theatre. But nobody at the Dramsko could match his English. There were subterranean rivalries between these two households that I never really fathomed. The G.O.M. of theatre in Zagreb was Dr. Branko Gavella, semi-retired from the Dramsko, who was responsible for my WINTER'S TALE translation. Nearly all the directors were his pupils. Spaic, struggling in Nottingham, and Ivo's boyfriend Vlado Habunek who already had an international reputation (he was currently at Covent Garden) of which some were a mite jealous. Therefore Habunek, when in Zagreb, directed at the Komedya, where I saw his extraordinary version of CHARLEY'S AUNT ('Charleyvna Tetka') with percussion accompaniment throughout. (Before Ayckbourn CHARLEY'S AUNT must have been our most regular theatrical export after Shakespeare.)

Ivo was likeable and astute. A charmer. I couldn't have wished for more emollient liaison. Though I could tell that he distanced himself from the political regime and was not all that welcome to Gavella and the other Dramsko high-ups.

I naturally tried to see something of the surrounding countryside but nobody, not even the Director of the theatre, had cars. It was possible, though, to take a tram from the centre of the city and walk up the mountains through a little village called Sestine where the women still scrubbed their washing on the flat stones of the fast-running mountain stream and spread it about the meadows to dry.

'The white sheet bleaching on the hedge,
With heigh, the sweet birds, O how they sing...'
Or...
'Na plotu vise kosuijice
Iju! i cvrkut ptica sad je blag...'
Zagreb old town, on the heights above the new, was attractive. In the market well-dressed women bargained for live chickens, stuffing them still squawking and flapping into their ordinary western style shopping bags.

My hotel, in the new town on the main square, was the Grand Hotel Dubrovnik, which was only mildly confusing. Every night at dinner our live three-piece band played, unfailingly, 'Embraceable you' and 'I'm getting sentimental over you'. Their signature tune was a jazzed-up version of Mendelssohn's Spring Song. Sometimes, as the slivovic and the music got under the Slavonic skin, the smash of a glass moodily thrown to the tiled floor punctuated the harmonies. A waiter would calmly sweep it up and add it to the final tally. I found the local red wine, served up in screw-cap bottles, attractive. This was before we had even heard back home of Lutomer Riesling. Long before Jugoslavia was opened up to the tourist trade. It was still, in spite of Tito's clever juggling between East and West, very much an Iron Curtain country.

I was very conscious of being the only Englishman in downtown Zagreb. The few other westerners were invisible in their various consulates. The representative of the British Council and his wife were impressively holed up in the main street beneath an imposing sign. But they gave me a wide berth to begin with because the Dramsko was looked upon as a hotbed of unreconstructed Communism and I perforce a Fellow Traveller. When I eventually made myself known to them (which I finally did under insistent pressure from Budak, the Dramsko director) they thawed gently and became quite kindly in a staid sort of way, inviting me to tea and lending me English detective novels to while away my increasingly sleepless nights. I had never known sleeplessness before this trip so I must have been under more strain than I allowed myself to realise. The actors were sometimes as noisy as children and, without the language, it wasn't always clear what they were being noisy about. Some of them were very talented. I had a lovely young Clown, Zorko Raicic, who could have been an international success if he had had any other language besides his own. They were not, generally speaking, linguists. Leontes spoke good English. Had relatives in the U.S. and was not looked on as politically 'serious', which Ivo lead me to believe could be quite dangerous for him. With my Hermione, and also with Pero Budak the Theatre Director, I was able to converse reasonably well in my Grange School Third Form French. Pero's was not much better, which made our conversations quite comically successful as we struggled with determination to communicate the experiences of our shared profession. For the rest I relied on Ivo all the way and if he wasn't present I became like a man with lockjaw. German was their natural second language and one became very aware that this had once been part of the Austro-Hungarian Empire.

Budak's attractive blonde wife Sonia, another English speaker, was an official government film censor. Censorship for political purposes she could accept but when I told her about our moral censorship she laughed with incomprehension. The English were strange. She had just sat through, in the course of duty, THE BELLES OF ST. TRINIAN'S, with Alastair Sim as the headmistress. What, please, was funny about this man dressed as a woman? This was grotesque. The English were impossible to understand. And didn't they keep their little boys in short trousers through the northern winter? This was barbaric.

As we get nearer the opening night Diary entries continue terse.

'8th April. Sunday. Lighting, It will all be terrible!'

'9th April. Monday. Rehearsal with music. Chaos! But good to hear Diccon's tunes.' (Diccon Shaw had composed music for all my Shakespearian productions since PERICLES.)

'10th April. Tuesday. 1st dress-rehearsal - without make-up. Not too bad a shambles.'

Anyway, it happened.

'14th April. Saturday. Morning - talked to Torbarina's students. Opening. Laden with gifts and kept up till 5 a.m.!'

At the party Ivo clasped me and said, 'John, you are a very nice man, but I have never seen you drunk. I would like just once to have seen you drunk.' That he didn't must have been a tribute to British phlegm or hollow legs.

I was only able to see two public performances before I had to hurry back to Nottingham, which I did this time via Venice where I spent a magical day walking the canals and left in a Turneresque thunderstorm.

What else?

Happy discussions with Professor Torbarina of Zagreb University who knew more about Shakespeare than many English scholars, and certainly than the Vice-Chancellor of Nottingham University. He would really have appreciated Caesar's entry in his nightgown.

Perdita who didn't speak English bursting into piping song whenever she saw me: 'Oh, Yonny, Oh Yonny, how you can lerv,' which as it happens I had no chance to demonstrate.

When I got back to England Kosta Spaic was still there having a look round and we met in London. He had had an amazing success in Nottingham with BLOOD WEDDING and was impressed by the way in which everybody had cracked on with the job. 'At home we just talk, talk, talk...'

One way and another I think the International Theatre Institute could feel pleased with the results of its exchange.

By January 1957 I decided I had had enough.

'Dear Mr. Hallward,

I feel it my duty to make known to the directors of the Nottingham Playhouse at this earliest opportunity that I do not seek re-appointment for the 1957-8 season. Five and a half of years of continuous (basically) fortnightly production have taxed my imagination to the uttermost and I feel in need of rest and change... the most I could hope to do under these continuing conditions would be a repetition. The new building is perhaps only a few years away, but, much as I should give to be its heir, I cannot - in honesty - believe that my work and health could do anything but deteriorate in the intervening years.

...I felt I must in fairness make my decision known as soon as it was known in my own mind, in order that the board may have ample time to plan for the future.

Yours faithfully...'

'Dear Harrison,

...I will not hide from you that I was distressed to receive your letter... I am sure that you would not have written (it) without most careful consideration and that you have weighed up all the pros and cons in coming to your decision. I am extremely grateful to you for your consideration of the interests of the Playhouse in making your decision so early in the season, so as to give us full time to find a successor.

I can see that it may be in your own interests and those of your wife to make a move now, though for personal reasons as well as from my position as Chairman of the Board I am genuinely very sorry to contemplate the thought of your both leaving us...

Yours sincerely...'
(As I said he and Daphne used to enjoy washing up.)

With still no offer coming from Bristol I began to let my thoughts run in a direction I had never intended. Michael Barry, head of BBC

TV Drama, had wanted me to join them after he had seen PERICLES. His was the one positive bite. But I arrogantly refused to take television seriously as a dramatic medium. I used to say things had been invented in the wrong order. If television had preceded the telephone in the mid nineteenth century, before film had given us preconceptions about screens, then we should all have become used to it as a means of visual communication - as an adjunct to, or substitute for, the telephone. That, after all, is how Shaw imagines it in his 1923 BACK TO METHUSELAH. I could see its value as a disseminator of news. For drama I thought it very small beer.

But Michael had kept up a gentle pressure over the years, as Daphne had become more and more of a household name. (She had had leave of absence from Nottingham for the JANE EYRE serial, for Mary Webb's PRECIOUS BANE and many others.) And now the idea of a total change of discipline began to seem very appealing. I still imagined, at this time, that the ultimate for a director, if that's what I was going to continue to be, must be film; and television, working with cameras, might be a step towards this. Also Michael was the one person who genuinely seemed to want me, which had its charms.

BBC 25th January 1957

Dear John,

When we met in Nottingham you said that you had it in mind to come South some time later in the year, and I would much like to think of our resuming our earlier talks about interesting you in Television.

There might be a chance of considering a training course in September and if this will fit in with your plans I will arrange to have a formal application form sent to you so that we could go through the preliminary arrangements.

With love to you both...

Obviously I was still at this stage less than committed, because:

BBC 1st February 1957

... I would like to make it clear, John, that I have no wish to press this suggestion unless you are really interested for I know the importance of the theatre to you and what you have to contribute to it, while on our side there is a press of applicants...

Letters were flying fairly quickly between us now and I was still playing for time.

BBC 7th February 1957

...Of course I understand how you feel and the considerable pressure under which you must be working. There is no doubt that November would be a more satisfactory date to aim for and I will see we make a note of this. We must certainly talk in detail before going much further and it seems doubtful if you will be able to leave Nottingham. Perhaps we might meet in Bristol during your production there in March.

Meantime you will have received an application form from our Appointments Department. This may have come a little out of the blue at this stage in our correspondence, but it is a piece of necessary machinery, the completion of which would help us should you decide to pursue the idea. It will in no way commit you and could always be destroyed should you so wish at a later stage...

I can't remember whether this Bristol meeting came off or not but by early summer skies had cleared sufficiently for me to take the plunge. Michael writes to me on my birthday.

BBC June 7th 1957

Dear John,

We are delighted that the future has cleared and allowed you to think of coming. I have put things in train and I think we can say that the November date is on...

BBC 16th July 1957

Dear Mr. Harrison,

Further to Mr. Barry's letter of 7th June, I am glad to be able to inform you that we are able to offer you a place on the six-month training course starting on 4th November 1957. You would be appointed at a training salary of £800.0.0d per annum and the Corporation would have the option of retaining your services as a Trainee Producer for a period of two years from 4th May 1958 at a salary of £1,500.0.0d per annum. You would be notified a month before the end of the training period whether or not the Corporation wished to exercise this option...

If you came to us, you would be attached to our Drama department for the first week of your time in order to get the feel of things here and would then attend a six-weeks Course at the Staff Training School from 11th November to 20th December. After that you would return to our Drama Department here.

Yours sincerely,

N. Kinchin Smith
(Assistant Establishment Officer, Television)

With this change in view we thought we would try living at the cottage from where I could commute. We'd long relinquished the London flat after several disheartening attempts at letting it. Every Summer we had spent a month at Wainhill and it was getting more and more under the skin. Now that I had a reliable Assistant Director in Peter Duguid we had also managed to wangle the occasional long weekend break. Stephen was three. A good age to start living in the country. And there was a large and comfortable German au pair called Erdmüthe Betzel who became a friend and, eventually, a Godmother.

I was into the Middle Years. Family and responsibilities. Yes I know I was only 32 but I've always had a tendency to feel older than I am while relishing looking younger. I've been complaining of old age since I was 50. I think it must be the Elizabethan time-scale.

This all entailed learning to drive. I always know if there's going to be any hope for me at a first lesson. I get a gut reaction that tells me to carry on or to cut my losses. The driving reaction was positive and I passed my test at the third go, having driven best at the first. I was so surprised to be failed that the second time I was in a lather of nerves and said to the examiner half way round 'Hadn't we better go straight home?' The third time I took a firm grip on events. I have now driven for nearly fifty years with one fine for speeding and one for failing to display a current licence. My first car (second-hand, of course, on my Nottingham salary) was a little grey Standard 8 Tourer with a collapsible hood. I used to have the driving seat extended so far back to accommodate my legs that when the hood was up it looked as if it was being driven by the Invisible Man.

The Arts Council rewarded my long service at Nottingham with a travel bursary which I decided to use for Sweden. I can't think quite why now but the Swedish cinema must have made it seem attractive at the time. All those semi-nude blonde 'flickas'.

The future began to look more relaxed.

On the last night of my last production (WAITING FOR GODOT: no significance. We always finished the season on a small cast play to save money.) Hugh came on stage and presented me with a typewriter for all the plays I was hoping to find time to write.

Sweden was a head-clearing experience leaving nothing particular to write home about except the rather dour coolness of the people after the wonderfully slavonic Serbo-Croatian bear-hug. Certainly no warm contact was established with the 'flickas'. I would arrive at a theatre armed with my letters of introduction and be granted a formal interview across a desk as if I were an insurance salesman. No carousing in bars into the small hours.

And so I settled into the BBC training course in November.

The lectures were a bit of a joke. R.D. Smith from radio was a colleague (the good-natured butt of his wife Olivia Manning's novels) and he and I used to pass rude notes in class. What it was all leading up to was the serious business in the Studio when we each of us did our exercise for the high-ups to watch on closed circuit.

I wrote mine myself, in a very cheeky vein, and called it EXERCISE CAMERA. I was able to call on the services of TV star Daphne Slater, along with John Turner, Bernard Kay and Julian Somers. We went into the studio on the 10th December for 24 hours camera rehearsal prior to a 30 minute closed circuit transmission.

(Excerpt from script)

'BERNARD: ...Closed circuit takes a load off your conscience. Those kids are drama students come to roost here. It's the kind of world into which they will be born, I reckon. Some of us may get fat in pictures. The happy chosen few may make a living on the stage. But for those of us who just like to eat regularly Television keeps an open table. (HE RISES AND KNOCKS ON A DOOR LABELLED 'SILENCE' 'KEEP OUT' 'TRANSMISSION') Overture and beginners, please!
JOHN AND DAPHNE: (BEHIND DOOR, A CHORUS OF HORROR) Impossible!
DAPHNE: (HAIR AWRY, HEAD ROUND DOOR) I don't remember a line! Not a line!
BERNARD: That's all right. So long as we see you. This is a visual medium.
DAPHNE: (PANIC) But I've got no costume. We can't have any costumes!
BERNARD AND JOHN: That's all right. So long as we see you. This is a visual medium.
DAPHNE: (UTTER DESPAIR) But I can't DO anything!!
BERNARD AND JOHN: (DISTORT, RISING TO SCREAM) That's all right. So long as we see you. This is a visual medium...'

...and more of the same. Including a modernised version of the balcony scene from ROMEO AND JULIET, after which -

BERNARD: Translation, you see, that's the thing. Not from the Ancient Greek, but from the English of Pre-Television to the English of Post-Television - distinguished as Pre-T and Po-T. Pre-T English is anachronistic, whereas Po-T English falls on the modern ear like muck into a sewer...

And we ended, as well we might, with a gale warning.

BERNARD: A strong gale of protest, arising from a ridge of low pressure in the Drama department, is moving swiftly in the direction of Portland Place.

Batten down all hatches.
Close all doors.

This is

THE END.'

It's a wonder I wasn't kicked out on my ear but the transmission was a nine days' wonder and ended with:

Dear Mr. Harrison,
I am writing to confirm formally the information I gave you this afternoon to the effect that the Corporation has decided to take up its option under your contract... to retain your services for a period of two years from 4th May 1958...

Yours sincerely,

(for Assistant Establishment Officer, Television)

I was now a television director. Or, as we still called them, producer.
The first script to come my way was YOU'RE A LONG TIME DEAD by Elaine Morgan. It was a Claude Chabrol kind of thriller so I gave it the full treatment with faces disappearing in baths of photographic acid and the like. Billie Whitelaw, Alfred Burke and Richard Pearson gave strong performances and it extended my days of wonder to at least eighteen.
The next script was more of a chore. I read dozens that the Corporation had bought and was finally down to Bill Naughton's MY FLESH, MY BLOOD. This wasn't really my dish of tea, being Northern and definitely High, but I said if I could get a genuine north country actor, say Eric Portman or Wilfrid Lawson, to take the lead I'd give it a go. It was a sort of contemporary northern Barretts of

Wimpole Street with a working class family dominated by a tyrannical paterfamilas.

I got Wilfrid. Which was a nerve-wracking start. Opposite him Marjorie Rhodes and the rebellious youngsters were headed by Andree Melly. (George's sister and a busy young actress then.)

Wilfrid was a fine actor but his alcoholism was a bore. He was wonderful in the mornings arriving dead on time with his little attaché case but useless after mid-day. Break for five minutes and he was round at the corner pub having a scotch and a chaser which was enough, given the advanced level of his blood-alcohol, to make him incoherent for the rest of the day. I tried not calling him after lunch but he was too intelligent not to see through that. One afternoon as he slumped at the head of the family table in our cheerless Paddington rehearsal room, more than five seas in liquor, he suddenly banged the table with his fist, raised his head and wailed 'I am a bloody fool!' which was not in the script. The young cast froze. Marjorie looked apprehensive. I gritted my teeth and waited for the lacerating self-revelation. He waved me over, as imperiously as his condition would allow, beckoning my ear to his lips. When I was close enough for his liking, which was pretty close, he carefully enunciated, 'Thash - wha' - he'sh - thinking - at - thish - moment - ishn't it?' Wilfrid was simply working. Somewhere in that fog the actor was still exercising his craft.

We used to have round table meetings of all the knights of the drama department (which then included Michael Elliott, Stuart Burge, Julian Amyes and many who went on to distinguish themselves) at which we were expected by Michael Barry to discuss each other's work over the preceding month. Of course the only directors' work to be freely criticised was that of those who for some reason or other weren't present at the meeting. But this time Michael launched off a rocket with 'What went wrong, John? Was it Wilfrid?' This winded me amidships because the play had received (I'd had it in my in-tray that afternoon) the highest ever Viewer Reaction Index in the department's history. 98 out of 100.

I burbled something incoherent about the front door having stuck during the final scene but this was clearly not what Michael had in mind. Nobody else said a word. My umpteen days allowance as Wonder Boy had obviously run out.

I was too stunned ever to find out what Michael so disliked about the production. But as, later, I reviewed the events of the day I began to feel a strange glow of comfort. After all these years of being sole boss and judge here was somebody who was actually going to tell me, fearlessly and frankly and not without affection, whether I had done well or badly. It felt like balm.

I think basically he was just disappointed that after the high jinks of EXERCISE CAMERA and the Chabrol-inspired everything-but-the-kitchen-sink treatment of YOU'RE A LONG TIME DEAD, the shooting of this one had been pretty plain and straightforward. Four-square, you might say. As always throughout my Ayliff-inspired directing life, my material dictated my method. Anyway I was pleased about the 98 Reaction Index which nobody seemed prepared to mention and the play went on to have a long and successful life in the theatre and on film with a happy change of title: SPRING AND PORT WINE.

Live television drama was truly amazing. You rehearsed quite normally with the actors in some Paddington or Shepherd's Bush barracks for two or three weeks, based on the length of the play, with the floor marked out and the furniture placed as it would be in the studio - hence the need for barracks. Towards the end of this period you made up your Camera Script, dividing the play into two or three hundred shots, depending on its complexity. To achieve this you had to work out what I always thought of as the Ballet of the Cameras. You would have an allowance of four cameras huddled in the centre of the studio with the half dozen different settings ranged round the walls. Your Number One camera, in drama, was a pretty elaborate job called the Mole-Richardson crane which could do anything that Orson Welles had done in CITIZEN KANE. It had a crew of three and could send the operator flying, hovering and swooping through the air like a lumbersome bird. Number Two was a motorised Vinten which basically tracked backwards and forwards like a tram but could also crank up and down. This had a crew of two. No zoom lenses then. The other two were the standard pedestal jobs handled by one man like you mostly see in the chat shows nowadays. Then you had three or four sound booms, high platforms on wheels with their microphone operators working devices like extended fishing rods, since all sound as well as vision was naturally live. And you had to arrange your cutting from camera to camera and your movements of camera and booms from set to set so that they all, literally, never got their wires crossed. You had to choose their cabling points from the detailed studio ground-plan. I used to spend hours at home with the ground-plan on the floor and flat cut-out scale-model cameras tied to pieces of string at the cabling outlets. To get your cables crossed in the studio was the most shaming thing that could happen. You'd feel like a defrocked arty among all those high-church technicians.

At the end of this process you would have one, two or three days in the studio, again depending on the length of the play from 30 to 90 minutes. The camera and sound crews had to learn the whole complicated ballet around the actors and then this ended up in a live transmission. You began at the beginning, calling the shots in the control room.

'Coming to you next, Camera One... Get ready shot number 22 on Two. That's the wrong lens, Three. Should be a 24 degree. Thank you... 22 on Two now, coming to you Four. Close-up of Wilfrid...'

And so you went on till you got to the end: 'Roll Credits.'

Then you'd go home and talk to people who had actually just switched off their sets. Fantastic.

Film was used for exteriors. There was no video-tape then. Your pre-shot and edited Telecine - say somebody driving up in a car outside the house, getting out, walking to the front door - had to be cued exactly from the Telecine Suite into the live broadcast.

'Run Telecine. 4 - 3 - 2 - 1. On Telecine now. Relax Studio. Thirty-seven seconds... Stand by Studio. Coming to you, Three, as Marjorie comes through the door. Shot 97 on Three. Cue Marjorie...'

So the commentary ran on into the technicians' headphones while the actors went about their business.

As Paul wrote to me with typical modesty and awareness after his first telly, 'the sureness of the technicians takes my breath away.'

In those balmy days the stop-watch didn't yet rule our lives. After our final run-through in the studio we would call up Presentation.

'Hallo, Presentation? Lime Grove Studio 4 here. YOU'RE A LONG TIME DEAD is over-running nineteen minutes.'

'Thank you,' they said. And adjusted the Epilogue.

The things we risked! When I did Barrie's MARY ROSE with Daphne I filled one studio with water and Kenneth Mackintosh rowed Daphne and Derek Godfrey out to the Island-That-Likes-To-Be-Visited, where they landed and carried on with the scene. All live. No chance of a re-take.

A much-admired colleague was Michael Elliott (later founder-director of the Manchester Royal Exchange). We would spend hours in the canteen doodling impossible shots on the formica-topped tables. I wanted to do a 360 degree pan on one show and we worked this out together. It meant of course the removal and replacement of lumps of scenery while the camera swivelled round, being dead careful not to get other cameras or the rest of the studio in your sights. And all without making a sound. Well, not too much sound anyway. When I watched a recent re-run of Joan Kemp-Welch's prize-winning production of Pinter's THE LOVER I was flabbergasted at the clonking and thumping. Presumably the sound reception in the home was that much less sensitive then.

I quite soon got my longed-for chance to write. Michael Barry called me into his office one day with a long face.

'Something's gone wrong with the schedules, John. I'm afraid we've got nothing for you to do for the next six weeks.' I looked suitably woebegone and shuffled out. The moment the door closed behind me I let out a metaphorical shout of joy, rushed back to the cottage and seized a clean sheet of paper. (Well, the back of a TV script actually. I wrote everything on the backs of TV scripts for many years, long before recycling became a laudable objective: I was just being canny.)

This was heaven. Money coming in. No worries about the immediate future. I was a subsidised writer at last. I'm no good at burning the midnight oil, can't well concentrate on two jobs at once. As a writer I like settled habits. I sit at my desk after breakfast and work solidly through till lunch with, if I'm lucky, someone to bring me a cup of coffee half way. In the afternoon I relax. Walk. Listen to music. Sometimes, as I get older, just read and doze. Then after a cup of tea I'm back at the desk for a couple of hours until supper-time. That way, if I've got a play to write, I can complete it in six weeks.

I had a play to write. It was called WINDMILL NEAR A FRONTIER. As I've already said, I'm not much good at potted plots.

If people ask me what something's about I tend to say 'Life and death.' ('You can't say that, John,' said Michael Attenborough crossly once.) Basically what I start from are situations and characters and, like many better-known playwrights from Shaw downwards, I don't always know where I'm going. I find out. And what's best is when it's a real surprise.

Anyway, the theme of this one was the Deadly Middle-Years. We were once again in the Balkans (this was very fashionable then, e.g. John Whiting's MARCHING SONG. It was a sort of imaginative no-man's land where you could expect European values to hold but against a more dangerous and shifting chiaroscuro.) A leader pursued from a revolutionary putsch in the capital holes up in a disused windmill, within tantalising sight of the heavily guarded frontier, which doubles as the afternoon love-nest of a young couple of conveniently opposite political persuasions; and then provides shelter from a violent storm for a married woman on holiday from her responsibilities. In true stage form they are trapped there by a flash flood, so with four characters and continuous action over three acts I was able to explore the Aristotelian Unities. I crammed in everything I thought about love, revolution, responsibility political and familial; and the deadly grind of the middle years - 'The expanding waist and the contracting vision.' I was a very word-conscious writer. Having begun as a poet and loving the Elizabethans above all I longed, at this time especially, for a renaissance of the word in the theatre: for plays to have a kinship with music.

'Word over all
Beautiful as the sky...'

But I was also a Shavian and loved argument.

I showed the results of my brief sabbatical to Michael Barry and to my amazement he asked me to direct it for the BBC. I had never thought of it in television terms. But Paul had also read it and liked it and was prepared to do it with me on the box. What had I got to lose?

The reviews were mostly cynical but the public response was a revelation. I had shoals of letters, from Biggar to Brighton. I must resist quoting from them or they'll begin to sound like testimonials for soap powder. But it was immensely heartening to discover that I had got through to so many ordinary people who felt sufficiently moved to put pen to paper - many of them over several pages. Particularly women, stuck in their own daily grind, who identified with my Henrietta who (as played by Margaret Johnston) 'echoed what I previously believed were my own private thoughts and feelings!' (Mrs. B. of Ealing). You see what I mean, it sounds like the Ads. Where does history begin and boasting end? But I am trying to be honest about my failures too. Oh well, let's record this treasured P. C., not from a housewife but from the Great Peter Hall, as yet un-knighted but running the Shakespeare Memorial Theatre (still so-called).

Stratford-upon-Avon Nov. 5th.

My dear John,

Have been meaning to say it all week, and I hope I'm not too late: <u>Did</u> enjoy your play on Sunday. Thought it sensitive, fascinating and beautifully written. It's such a change to get away from slice-of-life grumblings and mumblings, and to hear dialogue with style. And it was beautifully directed. Do write more.

Ever,

Peter

And for the other side of the coin, a bad review... Can't find one. I must have thrown them all away. There are times when you can do without discouragement.

My BBC contract was extended into a third year and I became a Jack-of-all-styles, from Pirandello to MAIGRET, from Barrie and Jean-Jacques Bernard to two Margery Allingham thriller serials which (cleverly adapted by John Hopkins of TALKING TO A STRANGER) became little cult successes. Even a comedy series written by Patrick Campbell and starring that delightful light comedian Brian Reece (never to be confused with the heavy comedian Brian Rix.)

In one episode the small part of a bartender was played by an immensely studious actor with wavy dark hair who spent his considerable waits studying Stanislavsky's AN ACTOR PREPARES. His name was Warren Mitchell.

The Pirandello was HENRY IV and Paul's television debut. My screen adaptor was Eric Crozier of unhappy Stratford memory but he was much more in his skin as a literary man and now a thoroughly interesting member of the Benjamin Britten circle. (He later co-wrote the libretto of BILLY BUDD with E.M. Forster.) We managed a good translation to the screen and had smashing designs by Guy Sheppard. The Daily Telegraph's R.P.M.G. said 'one was constantly being reminded of Renaissance painting'. Paul wanted the low-down on television acting. I said there was no mystique. A good stage actor usually adapts easily to any medium (although a good, primarily screen, actor rarely adapts well to the stage). I said the main thing to remember was that, however many millions they tell you are watching, you are basically playing to an audience of two or three. But if he wanted to go for the big effect I could pull back and shoot in long-shot: when he wanted to be really intimate I could get between his ears. The play was 'telerecorded', i.e. filmed on 35mm off the screen during transmission - long before the invention of videotape - and some fifty years later I acquired a video copy made for me by the Beeb. I sat down to watch in some trepidation, but I have to say I was not ashamed.

When George Devine learned what we were rehearsing he wanted us to take it to the Royal Court but Paul said no. It was being planned and rehearsed for television and that's the way it should stay. I was a bit sad about that. I could have done with a foot in that door. Because there's no doubt about it, television didn't satisfy me. I longed to be back in the theatre. Preferably as a writer.

Somehow I found time to complete another play (probably during my annual 'leave': the BBC was very militaristic in its use of terms.)

I had been fascinated by what had just happened to that now-forgotten figure in Soviet history, Malenkov. From being P.M., in a spectacular fall from grace he had, instead of (for the first time in Soviet history) being shot, been demoted to be head of a power station. I thought this giddy-making example of political snakes and ladders would make a wonderful play for Paul. He would be Saul Tarn, once leader of a nameless communist state, demoted to be Inspector of Mines in a remote hinterland. The play was called GONE TO GROUND and I wrote it at Wainhill on the back of a TV script in six weeks.

Paul really liked it and showed it to Wolf Mankowitz who was then for a while in management and currently presenting him in EXPRESSO BONGO, Paul's only musical. Mankowitz was excited and bought a two-year option on the rights. I was certainly excited. The small print in the contract looked so real. All that stuff about film rights, U.S. rights, translation rights etc., etc...

I also sent a copy to my admirer Peter Hall.

7th November, 1960

...enjoyed it enormously. I'm not a bit surprised Mankowitz has bought it. It's a beautifully professional bit of work, and Tarn is a dream of a star part...

I do congratulate you on it, and I'm thrilled about Mankowitz' interest. I hope it will be a real hit – and I think it might.

Yours ever,

Peter

The observant reader will have wondered perhaps why Mankowitz had to buy an option for as long as two years?

Paul had a prior commitment to a play for H.M. Tennent. Neither he nor anybody else expected it to run but he liked the part. Daphne and I saw it on its out of town tour at Oxford and were comfortably sure it wouldn't run. It opened in the West End to decidedly lukewarm reviews and less than crowded houses, until Sunday Times critic Harold Hobson took up the cudgels on its behalf. In those days a strong management like Tennents could still afford to 'nurse' a play to see if the patient would recover. And slowly and inexorably it did. It sat up and took nourishment. The play was A MAN FOR ALL SEASONS and after the London run there was the Broadway run and after the Broadway run there was the film...

And then just to put the boot in my fan Peter Hall offered Paul something that was rather difficult to turn down: LEAR with Peter Brook.

Nothing dates quicker than a play with a political theme and my GONE TO GROUND lay washed up on the tide. I sold it to BBC TV for something called Theatre 625, but they never produced it. 'Too many Russian plays,' they eventually said. It finally had an airing, long past its sell-by date, at the Colchester Rep directed by David Buxton. It was small comfort to see that it held up well on the stage.

That small print had been so convincing. At last I was going to be able to relinquish the directing and do what I really wanted to do.

But no, but no.

We now had two children. William Alexander Harrison, conceived in the heady aftermath of my visit to Sweden, had been born on the 5th July 1958. Our socialist dreams of State education became nightmares when we enquired into Chinnor village school which turned out to have one of the lowest levels of attainment in Oxfordshire. Ours were bright boys who could already read by the age of four and were not going to be content puddling about with plasticine. It's really no good having theories about education until you know who your children are going to be. So long as there is the possibility of choice you are not going to condemn them to the educational equivalent of leg-irons. We had to face the fact that their schooling would need to be paid for. So it was no good me sitting down like Wordsworth in the Lake District and pretending to be a writer. I had to make a steady income.

Daphne was earning less and less as she willingly devoted more time to being a mother. She became known as a 'term-time actress'. She began to turn down jobs that fell over the school holidays. This (and where we lived) ruled out theatre and meant accepting only convenient tellies, which eventually pisses-off the casting directors.

Because of the writing hopes I was now doing shows for the Beeb on one-off contracts. Mostly episodes of the original MAIGRET series starring Rupert Davies. (The nice thing about that was that it introduced me to Paris where we used to do all our insert filming.) But this was an unreliable way of earning one's living. And TV was changing.

Commercial had happened. After having considered ourselves, in Michael's words, 'the National Theatre of the Air' - because we were subsidised and there was no other National Theatre yet - we were suddenly gathered together and told that we were going to compete for the mass audience. Also video-tape had been perfected, live transmission of drama was becoming the exception, and the whole thing was moving more in the direction of film. I had now had opportunities to try my hand at filming (one whole week on a tricky dialogue scene in Ealing studios for the Brian Reece series) and discovered that I couldn't do it. I couldn't control the pacing. I'd always allowed the tempo to grow naturally between the actors out of rehearsal, though under my control, as in the theatre, and I turned out to have no skill or interest in pasting it on or cutting it in afterwards. So film directing would not be a happy way forward.

About this time I was invited back to Birmingham Rep to do a guest production of SHE STOOPS TO CONQUER. Derek Jacobi, Rosemary Leach, Elizabeth Spriggs and Arthur Pentelow all in the company. Sir Barry died a few days into the run. According to Tom English, his personal secretary, this was the last letter he signed from his hospital bed.

Dear John,

It is perhaps unnecessary to say what infinite pleasure I have had from the knowledge that you were returning to BRT as producer. You have done well since those not so far distant days of your debut, and I have not the slightest doubt that your work with "She Stoops" will be of highest order.

I had hoped to see you last week, but I was allowed home for a few days and so missed the chance.

All good wishes for tonight and many more first nights,

Sincerely yours,

Barry Jackson

How formal. How from another theatrical age. But how touching too for me because this man had been my theatrical Alpha and Omega. This was dated 21st March 1961. He died on April 3rd, aged 81. A good innings, as they say. A history book innings. The Birmingham Rep, the Royal Court seasons, modern dress Shakespeare, BACK TO METHUSELAH, the Malvern Festival; not to mention box office hits like THE BARRETTS OF WIMPOLE STREET, THE FARMER'S WIFE, and Rutland Boughton's fairy tale opera THE IMMORTAL HOUR. 'To serve an art, rather than to let that art serve a commercial purpose.' A battle cry from another age.

SHE STOOPS went well and I persuaded the BBC to let me do it on the box with some of the Birmingham cast (I particularly looked forward to showing the young Derek Jacobi to the nation), but with Daphne replacing Rosemary Leach as Kate. You have to remember that nobody had heard of Rosemary Leach whereas Daphne was still TV audience bait. I also brought in a rising young actor called Dinsdale Landen as Tony Lumpkin and actors of the right years (Arthur Brough and Marjorie Rhodes) for the Hardcastles. We did it, aptly, in the BBC's Birmingham studios and memory insists it was a live transmission. The Radio Times billing says very firmly 'from the Midlands'. And 'Introducing Derek Jacobi'. Two of the people it introduced him to were Laurence Olivier and Joan Plowright. For some reason I forget they were locked out of their Brighton home and had to take refuge in a hotel where 'Joanie' switched on the television... And that's basically how, eventually, a way opened up for Jacobi at Chichester and the National.

Nancy Burman was now administrator of the Rep and Bernard Hepton Director of Productions. I had known Nancy since she was our wondrously human and reliable production manager at Stratford in 1947. An immensely able woman. Her mother, May Burman, had been an actress with Barry Jackson's original Pilgrim Players (the amateur group that transformed themselves into the first Birmingham Repertory Company in 1913). Sir Barry had come to rely on her more and more and, with his death, she found herself in sole charge.

I was invited to do two more productions in the Autumn of 1961, Anouilh's TRAVELLER WITHOUT LUGGAGE and THE WAY OF THE WORLD (Hepton as Mirabell, Jacobi as Fainall); and then one day she took me out to lunch and wooed me to come back to Birmingham as full-time Artistic Director. I muttered about my antipathy towards theatre boards. 'Don't worry your head about them,' she said. 'I'll deal with all that. You'll hardly even have to meet them. It'll just be you and me.'

Daphne was not for moving to Birmingham. She didn't want to

upheave the boys from their local private schools. It was then just over two hours drive to the midlands from the cottage. I could come home at weekends: Nancy was prepared to connive at my having no engagements on Monday mornings. It would be a reliable, if hardly generous, income. And it was the theatre. What's more a theatre I loved. To return to the old school as headmaster? Irresistible really.

I said yes. Provided I didn't have to cope with the board. And I started to look for digs in Birmingham.

Birmingham has twice been a cross-roads in my life. I should have known.

I plunged in headlong in my usual way with THE TEMPEST (Jacobi as Ferdinand, Jennifer Hilary as Miranda) and the second professional production of John Whiting's enigmatic and controversial SAINT'S DAY. I had kept Derek Jacobi and Arthur Pentelow from the previous company and added Jennifer Hilary, Lesley Nunnerley, Georgine Anderson and Ralph Nossek among others. I set to and wrote the libretto for a musical, music by Christopher Whelen with whom I had been working a lot at the BBC, of J.M. Barrie's little known first play, WALKER, LONDON for our Summer slot. (An impenetrable title which I foolishly didn't change.) It's a charming, fluff-light little Edwardian farce, enticingly set on a house-boat on the Thames. The cast needed bumping up with musical talent so Chris and I auditioned in London. He wanted me to see a girl who had impressed him in the chorus of his previous musical SCHOOL, but he wasn't sure of her name. Linda Blacklegs or something. It transpired that she had in fact been born Linda Blackledge but had been given twenty-four hours to change her name when she was chosen by Binkie Beaumont of Tennents to take over from Juliet Mills in Peter Shaffer's first play FIVE FINGER EXERCISE at the Comedy Theatre. In the late 1950s you couldn't put a name like Blackledge on a Tennent poster. The Tushinghams and Whitelaws of the Royal Court revolution had not happened yet. Stage names had to be euphonious even if phoney. So she had become Linda Gardner (which was actually a family name on her father's side). Chris winkled her out and she duly appeared before us on the stage of the Fortune Theatre. She did a restoration piece with sparky confidence and sang with full double-cream charm. I turned to Chris. 'That's our Nanny,' I whispered. Which was the character's name, not her function. She was so streets ahead of the rest in terms of musical theatre, of which she had already done a fair bit, that we wrote her in an extra solo. There seemed no end to her talents. One day in rehearsal at the end of her number she said, 'Would you like me to do the splits?' I'd never had anybody do the splits for me before. She was quite captivating. In her Edwardian costume she looked like a sturdy piece of decorative porcelain. When I introduced her to Daphne at the first night party I said, with then acceptable male chauvinism, 'I'd like one of these for my mantelpiece.'

I had discovered, browsing in the Birmingham Reference library, an old comedy which had lain unproduced and unprinted since 1735, THE DOUBLE DECEIT, or A CURE FOR JEALOUSY, by the delightfully named William Popple. This was the kind of novelty Sir Barry would have loved so I determined to resurrect it. Later, more famous, plays owe an unacknowledged debt to Popple. You can hear Sheridan's Sir Anthony Absolute in Popple's Sir William Courtlove. Yet Sheridan didn't write THE RIVALS until 1775. And as two young heiresses come to the end of their masquerade as their own maidservants the way is laid down for Kate who stooped to conquer - in 1773. When Gaylife says, 'You surprise us still more... that you, bred up in the country...' we already hear Young Marlow: 'This girl every minute improves upon me...' nearly forty years later. Not only as a precursor but as a stylist in his own right Popple deserves consideration: 'I'll be hanged if this old Winterpiece has not a mind to melt her snow in the spring of your embraces...' And old Sir William's '...you wanton little hussies. Stand fair, let me kiss you till your ears crack.'

There was a typical pert maid, Lettice, for whom Linda would be perfection. Not a lead, but a vital cog. But she was much in demand and her agent hesitated to commit her to something in mid-Autumn. She had only really come for the musical in hopes of a London transfer; Whelen was a warmish property in those days (soon to be refrigerated by the disaster of Osborne's THE WORLD OF PAUL SLICKEY). But I had a ploy.

I was about to direct, on another one-off contract, yet another MAIGRET episode. Nancy liked me to keep one foot in television, which she thought was good for the theatre, although I was more and more reluctant. However there was a part in this one that Miss Gardner could do, which would keep her nicely on the back burner until I needed her to Popple in October. Being telly naturally the agent fell for it. Wearing two hats I was clearly a director to keep in with.

I had a bit of trouble with Miss G. during the pre-filming in Paris. Because of her basically stage and musical comedy background she tended to step off a Paris pavement like Cicely Courtneidge in a show-stopper. However we finally subdued her and got it in the can. I remember thinking afterwards in my lonely Paris hotel room, as I gazed out over the vie de Boheme rooftops, there's this glorious girl out there somewhere: why hadn't I at least tried to date her? But I had no means of getting in touch, she was due to fly back next morning and I had a whole further week's filming to complete. Including a day in a sewage disposal plant where a vital clue would be found.

For Christmas I was reviving an adaptation I had made for Nottingham of ALICE IN WONDERLAND with music again by Diccon Shaw. I discussed the casting with Daphne who had been my grave and lovely Alice then. I was beginning to think that to look like the Tenniel drawings (which Jennifer Hilary, who was expecting to play it, did to the life) was less important than being able to carry what I more and more came to see as 'The Alice Show'. I thought it demanded someone like Linda. Daphne agreed. Someone who could bounce on and deliver a number. Who could dance (because she had trained at Elmhurst and the Royal Ballet School) and even look after the choreography. Someone the audience could warm their hands at. So Miss Gardner was offered the part and duly accepted. A plump little Alice she would be, perhaps (I begged her to lose a little weight), but a fresh and funny one.

Through all this time you must believe our relationship was straightforwardly professional. If I was flirting seriously with anybody it was my resident designer who had a convenient flat in the Y.W.C.A. (where young Christian men were also occasionally to be seen in the lift, though strictly against house regs.).

Daphne believed flirtation, even affairs, were good for our marriage so long as they didn't rock the boat and I had, very reluctantly, come to accept her view, although at heart I was an old-fashioned monogamist who agonised over every lapse. My score was still a modest two. She didn't believe it possible that two people could be everything to each other. She thought if I looked elsewhere I was seeking something that she couldn't provide, and vice versa. And that this was good for us both. She had never wanted anybody but me to be the father of her children and our relationship of fifteen years had a lot going for it. I was cynical, rather than seriously unhappy, though carrying somewhere inside a sense of loss. And now of course she was falling into the old trap of letting the children occupy most of her waking thoughts. I wasn't excluded exactly but I was beginning to be a bit spare. It happens in the young parenting stage of most marriages, doesn't it? Unless the father has a strongly domestic streak, which I haven't. At the first sight of nappies I bought our first washing machine. If only children flew the nest as soon as blackbirds there might be less disturbance to the mated pair. My son William tells me blackbirds are regular Darbies and Joans.

Throughout rehearsals everything between Miss Gardner and myself was strictly professional. We agonised together over her performance and her choreography. We took a night off to go to Stratford to see John Whiting's THE DEVILS (Dorothy Tutin marvellous) and stopped for fish and chips in the car coming back. She said she lived a lot in the past, which was perplexing at 23.

At the final dress rehearsal I came down with a most appalling knock-out 'flu. I could hardly stand. I certainly couldn't drive myself home. Linda was in the same digs so she leapt into the driving seat of my Hillman Husky (the only car I ever bought from new, with my TV pickings) and whisked me back to Mr. Smerdon's where I collapsed shivering into bed. At that stage of my driving career I was still disproportionately impressed by anybody who could, without hesitation or grinding of gears, drive any car other than their own. Fevered as I was she went up several notches that night.

I was too ill to attend the first night. Linda and Diccon came in and sat on the foot of my bed and told me how it had gone. It was three days before I could drag myself out of bed to see the production. I sat in the balcony, as I had done all those years ago for Margaret Leighton. Linda was radiant. Totally in command of the show and the audience. We went back to the digs and sat in front of my hissing gas fire with what Mr. Smerdon called 'Milky drinks'.

I now knew I loved this person. I've always believed, since I read it somewhere, that you should tell someone if you love them. 'It might make a difference to them,' the writer had said. So I told her. As I held her in my arms she shook like a leaf. 'I'm so lucky,' she kept repeating. I said I thought not. I could never desert the family.

'Make no mistake.

Be my love

Is the only proposal I can make...'

She still insisted on her luck. But I'm afraid the luck was mine.

She was just 23. I 39. A magical gap. Time may have done cruel things to it if Time had been allowed to try. I asked if she'd had many lovers. Swinging 60s remember. She said none in the way I meant. She had carried a hopeless passion for Jeremy Brett since she had been his Ophelia at the age of 17. This had blocked her off from casual experiences. And made her live in her still-brief past.

Greatly daring, treading on egg-shells, we had a few weekends at hotels in Knowle and Warwick. 'Will you think less of me if I come with you?' she had asked. Mindful of her virginity I said we didn't have to do anything about it. I just wanted to be with her. But she was ripe for experience and from the beginning the most natural lover.

I left Mr. Smerdon's and rented a flat in Edgbaston. Linda took one in Harborne. This was just a blind. She was never there. But the Birmingham Rep, from Sir Barry to Nancy, was a puritan stronghold. He had never even allowed the ladies of his companies to be seen in trousers in public. Nancy too had an old-maidish innocence. About the new theatre proposed eventually to replace the Rep she used loudly to say, 'What Sir Barry always wanted was a splendid erection up by the War Memorial.'

If Nancy had suspected I was playing Daphne false my contract wouldn't have been worth a hoot.

You know the old song?

'At seventeen

He fell in love quite madly

With eyes of a tender blue...'

and so on through the Seven Ages until

'But just when he thinks he's past love,
Why it's then he meets his last love,
And he loves her as he's never loved befo-o-ore.'

Or as Shakespeare breathlessly puts it

'O coz, coz, coz, my pretty little coz, that thou didst know how many
fathoms deep I am in love. But my affection hath an unknown bottom,
like the Bay of Portugal... I tell thee Aliena, I cannot be out of the sight
of Orlando. I'll go find a shadow and sigh till he come...'

Just transpose the sexes.

Our cover started to be blown when, in the summer, we took our
Rep production of THE COUNTRY WIFE (in which Linda played
Margery Pinchwife like an English Giulietta Massina) on tour to the
Antwerp and Zurich Festivals. The lovely Julie Christie, who played
Alithea, said afterwards she suspected there had been something
between us, but somewhere in the past. We covered it that well. But
not well enough. We were seen together more than was natural and
news somehow reached Nancy in Birmingham. I was for the hot seat
on my return.

By now of course Daphne knew about the whole thing. I could never
be a secret philanderer. And she knew how serious it was. But she still
rejected moving to Birmingham. That may not have saved the marriage
anyway. I was far too deeply in.

I had an Arts Council bursary to look at new theatre architecture in
Germany and Finland and proposed to take Linda with me after Zurich.
Daphne even encouraged us. I think she hoped the thing would burn
itself out, as had been her own previous experience. But as she waited
hopefully for that to happen the relationship just put down stronger and
stronger roots. Linda had visited the cottage on several weekends and
taken charge of the boys when they came to Birmingham to see
ALICE. She was burrowing into the family in the most innocent way.
There was no calculation about it. She had too much simplicity to

scheme. She accepted where my first duty lay and just somehow went with the flow. But from the very first she and Daphne got on like a house on fire. There was never any confrontation between them.

Daphne summed it up wryly: 'Poor you. Sixteen years with the wrong woman.' Which was not entirely true. I had married in good faith and in an almost adolescent lather of loving. I had been too desperate. Men take so much longer to mature. In a way she herself was looking for some sort of change in our way of life which had fallen pretty much into the sere. But she believed that whatever was to happen must be designed around the children. She thought rather than the family flying apart it should somehow expand to include this other person. I don't mean anything Mohammedan. There was no question of concubinage. We had been married, moderately successfully in the modern manner, for sixteen years. We were close friends. And amazingly there was no jealousy between the two women. I can't explain it. Most people boggle at the story. I just say they were two very remarkable women and I was an undeservedly lucky man. We had a thoroughly conniving divorce in which Hugh Willatt wearing his solicitor's hat acted for both parties. The boys had been gently brought into the picture. Stephen, seven years old and rather old-fashioned, greeted me one weekend rather archly reproving with 'Dada, I hear you have been getting mixed up in love affairs.' William's four year old reaction was the enchanting 'Shall we be able to call her Linda Harrison?'

Two days after Linda and I were married we joined Daphne and the boys in a rented house for the annual summer fortnight by the sea. The cine film records a very happy-looking bunch of people.

'Nothing extenuate, nor set down ought in malice...' I tell it simply as it was.

When I left Birmingham in 1966 Linda and I bought a house in High Wycombe to be near Wainhill. She and Daphne alternated Sunday lunches. Our Wycombe house became a staging post for the boys between Wainhill and their day school in Beaconsfield and for their music lessons in High Wycombe. Stephen was becoming proficient on clarinet and piano. William, never to be outfaced, chose the biggest instrument he could think of, the horn.

We were still a family.

CHAPTER ELEVEN

TV nuns etcetera

'It was, of course, a grave misfortune that he left Birmingham...
at a time when there was not often much to choose between the
governing boards of football clubs and repertory theatres.
Football managers and repertory directors alike were having a
bad time; and I remember quoting Vindice in THE REVENGER'S
TRAGEDY: "As fast as they pop up, let's cut 'em down."

J.C. TREWIN. The Birmingham Post. 18/1/1975

After I'd been cosily settled at the Rep for a couple of years Nancy took me aside one day and told me she was going to retire. An independently wealthy woman she had no need to work. She lived in a lovely Manor House at Loxley near Stratford and just wasn't seeing enough of it.

'Now that you're here,' she said, 'I feel I can safely step down.'

She couldn't more unexpectedly have pulled the chair from under me.

'But what about the board?' I expostulated.

'You'll have no trouble,' she said. 'They're bound to invite me to be a member and I'll see you're all right.'

But of course they didn't. A bunch of Yes-men, carefully chosen by Sir Barry for their nonentity, they suddenly felt the bit between their teeth and the last thing they wanted was Nancy sitting in their midst knowing all the answers. It was a scandal not to reward her years of service, but there you are.

With Nancy gone, gone, gone, I was disarmed and naked, and, what's more, harbouring a snake in the grass in the person of my General Manager who, having risen to this position from humble third electrician, saw himself as the new Sir Barry. I think he was slightly demented. Greenly jealous and seeing imaginary slights all over the place. But he was a good-looking plausible fellow and very successful at ingratiating himself with the board to whom we were jointly responsible.

I seriously tried to woo them but they slipped from my embraces. Let's face it, I'm no good with boards. I don't tell them enough. I don't, as the saying goes, 'take them into my confidence'. I'm too busy running the place. In my view theatre does best as a dictatorship, preferably benevolent, but even maleficent will give you better theatre than any committee. Someone has to put the 'face' on the building and the programme.

Unless you're as consummate and natural a politician as Peter Hall it's a pain to drag this protesting collection of amateurs along with you. After all I always tell myself they have the ultimate sanction of being able to sack me if the work isn't up to scratch.

Richard Hoggart was the one board member I hoped might prove a kindred spirit, of the kidney of Hugh Willatt at Nottingham. Wrong. He was patently hung-up on my mystifying class origins. My Uses of Literacy were my undoing. And I didn't exactly want to preface every report with 'Look, mate, my Dad was a baker. I grew up in Battersea.' There's a particular kind of inverted snobbery that is just as frightening as the verted kind. One of the glories of working in the theatre for me has always been that it's as near as dammit a classless milieu.

Once again a new theatre was on the drawing-board. I was highly suspicious of the design which had been awarded to the junior partner of another board member long before I arrived on the scene and was already far too advanced for me to do much about. It fell victim to a number of axioms.

(1) Sums showed that you needed 900 seats to be financially viable.
(2) The old Rep proved the advantages of a steeply raked auditorium.
(3) In the egalitarian sixties you could not have second class citizens sitting in balconies.

Ergo what you wanted were 900 seats in one steep rake. But the stage area had not been re-thought so at the bottom of this rake you had, not the enchanted ground of Epidavros, but a small neat opening like a peep-show surrounded by void. I called in the theatre consultants Theatre Projects in the person of excellent Richard Pilbrow and at least insisted that the proscenium width should match the auditorium. But it was too late to compensate for the resulting lack of wing space or to get any corresponding depth. The finished theatre is a true bastard and a monument to provincial nepotism.

There had been no need for me to have a written contract with Nancy but the board now proposed putting me on an annually renewable one. I felt strongly that if I was going to be expected to work with the architect and consultants to minimise this up-coming disaster I needed a long-term agreement at least guaranteeing my presence in the new building. They were not prepared for this. In their new-found importance they seemed eager to have any excuse for losing the last of the old regime. I steadfastly refused to sign on an annual basis. They as firmly dug their heels in and refused to offer me anything better. The Snake, busy in-the grass, waited expectantly to become the new Sir Barry.

I went out with a bang with three plays in repertoire. Marlowe's EDWARD II, Shaw's THE SIMPLETON OF THE UNEXPECTED ISLES and a new play from a Henry James novella by Ronald Gow, THE BOSTON STORY. This had a lovely part for Linda. Other members of the company were Patrick Mower, Gabrielle Drake, Benjamin Whitrow and Linda Marlowe. In a final splurge I directed them all myself.

The EDWARD II was the first of those productions where the whole cast sits round a circular raked rostrum dressed in basic garb with a semi-circular clothes-rack behind them to bear their changes of costume. A solitary crown hung above them in a beautifully simple design by Finlay James. Everything happened in full view of the audience. As the actors spoke so they emerged on to the rostrum and into the light. Ken Tynan, now Literary Manager for Olivier at the National Theatre, saw it and was fascinated. Not long after he returned to London something similar was attempted at the National with Osborne's A BOND HONOURED. And before long it was a theatrical cliché.

How many times those of us who toil in the regions have seen our clothes stolen! So all right. You can cover yourself with a blanket. It's the lack of recognition that hurts. The centralisation of our theatre, with the immovable presence of all the senior drama critics in London, has been continuously demoralising to workers in the provincial field. In Germany Hamburg is as important as Cologne as Dresden as Düsseldorf. Here we insist on prostrating ourselves before the capital.

My chosen successor at Birmingham was Peter Dews. I thought it fair to warn him of the snake.

'Don't worry,' he said, in his blunt Yorkshire way, 'I'll see him off.'

And within a year he had.

Before I leave Birmingham for the last time there is a clutch of names which ought at least to grace the Index.

Julie Christie (who popped in disgracefully paranthetically a few pages back) discovering a rare freedom assuming a convincing Brummie accent for a production of James Saunders's NEXT TIME I'LL SING TO YOU... She proved again much later with the film McCABE AND MRS.MILLER that her beauty had lost us a spunky character actress. She was not often fully herself on stage but it was uncanny the way she opened up whenever a camera was in the offing, even if it was only accompanying a reporter from the Birmingham Post...a very young Sheila Gash (sic) going on for Linda, who-was running a temperature of 104, at a moment's notice as Anouilh's COLOMBE and making a good fist of it. I had returned from holiday one year to nudges and winks from all the male staff about this new page 3 bird I'd engaged who'd been photographed for the Mirror in brief bikini on an Algarve beach. 'Sheila Gash who is shortly joining the Birmingham Rep.' This was news to me. Naturally I sent for her and gave her an audition. Which of course was just what she'd planned. Her cheek was rewarded by a lowly place in the company where she played maidservants from many centuries. With practice and a subtle change of name she eventually took her stand as one of our theatre's more bravura leading ladies.

...Malcolm Bradbury and David Lodge, novelists in cocoon, then teaching at Birmingham University, who co-wrote with a gifted student of theirs, Jim Duckett, two satirical revues for me, BETWEEN THESE FOUR WALLS and SLAP IN THE MIDDLE, in which Linda was in her element and Julie took lively part. Ms. Christie even sang, not very successfully. But she was certainly sexy. Our authors could only be kept from rehearsals with difficulty. This was not my first meeting with one of them. Many years back at Nottingham a play had been submitted with a local postmark which, though a pastiche of then fashionable Anouilh, stood out from the ruck. I thought I should at least talk to the author. A wan and reedy sixth-former presented himself... M. Bradbury...

Our accompanist for the second revue was a nice shy chap who was studying music at the University called Christopher Hogwood...

...Angela Pleasance, a swaying, hypnotic, incantatory Titania... John Shrapnel brooding in the background in several plays... Derek Smith always valuably over the top... Jeremy Brett and Wendy Hiller, incomparable paring, in a play which nearly made it to London, A MEASURE OF CRUELTY (Translated by Yvonne Mitchell from Steve Passeur). This began a much-valued friendship with Wendy of which more in its proper place when I write a play for her...

...Evan Hunter (Author of THE BLACKBOARD JUNGLE, also widely known as Ed McBain of the 87th Precinct novels) of whose play THE EASTER MAN we gave the English premiere. Starring Ian McShane it moved from an enthusiastic sell-out season in Birmingham to fizzle out ignominiously at London's Globe after three weeks: Evan, slumped in the taxi on our way to the first-night party: 'I guess I flopped.'

I didn't seem to have the Midas touch where transfers were concerned.

And Derek Jacobi 'partout'...quiveringly sincere as poor TROILUS opposite Jennifer Hilary's self-betrayed Cressida...a bloat HENRY VIII showing the flair for character beneath make-up that would later make him famous as TV's CLAUDIUS ....a febrile Jimmy Porter ...a dashing 18th Century buck in THE DOUBLE DECEIT... The last of our major actors to train himself classically for the job in Rep. 'And what shall the robin do now, poor thing?'

Goodbye to Brum. I left, heavily mourned by John Trewin in the Birmingham Post, in the summer of 1966.

James Sharkey, such a cherishable name for a theatrical agent, had been friendly since I had first known him as a junior in the Al Parker agency. He was now in business on his own and asked if he might look out for something for me. As I said, I have only twice in my life found work, and memorable work at that, through agents. This was to be the second time.

I soon got a call to go down to London to meet Stella Richman, Head of Series for Associated Rediffusion Television, then one of the most go-ahead of the independent companies for drama. Stella was a very sparky lady who also ran a restaurant, the White Elephant. Her theatrical involvement went back to being Alec Clunes's assistant at the Arts Theatre Club. We had a convivial coffee morning in her north London home.

'What did you do to her?' Mr. Sharkey asked on the telephone. 'She's mad about you!'

A Format arrived for me in the post. A Format is a twenty-odd page document outlining the idea for a television series. This includes the basic premise (doctors or waitresses or whatever), the regular characters with their potted life histories, specimen stories, locations and so on. This one, called SANCTUARY, was based in a convent of Roman Catholic nuns who were not contemplatives but worked in the community. I liked it. I thought that, treated with gritty naturalism, it could do for nuns what Z CARS had done for the police. I wired back in some enthusiasm. (What a pity we no longer have telegrams. I suppose we have Fax. But it's not the same. Telegrams had a whole pithy language of their own, based on the financial pressure to keep it short. A Fax can maunder on for ever and nobody seems to mind.) The notion was that I should *produce* the series, (producing and directing having finally been differentiated as in films), that is to say mastermind it from an office in Rediffusion's Kingsway HQ, not direct it on the floor. Stella thought there were plenty enough television directors around but not many people with the experience or the clout to produce. This appealed to me as I was all for a change of emphasis if I was to re-enter the television arena. (The Snake's amazed reaction when he heard was 'My God! You do land on your feet, don't you!')

But to work my way into a new company, particularly as I had a BBC past, Stella thought it would be a good idea if I directed something first, just to prove I knew my onions.

I did a good script by John Hawkesworth (later producer of

UPSTAIRS, DOWNSTAIRS) called THE CREAM OFF THE TOP for a series they were running called BLACKMAIL. And I had James Maxwell giving a first-rate performance in one of the two leading parts. The chap who had been cast opposite him wasn't in the same league, yet the script needed performances of equal weight. I just gave the lesser actor more close-ups. You have to use these unfair dodges. Almost anybody can be an actor in TV close-up. Which is why I will never engage an actor for the theatre on the basis of a television performance. I need to see him on a stage, even if it's only a few planks in a church hall.

Round about the same time a television play I had written myself during my last quiet months at Birmingham went out on ABC Armchair Theatre. I'd called it THE WAR GAME but the BBC anticipated my title with a famous documentary so it was changed to the somewhat tired sounding ANY NUMBER CAN PLAY. The idea had come to me sitting in the chair at my old-fashioned scissor-wielding barber's at Five Ways in Birmingham.

As I can't tell stories I'll leave it to Maurice Wiggin in the Sunday Times:

'An unusually vivid and lively play of ideas was ANY NUMBER CAN PLAY, by John Harrison, which ABC's "Armchair Theatre" put out last weekend. Mr. Harrison took us into a World State of the future, at peace and run by a committee of benevolent egg-heads, in which limited war within a limited zone was preserved as a therapeutic "game". Some played the game because they wanted to - incurably aggressive; some were sent for a cure, to release their inner tensions; some were sentenced to the war for short periods, as delinquents of the peaceful society. The area in which the formal killing went on was delimited by some sort of "nuclear curtain" which prevented the warlovers from breaking out. Ah, but what if the atavists could secure the services of an electronic-nuclear technician and break out in good earnest? Then they could put the clock back and revert to what they really enjoyed - savagery and bullying on the global scale, fighting for the love of fighting and dominion unimaginable.

A melodramatic sci-fi notion, perhaps; and of course there was the odd practical question about ways and means which tended to ask itself at inconvenient moments. Nevertheless, a thought-provoking play of some dramatic power and not inconsiderable psychological penetration.'

He doesn't mention that the cast was led by Donald Houston and Adrienne Corrie.

Terence Feely, who was Script Editor for Armchair Theatre, said afterwards that I should have held on to the property for a film. But I wasn't geared to thinking of things I'd written as 'properties'. It had arrived in my head beneath the scissors as an idea for a television play. I'd written it as such and submitted it to Leonard White (Once Bad Angel to my Good in FAUSTUS at Stratford) who was now conveniently Armchair Theatre's producer. The director Don Leaver had filched it from the top of Leonard's pile and become passionate to direct it. That seems to me a properly organic process. Nothing to do with touting properties.

Anyhow one way and another I returned to television with a certain éclat.

But I'm afraid I didn't really enjoy being a producer. It was the best paid job I've ever held and a fortuitous bit of timing with two homes to maintain but I prefer to have some sort of hands-on involvement with what I'm doing. Mostly the new job seemed to be about sitting behind a big desk and swanning around London in taxis. Also a lot of kow-towing to those above me in the corridors of power was expected which delicate art, like flower arranging, had never been included in my training and came hard. I don't arrange flowers too well either.

We had an extraordinary cast: Joanna Dunham, Peggy Thorpe-Bates, Alison Leggatt and Fay Compton were all above the title every week and guest artists for particular episodes drew on the cream of the profession. But the scripts were rarely good enough (except those written by Elaine Morgan and G.W. Target) and I was mostly forced by the budget to use contracted staff directors who were not good enough either. Whenever I was able to go a bust on a Joan Kemp-Welch or a Tania Lieven or a Marc Miller the thing took off. But it was very uneven. We were a so-so success. Good enough to go into a second series. 26 fifty-minute episodes in all. But we were buggered about the schedules. In some ITV areas we went out at 7.30 and in others at 10.30. It was difficult to know which audience to aim for. We were saddled (more nepotism) with a dreadfully inappropriate script editor (a Jewish veteran of 'B' movies) for the first series but for the second I was in a strong enough position to stick out for the man I wanted. I'd met Alfred Shaughnessy in the corridors at Kingsway where he was working on a series for John Whitney (later Director of the I.T.A.). In our brief encounters I recognised a kindred spirit.

Under Freddy things got better. He was a Catholic and took the professionally Religious seriously. A large, nervous bear of a man, blinking anxiously, talking animatedly: a self-confessed snob, staunchly of the political Right. But there was more to Freddy than a stuffed shirt. Eton and the Guards may have created the mould but there was a crab's tender vulnerability beneath the shell. One of the prides of his life had been to be made officer in charge of re-starting opera in the devastated Rhineland after the war. His snobbery was a reflex action: his instincts were as liberal and buccaneering as the origins of his great-grandfather's fortune in the Canadian railways might suggest. And privately he was a charming doodler and songster at the piano in the 'Hutch'/Coward mould. Evenings at Freddy and Jean's always ended with a crooning session at the keyboard which Linda used to adore. It was good to find that past forty one could still make new friends. My third Old Etonian, (perhaps I am the snob?), he has written his own fascinating autobiography, BOTH ENDS OF THE CANDLE, which sold on the back of the fact that he later became script editor of the fabulously successful UPSTAIRS, DOWNSTAIRS.

Freddy cleverly persuaded me to write the first episode of the new Sanctuary series myself, thereby giving me the hands-an connection that I so sorely missed. I hadn't imagined I would ever be able to script to a format but, with Freddy's encouragement, and having lived with the convent and its characters for nearly a year, I came up with quite a tolerable episode in which I cast Gemma Jones and a then very un-fledged but obviously promising Martin Shaw. It was a talky script, which worried the director. But when I suggested he might shoot one of the scenes on top of a moving bus he was happy. As long as they can feel themselves to be playing movies television directors are easily mollified.

Peter Black in the Daily Mail:

'The new SANCTUARY series (Rediffusion) promises to consider the more controversial aspects of nunnish life. THE NOVICE, written by John Harrison, made good the promise by dramatising with reasonable honesty the situation of a novice nun whose motives for joining proved unsatisfactory.

When the senior Sister Paul went off to talk to the girl's parents in Birmingham and her ex-fiancé in London, we got quite a fair clash between the Christian and the humanist view of conventual life, and in the student a good sketch of the religious temperament that cannot stand religion.

The question: Who will get the girl, the fiancé or the church? was resolved without sentimentality. It was the glossified look and talk of the nuns, as usual, that supplied the false note.

We seemed to be watching a commercial for nuns. But this problem is insoluble.'

The glossified look of the nuns! So much for my efforts at gritty realism! Dear 'Faydie' (Compton) would never go on screen without her make-up. However many times it was wiped off she would always repair it behind a flat before going on camera. 'I'm not appearing naked, darling.' Barrie's original Mary Rose was now an outspoken old lady whose salty language caused many a raised eyebrow in the canteen where she sat drinking white wine in her nun's habit.

We often had groups of real nuns to the Studio as a P.R. exercise and one party had been allowed to watch a take of Fay doing a particularly affecting sick-bed scene. At the end of it even the stony-hearted technicians applauded and I went on the floor to congratulate her.

'I should bloody think so,' she grumbled loudly, 'with that effing lot looking on!'

One of the perks of the job was getting on the inside of many London convents for 'research'. The real nuns loved the series and found their glamourised selves 'very true to life'. Never mind. In all other respects I found them splendidly practical and business-like.

Perhaps, as an atheist in charge of a series about nuns, this is the moment to say something about me and religion.

As a youth I had passionately wanted a faith. Somehow going to church never seemed to be any part of this, even when I went regularly with the Grange School boys to St. Nicholas's, Combe Raleigh and read the lessons. This was just some sort of ritual that went with the job. And most of the Creed stuck in my craw. No way could I believe that he was conceived of the virgin or rose on the third day. Or, I'm afraid, that he'd made heaven and earth. Depends what you meant by Him. In those days I was reading Sir Arthur Eddington's THE EXPANDING UNIVERSE which didn't exactly chime with the first chapter of Genesis; and I was imbibing Wells and Shaw's and Bertrand Russell's rationalism along with their social theories. But to be a creature of Shaw or Russell was as anathematic to me as to be brainwashed by the 39 articles. We were living in a miraculous world, that was always clear. I had no difficulty in seeing heaven in a grain of sand or eternity in an hour. And I could go along with the whole of the New Testament if you left out the conjuring tricks. The sermon on the mount seemed to me then, and seems to me still, the most stunning blueprint for life on earth. Perhaps its very perfectionism has been its downfall because at very few points in the history of the Christian church have its adherents been able to turn the other cheek, or bless those that cursed them. 'Lay not up for yourselves treasures upon earth...' No, not even in Lambeth Palace or the Vatican. 'Judge not, that ye be not judged...' Oh, hard, hard. And the ultimate masochism: '...resist not evil: but whosoever shall smite thee on thy right cheek, turn to him the other also... bless them that curse you, do good to them that hate you... For if ye love them which love you, what reward have ye?' There was no way in which I could be superhuman enough to be a Christian and I could see no point in joining in the general sham.

I started reading the other World Religions. I bought a big fat book called The Bible of the World. The Hindu scriptures seemed, when not making fanciful poems about the creation, to be largely about hygiene in hot countries. Confucianism was a philosophy rather than a religion. I began to be at home, as so many people a couple of decades later, with Buddhism, particularly the Taoist branch. 'Tao, the way...'

'Without going out of the door
One can know the whole world;

Without peeping out of the window
One can see the Tao of heaven.
The further one travels
The less one knows.
Therefore the sage knows everything without travelling;
He names everything without seeing it;
He accomplishes everything without doing it.'

But this is not a recipe for action, or even worship.

'That which we look at and cannot see is called plainness.
That which we listen to and cannot hear is called rareness.
That which we grope for and cannot get is called minuteness.

These three cannot be closely examined;
So they blend into One
 Revealed, it is not dazzling;
Hidden, it is not dark.
Infinite, it cannot be defined.
It goes back to non-existence.
It is called mystery.
Meet it, you cannot see its face;
Follow it, you cannot see its back.

By adhering to the Tao of the past
You will master the existence of the present
And be able to know the origin of the past.
This is called the clue of Tao.'

And is not so far removed from Wordsworth's Ode on the
Intimations of Immortality - 'a sense of something far more deeply
interfused...'
I did not become a Taoist. But I do still like

'He who knows the masculine and yet keeps to the feminine
Will become a channel drawing all the world towards it...'

Mohammedanism, the most modern religion, seemed the most backward: tribal, battle obsessed. As we have since had good reason to observe.

When I had covered the ground the one thing that stood out a mile was man's deep psychological need to believe something irrational that would confirm his own idea of his importance in the universe. The most amazing thing about religions, great and small, is their sameness.

After pussyfooting about for many years keeping my options open by saying I was an agnostic, I finally woke up to the fact that I wasn't at all. I was a convinced atheist. I am happy with it and feel no compulsion to convert anybody else. Simply, as the amazing Charles Bradlaugh put it in 1880, 'I am without God.' I can manage without the comforts of an afterlife. Though I felt the desperate human pressure to believe in one when the dearest person in life to me died cruelly before her time.

But it's no good. I still stick with what Grandma, peasantly earthbound, said to me long ago. 'I believe that when you die you die and there's an end on't.'

I am content with that.

We seem to have come a long way from SANCTUARY and Rediffusion Television.

Right at the start of my job Linda and I had a bit of a crisis. She had been auditioning for the part of Hodel in the new Jerome Robbins musical FIDDLER ON THE ROOF. The candidates had been whittled down from about two hundred to two. It was now between her and Dilys Watling. It's quite a featured role with its own solo number, 'Far from the home I love'. The week of the final eliminatory auditions I had to fly to India. More about that in a moment. We were on the horns of a dilemma. We'd just moved into our new house in High Wycombe. I was earning more than enough for two. We really didn't want or need her to work in the theatre immediately. TV, with its shorter time commitment, would have been perfect. We would see very little of each other if she got the part.

I went off to India for a week at the invitation of the International

Theatre Institute to be the British delegate to an East-West Theatre Seminar in New Delhi. The Indians had asked for the great Joan Littlewood but nobody could find her. In the end she turned up on the aircraft and we became a delegation of two.

Delhi in October was very, very hot. Temperatures in the upper 90s Fahrenheit which don't suit me at all. Even at 8.30 a.m. with the sun not yet a quarter of the way up the sky I was regularly defeated in my attempts to reach the nearest street market from the hotel in search of a little local colour. I was reduced to sitting gasping like a fish in the shade of a tree while a gardener watered all around me from a great bolster slung across his back, regulating the flow by squeeze control of the open corner. There I waited for the conference bus to honk explosively into the yard and convey our hotch-potch of delegates to the mercifully air-conditioned hall.

Joan and I must have made an odd couple as we sat together behind our individual microphones and the sign reading United Kingdom, for all the world like a toy United Nations. Various U.S.S.R. satellites read long and boring papers while the big grey men from Moscow leaned forward intently, hanging on the words of the East German ladies as they paid reverent lip-service to Karl Marx. American academics riposted with learned hecadecasyllables. I spoke up from time to time to justify my air fare. Joan made much mock of my 'whispering baritone' as she sat there silently taking sheaf after sheaf of notes. There was much banqueting after dark in the blessed cool beneath the stars which Joan ignored, preferring to roam the beggar-infested streets of Delhi. The rest of us hedonists meanwhile dined with princesses and the Minister for Railways who, by some oriental subtlety, was the patron of the seminar.

I discovered the delights of true Indian food, so much more subtly spiced and coloured than our average High Street curry pavilion and, by the end of the week, the miseries of Delhi belly.

On the penultimate day Joan delighted the delegates by taking to the microphone. For this they had waited with polite Indian patience all week. But they were ill prepared for what she had to say. Incoherent, passionate, with several 'bloodies' and one 'bugger' she lambasted them for wasting money on a theatre conference at all when they had not even begun to address the problems of their poor and hungry. She was like an uncensored Major Barbara. She sat down to an embarrassed silence.

'Fantastic,' I whispered, 'but what's that got to do with all those notes you've been taking?'

'I'm just a compulsive note-taker ducky,' she replied.

On the last day I began to fall under her spell. This time there was no rant. Forgetting her taunts of my whispering baritone she herself leaned close into the mike and spoke with humbling sincerity of her beloved 'Fun Palace'. It is tragic that the British Theatre Establishment could find no place for her. But then even Peter Brook was driven eventually to seek his funding in France. These great prophets fundamentally embarrass us. They resist classification. We like to tame our artists with a lick of the commercial cat o' nine tails.

I found time with a bunch of Americans in a shared taxi (hair-raisingly overtaking a mile of slow-moving army lorries via the on-coming carriageway) to see the Taj Mahal which was disappointingly like the biscuit tins. Even going back to my first sight of the rock of Gibraltar in 1949 I've always felt a sense of déjà vu when confronted by the actual evidence of something you've seen in photograph after photograph. But braving the brain-oppressing heat we pressed on to Fatehpur Sikri about which I knew nothing and were rewarded by the mind-bendingly wonderful. An empty city of red sandstone inlaid with marble, built while Shakespeare was still at his half-timbered Grammar school in Stratford by the Moghul Emperor Akbar in extravagant celebration of a local mystic's successful prophecy of the birth of a royal son. And then deserted for some reason after only sixteen years. Yet there it stands before us still: palaces, courtyards, a fort, a mosque which once housed the remains of Salim Chisti, the honoured mystic. Breathtakingly preserved as if the inhabitants had left it yesterday rather than before the first production of Hamlet. Even an open-air chess-board made of marble squares on which the ladies of the harem sat as pieces to be moved at the Emperor's behest...

Linda met me off the plane with a long face. 'I've got it,' she said. It might have been measles.

FIDDLER ON THE ROOF for which, having read the script and listened to the Broadway album, I had hopefully predicted a short run, settled into Her Majesty's for life. Linda's and my trains passed each other going in opposite directions just outside High Wycombe station. Our communication was by notes left in the kitchen. I was too tired from my daytime job to wait up for her to get home after midnight. She was sleeping when I left in the morning. It was a very trying time. For this we had gone through all the paraphernalia of divorce? (The fat private eye had sat drinking coffee in my Birmingham flat making notes. 'I see there's a double bed,' he said to us. 'I shan't need you to get in to it.')

After about four months Linda sought release from her contract. A bad career move. But surely life had to come first? It would have been near impossible for me to get out of mine with Rediffusion. I was the boss man; I could have been sued. She was with the show long enough to feature on the original London cast recording with Topol and Miriam Karlin which has brought in steady royalties ever since. Synchronicity, when it comes to job offers, rarely happens in the theatre. In a couple of years time when I had settled down to full-time writing and working at home we'd have fallen on FIDDLER with open arms. But four or five months of sharing the same roof without ever meeting each other in a waking state was a kind of hell. A year of it, which was the contractual obligation, was unimaginable.

Perhaps we should have been brave and stuck it out. But 'Time travels in divers paces...' He trots, he ambles and he stays still withal. For those few months he stayed still withal. He expanded. He became gross. But I know I should have been stronger. I know she later sometimes regretted not having followed where that particular road was leading. She loved musicals. Director Ronald Eyre, when he saw it, said glowingly 'She's a kind of star.' And I think she could have been.

I can't escape the responsibility for having now connived at the abortion of two notable careers.

CHAPTER TWELVE

In which I try to become a Playwright

'ONE WILD NIGHT IN THE LIFE OF A SPINSTER'

Headline in The Windsor, Slough and Eton Express. October 16th, 1970.

This is the chapter where I really do confidently set out to be a full-time writer.

I was doing nicely enough at Associated Rediffusion. Stella, my boss, was pleased with me. One day in a taxi (if everything at the old Birmingham Rep happened on the stairs, everything at A.R. happened in taxis) she said she was planning to challenge the BBC's monopoly of Classic Serials - you know, the Dickens, Jane Austen Sunday slot. Would I take charge?

'But supposing,' I said, as we whirled through Regent's Park, 'supposing we don't get the franchise?'

1968. The commercial franchises were up for grabs for only the second time in the history of British television. The first time round nobody in politics had had the nerve to disturb the status quo.

'Of course we shall get the franchise,' she said. 'What do you think about Sir Walter Scott?'

The new Postmaster-General, charged with responsibility for the dispensations, was Dr. Charles Hill, the one-time 'Radio Doctor' who throughout the war had always been so laudably concerned about the movement of the nation's bowels. Now Lord Hill, and (unlike Charity) considerably 'puffed-up', he didn't relish his cavalier treatment at the hands of the doughty ex-Admiral who by some quirk was chairman of Associated Rediffusion. The Admiral, it was said, refused to be brow-beaten on his own quarter-deck. So Hill decided, in good old medical fashion, on a purge. Rediffusion lost its franchise. Two new companies were created, London Weekend and Thames.

When dawn broke (to change the metaphor) and we looked round to see who was clinging to the wreckage Stella wasn't among the survivors. My new job was gone before it was given.

So now I really would be a writer. There was money saved from the overpaid job. With my new-found contacts I should be able to get enough commissions for series episodes to keep the wolf from the door. Freddy had gone off to script-edit something called HADLEIGH, starring Gerald Harper, for Yorkshire TV. I could probably count on a couple of those.

And once again I had a play of my own to write.

The notes for it had been sitting in the memo pages of a pocket diary for a couple of years waiting for a patch of time. They read as follows: KNIGHT IN FOUR ACTS. 1:PRE-RAPHAELITE SPRING. 2:RENAISSANCE SUMMER. 3:EDWARDIAN AUTUMN. 4:CONTEMPORARY WINTER.

The idea was to take a politician through the phases of his life from the idealism of a young Knight Errant to the disillusion of a washed-out apology like Ramsay Macdonald. And to heighten the theatricality I thought I would move the same characters through the centuries whilst telling a continuous story. There would be a false-friend villain figure who would begin Act One in black armour and end the play as a TV pundit. There would be an idyllic rescuing of a damsel in distress which would lead to the disillusion of a complaisant marriage in the Elizabethan act and the acquisition of a new mistress in the Edwardian one. Our hero the Knight, William Knight, ultimately Sir William Knight and an Edwardian Prime Minister, would be a hollow man who could only define himself through his womenfolk. After a full-blown Edwardian scandal we would pick him up in contemporary London living in parliamentary exile with his 'supposed' daughter, only to have that comfortable illusion finally taken from him.

The first act would be pastiche Malory, the second pastiche Tudor, the third pastiche Pinero, the fourth, I hoped, in my own style. Why be so complicated? Because that was the whole point really. After two years of television I wanted to write something overtly theatrical. And having directed so many plays I had a good ear for period and relished the self-imposed challenge.

Paul, always my first reader after Linda, loved it but couldn't see himself playing Knight. 'I can hear myself doing the last act,' he said, 'but not the others.' But he thought I should show it to anybody and everybody, 'provided they can read.'

I started to push it about.

Ken Tynan at the National:

'It's *very* suavely written and has a nice shape, but I'm not sure that the content really justifies the elaborate chronological jump-technique. Above all, it's part of our policy to avoid overlapping, where possible, with the commercial theatre; and I feel your play might probably get its chance there...'

Commercial Manager Peter Bridge, just then preparing Ayckbourn's first West End hit HOW THE OTHER HALF LOVES:

'I am sorry to say that I do not really feel this is a play for the hard, commercial world we live in at the moment and strongly disagree with Kenneth Tynan's reaction that it should be in the commercial theatre to start with. I am sure that your chance will come from someone like Peter Dews at Birmingham...'

Peter Dews at Birmingham:

'I did enjoy reading it very much but I have some reservations about the staging of it... For an idea so delicate it's a very thick script. The four-act structure is fine but each of the acts would very nearly warrant an interval - indeed between three and four Samela and William will surely need one for the change. I think, too, the Narrator-figure whose name we won't mention' (I had christened the villain after the Snake) 'should, if he brings the curtain down, play a more active part sometimes in taking it up... If, as I hope, they decide on the new theatre, it might be nice to do a farewell season here, and I'd be very keen for you to be a participant. What about the idea of doing this play as part of it? But I do think it needs the pruning shears, if not the billhook. If the idea strikes you as being worth following up, let's meet and have a talk...'

This seemed perfect to me. Birmingham... The Alma Mater... as actor, director, and now, the greatest of these, as playwright. I warmly followed up Peter's approach. In those days I still foolishly thought there was something immoral about directing your own work so I said

I would prefer him to do it which he was more than happy about. I'd finished the play in August. This was now September. Not bad going. I excitedly told John Trewin, who had of course been an early and enthusiastic reader, and he asked if he could publish it in PLAYS OF THE YEAR which he edited, to coincide with the Birmingham premiere, which looked like being volume 38.

In December 1968 I had another call from the International Theatre Institute. Would I like to go to Chicago for three months to direct a play at the Goodman Theatre and to teach at the Goodman School? My natural reaction to all such requests is yes. If I'm asked to go round the corner to direct I may hum and haw and cavil but if somebody says come to Timbuctoo I'm on my way. We settled the most important thing: Linda would be able to come with me. Next the play. After several transatlantic phone negotiations by dawn's early light THE RECRUITING OFFICER was decided upon. And I would teach directing. In England, again, I would have raised all kinds of objections to the notion of teaching directing, but when it's the price of a ticket to foreign parts...

Let's keep on with KNIGHT IN FOUR ACTS though.

Peter writes to me in Chicago in February:

'I hope you're both enjoying life in the snow... Work has actually started on the site and the estimate is for an opening in Autumn 1971. That means I'd begin the Farewell Year in Autumn 1970 so I think that's the date to be moving towards!'

When we came back from Chicago I got out the shears as he advised. To help me prune I had persuaded a group of friends to record it for me in all its efflorescence.

Peter:
'Let me know how the taping goes, and when you've done your cuts we'll rendezvous again. In the meantime, if you want to tell Fred' (Birmingham Post Theatre Reporter) 'about it, please do, by all means.'

Linda laid on a staggering lunch in High Wycombe and Derek Smith brought his smart new tape-recorder. Our cast was Bernard Horsfall, Geoffrey Palmer, Daphne Slater, Derek Smith, Linda Gardner, Georgine Anderson, Robert Grange and Chrys Salt. (Geoff Palmer had just played Torvald opposite Linda's Nora in a tour of A DOLL'S HOUSE. Chrys Salt, striking poet, was her close friend. Bernard dated back to Nottingham for me and the others had all worked with us in Brum.)

'Glad to hear the taping went well - very distinguished troupe - and I look forward to the cut version...The plan is still to do it this next Autumn... Business has picked up since you-know-who left... See you soon...'

That was the 31st of January 1969. On the 10th of May Peter writes from Chichester where he is directing a play in the Festival.

'I had to go up to the Rep yesterday to have a meeting ...One of the results of costing the Farewell season was that although we tried every permutation we know, we just can't afford to do your play... But I do hope that by our releasing it the minute we got wind of the financial situation it will enable you to get it presented this Autumn somewhere else. I'm delighted about its publication. This should help its chances enormously. Please forgive me for letting you down. We were all very keen about it, but the perpetual chase for cash has thwarted us...'

Get it presented this Autumn somewhere else? Some hope. It was already the not so merry month of May.

I tried the Bristol Old Vic, now run by Val May who had been my successor at Nottingham.

'I considered this very seriously for our Autumn season and hoped very much to be able to suggest a production to you, but in the end I had to decide against it for a variety of reasons. I enjoyed reading the play very much and I think it is a fascinating idea worked out with great originality... and although I would have loved to have suggested to you that we might work on the play together I felt eventually that there wouldn't really be the time ...as we are already committed to two new plays ...I am sorry about this, John ...I do hope it has a very successful production somewhere else...'

Braham Murray at the Royal Exchange. 'I enjoyed reading it very much although I did have some slight reservations about the last episode. The situation is that we are fully committed up to October 1971...I imagine you are looking for something rather sooner...'

You begin to get the picture. I won't delve much deeper into the file. A year later I was still beavering away. That gifted playwright, the late Cecil P. Taylor (AND A NIGHTINGALE SANG; GOOD) writing from the Tyneside Theatre Company where he was literary advisor:

1/ Nov./71.

...I honestly read it with interest and enjoyment. I think you have hit on a very interesting idea and there is some lovely writing in it. At this stage in the development of our theatre, I can't see it in the main theatre for a number of reasons. I am passing it on to Gareth Morgan as a possible production for our studio theatre...'

Gareth Morgan: 'I agree with Cecil that it may well be a possibility for the Gulbenkian Studio Theatre. This could not be until the Autumn/New Year of 1972-73... I am quite certain there is the strong possibility of a play here...'

And in response to my nervous enquiry in February 1972:

'We have not lost track of your KNIGHT IN FOUR ACTS, but it will be some time before we finalise plans...
I will be in touch with you again...'

Here I shall close the melancholy file. John Trewin, undaunted, duly published the text in PLAYS OF THE YEAR, Volume 38, along with David Storey's IN CELEBRATION and John Hale's SPITHEAD. Just to finish the story. In 1973, when I was running the Leeds Playhouse, my associate director David Carson begged me to let him do it. We opened during a newspaper strike. Very few people know there is such a play at all.

A happier break was to be chosen as one of the initial four writers for a series that became one of television's standing stones, UPSTAIRS, DOWNSTAIRS. Once again Freddy Shaughnessy was the script editor. Somehow I could write for telly when it was for Freddy. It was as if I knew how to enter into his game. And the subject, life above and below stairs in an Edwardian household, had special appeal for me. If Freddy (and John Hawksworth producing) knew all about UPSTAIRS, I, through Grandma, knew all about DOWNSTAIRS. She had been that very thing, a lady's maid in Edwardian London. And what a classic notion for a successful series with appeal to all ages and wages!

But there's a nice cautionary tale here for anyone who sits at home trying to dream up a format for a new TV series, thinking 'If only I could come up with a winner like UP/DOWN...'(as it came to be known to the initiates). Because I have to tell you that's not really how it came about at all.

To begin with, yes, buddies and budding actresses Eileen Atkins and Jean Marsh had originally hit on the idea to keep themselves in work together, during a holiday in the South of France. Whether or not they had come across a book called 'Below Stairs' by Margaret Powell about being a kitchen maid in the twenties, they saw themselves as two nicely contrasted such misses in the Victorian era. They took the idea to John Hawksworth and John Whitney, now in independent business as Sagitta Productions. With a few subtle developments like moving the setting to Edwardian London and making the series as much about above stairs as below they in turn took it to London Weekend Television. Now Eileen Atkins at that time was a hot property. LWT leaped at the idea of a starring vehicle for her. Jean Marsh was a nobody by comparison but they bought the whole ticket and Hawkesworth and Freddy Shaughnessy began to flesh out the format.

Then, as luck would have it, Eileen Atkins was offered a new Robert Bolt play at the Chichester Festival and wanted to pull out. LWT immediately lost interest in the series (called, at this juncture, 81 EATON PLACE). Eileen didn't want to do her friend Jean out of a good job so she shuffled her schedule and offered to make the first three episodes. After which the part could be safely written out as the audience would by now be hooked. LWT signed up again. Anything, apparently, to get Miss Atkins on their screens. How do I know all this? Because I had the task of writing episode four. A vital new character would be introduced to take the audience's minds off the disappearance of Miss A. The daughter of the household, Elizabeth, to be played by Nicola Pagett, would return from finishing school in Germany and I had the rare joy for a series writer of creating her character.

Once the wheels were safely and irrevocably in motion Eileen Atkins pulled out completely. It was too late to stop it now. 81 EATON PLACE, with a blissful last second change of title to UPSTAIRS, DOWNSTAIRS, was rolling. Curses not loud but deep must have echoed in the corridors of LWT as they handled this hot potato and cursorily replaced Eileen Atkins with a fairly unknown actress for the first three episodes. Pauline Collins made such a hit that the character had to be dragged back at the earliest opportunity.

The series went on gathering strength and golden opinions for many years.

That's how it really happens.

No entrepreneurial wizards sit behind those big desks with judges' noses for the winning idea.

One of the best things about the job in Chicago was that the Goodman School and Theatre were housed in the Art Institute, which is where all those well-known Renoirs are, and the Seurats (including what I suppose we must now call 'Sunday in the Park with George') and practically all the Impressionist paintings we know and love from picture postcards and illustrations. It was a magnetic experience to be able to enjoy them in the reality, drawing me always to walk the long way round through the Art Institute to work.

Being in the U.S. of A. and teaching gave me an idea for a play for Wendy Hiller. We'd became neighbourly since moving to High Wycombe as she and her husband Ronald Gow lived nearby in Beaconsfield. They had moved there in her early days as a Denham film star and taken root. 'Mrs. Gow', as she always announced herself on the telephone, and Linda had become close, and of course I'd directed her in A MEASURE OF CRUELTY at Birmingham and also directed Ronald's play A BOSTON STORY. At this time Wendy was getting very typecast in suffering roles and I wanted to remind the world what a brilliant comedy actress she was.

She would be a north British spinster, an Oxford Don teaching for a semester at a large mid-western university. Was this before the Bradbury/Lodge transatlantic campus novels? 1969. I think so. And she would tangle with a couple of her students, one of each sex, during a long night in a beach-house by the Great Lake. I'd be able to get in plenty of comment on the U.S./British cousinship. There would be fantasy sequences and the piece - because I intended it as a bravura part for Wendy - was called UNACCOMPANIED CELLO. Why couldn't I stop playing clever with titles? Wouldn't ONE WILD NIGHT IN THE LIFE OF A SPINSTER have served me better?

I started soon after we got back to England (at a time, quite the professional writer now, when I was still confidently expecting KNIGHT to be baptised in Birmingham) finishing it on Christmas Day in time for us to whizz over to Wainhill for family Christmas lunch.

The first act had just rattled along but I must confess to having had some unaccustomed trouble with the rest, which was perhaps an omen.

My Mr. Sharkey was keen on the piece though and Wendy was game (though Ronald was critical, which was another omen. He'd admired KNIGHT but withheld his approval from this one beyond the first act.) The first bite for a prior-to-London try-out came from Tony Church, then running the Northcott Theatre, Exeter. They had just successfully transferred ABELARD AND HELOISE to the West End with Diana Rigg. (Though he was leary of the title: 'UNACCOMPANIED CELLO - I have tried the title out on everybody here and nobody likes it. Can we have some alternatives? I'm stuck!')

One of the many things that drew me to Mr. and Mrs. Gow was that for decades they had holidayed in Sidmouth and knew it nearly as well as I did. On one of their little breaks Wendy popped in to Exeter to give the Northcott the once over. I'm sorry to say she took against it. It is, of course, a thrust stage without the old-fashioned trappings of a curtain. 'Oh, no, dearest,' said Wendy, 'I couldn't possibly have all those people sitting in my lap.' She wanted a more conventional house. James went on putting the play about and eventually it landed on the desk of the legendary 'Binkie' Beaumont of H.M. Tennent.

It's hard to convey the force this man was in the post-war London Theatre. Everything of any class that went on was presented by H.M.T. Gielgud, Olivier, Richardson, Vivien Leigh, Edith Evans, Scofield: all the new plays of Rattigan, Fry, Anouilh: all the starry classic revivals: all the major U.S. imports: all the productions of Peter Brook... 'Binkie' was a one-man National Theatre. If you weren't 'in' with Tennents you could kiss any interesting London career goodbye.

He had a rather camp voice but was otherwise totally unflamboyant and anonymous and ran his empire from an office at the top of the Globe Theatre in Shaftesbury Avenue which was eccentrically reached by a claustrophobic one-person lift from the foyer.

I had twice had a brief working relationship with him. He it was who had initially introduced me to Wendy and to the play A MEASURE OF CRUELTY. (I had been vetted by the Gows over dinner at Brown's Hotel.) When he saw it at Birmingham he decided against a transfer. I can't remember if he gave me any reason. But then you don't ask for reasons of the oracle. And he had a share in the management of Evan Hunter's THE EASTER MAN when it landed up at his Globe Theatre. He was reputed to be able to transform a production with a few devastatingly chosen words at the dress rehearsal. I can't remember, alas, what he said on that occasion. Perhaps he thought it was past cure.

However...

Globe Theatre. 17th June, 1970

Dear John Harrison,

It was with great pleasure that I read 'Unaccompanied Cello', sent to me by James Sharkey. I had a long talk with him on the telephone about the play, but I particularly wanted you to know of the enthusiasm I had for the creation of your characters.

My frank opinion is that you had set yourself a very difficult task. The first half of the play I thought was really gripping and full of exciting ideas, with a great gift of amusing dialogue, but it seemed the moment the girl appears we get into a difficult area and I think the brilliance of the first part of the play is not sustained. I enormously enjoyed the character creation of the English teacher, but somehow I felt that the play centred as it is around the women and the boy needs a little more to sustain it as a full evening's play.

I don't know what plans you may have, but it does seem to me that the play has so many qualities perhaps one could arrange, if the idea appeals to you, for a production with Wendy Hiller playing 'Violet' at say the Theatre Royal, Windsor.

However, the main point of my letter is to convey my enthusiasm and admiration and if you think anything of my suggestion, do let us be in touch.

Kind regards,

Yours sincerely,

Binkie
(Hugh Beamont)

Hurrah, hurrah, and general amazement. We were off again.

The first night at Windsor had all the feel of an outsize hit. The audience had laughed and applauded. I remember appealing rather desperately to Mr. Sharkey after several glasses of champagne at the party, 'Please, Jim, can I now be a success?' Oh, a long way from the hermit of Combe Raleigh!

But Binkie was still worried about the way the play developed, moving from a totally naturalistic first act to the fantasy areas of the second half. He thought I should re-write the second half.

'How?' I begged to know.

'Oh, that's your job, dear boy,' the great man said sweetly.

His idea was that I had three weeks in which to get it right if the play was to have a future. But I couldn't see for looking. I was too close to the thing. Richard Digby-Day, the director, didn't share the view that changes were necessary. I had nobody else to guide me. Richard and I tinkered. Every time I saw the play the audience seemed to be having such a whale of a time that it was hard to see what more I could do. Binkie came again in the last week and was closeted with Wendy and Ronald in her dressing-room for a long time.

Globe Theatre. 5th November, 1970.

Dear John,

I went last Wednesday night to Windsor to see the rearranged second act of the play.

I am afraid I must be quite honest with you and say that in spite of tightening done by you and Digby-Day, the second act is still not strong enough. I am only hopeful that seeing the play performed before an audience may stimulate you to come up with an entirely new second act...

...I still feel there is something in this property which could be very valuable and more than worth another attempt to re-write act II...

...I hope you can come up with either a brilliant rewrite or a new play for Wendy.

Kind regards,

Yours,

Binkie

But nobody would tell me how.

As it was a try-out there had been no invitations to the London drama critics. Once again I had written a play, had it performed, and nobody knew.

Dear John Trewin, bless him, published it in PLAYS OF THE YEAR Vol. 40. This time my bed-fellows between the covers included William Douglas-Home and again David Storey, now with THE CONTRACTOR. Publication led at least to a successful production of CELLO in Sydney, Australia, which I never saw.

But it has to be said that my writing career was not exactly rocket-propelled. I was by now pretty disheartened.

Towards the end of 1971 'Dick' (N.V.) Linklater, Drama Director of the Arts Council, who had been a friend since Nottingham days, started talking to me about the new Playhouse in Leeds. It had been open two years and had just sacked its director. I really didn't want to know. I'd done my time in Nottingham and Birmingham and couldn't see myself coping with yet another board. But Dick wouldn't leave it alone. He kept dropping it in my ear. Every few weeks, 'They're still looking for somebody for Leeds.' And finally late on a Friday an urgent phone call: 'They're interviewing for the last time this Sunday.'

'But I haven't applied.'

'That doesn't matter. I can organise that.'

When I put the phone down I said to Linda, 'I think the Arts Council will write me off as past it if I don't at least go for an interview.'

The M1 seemed never ending. Linda did most of the driving. Could anywhere be as far north as this? We ran out of petrol just south of Leicester, fortunately within walking distance of Leicester Forest East.

Leeds on a Sunday in those days was not exactly throbbing. We munched our sandwiches on the steps outside the threateningly northern town hall. The interviews were being held in strict camera at the deserted University. The first person I saw when I walked into the room was Nancy Burman, placed there by the Arts Council to represent an independent view. We greeted like long lost brother and sister. The interview proceeded amicably. I can't remember what we talked about. They seemed a pleasant enough group of people, just five men representing the board, including the brilliant artist Lawrence Gowing whose agonising stutter was breath-taking in an interview situation. He wasn't at all embarrassed by it. You just had to wait. A young hopeful came out before me and another went in after me. 'It's all right,' I said to Linda when I rejoined her in the car, 'plenty of young people up for the job.' I was now 48. Over the hill, surely, for running a repertory theatre. We drove the long miles back. Scarcely had we switched on the lights in High Wycombe when the telephone rang. It was the Chairman Arthur Dower offering me the job. Hold on, hold on. I hadn't even seen the theatre!

Back we went a few days later and I met the committee again. They continued friendly. We were housed, dined and taken to the play. (It was a rather ragged new piece by Barry Collins called AND WAS JERUSALEM.)

The salary offered was a joke after what I'd been getting at Rediffusion. I said I would need them to double it. They doubled it.

'As your wife's an actress,' they asked, 'would you expect to cast her in the company?'

'Yes,' I said firmly, anticipating cries of Shame! If we were going to commit this madness we were going to commit it together.

'You've said you're a playwright. Would you programme your own plays?'

'Yes,' very firmly indeed. At the time I perhaps had no such intention but I was anxiously putting every obstacle between me and the job.

I really was desperate now because having seen the Playhouse I had fallen in love with it. Here, miraculously, was another of those places where you could 'do it'. I'd never directed on a thrust stage, which was another challenge. Above all Leeds was then committed to running a permanent ensemble in true repertoire (the same actors in a group of plays which alternate from day to day) which, for me, is a director's dream. There was the other challenge to vanity of taking on a foundering theatre after two years, just as at Nottingham, and seeing what I could make of it.

I made one last pitch for rescue.

'Can you assure me,' I asked, 'that the group I shall be working to is you, this committee which has been interviewing me, and not the full board?'

They thought long and hard about this one but finally Arthur Dower gave me the assurance. It later transpired that he'd had no right to do so. But for the moment I didn't know this. He'd said 'Yes.'

As we drove back down the Ml after about the third visit I said to Linda 'They've left me no reason to turn the job down. Are you game for us to do it together?'

Since FIDDLER Linda had kept moderately busy. There had been the tour of A DOLL'S HOUSE, a revival of Bridie's weird MEETING AT NIGHT starring Wilfrid Hyde-White at the Duke of York's, an unexpected drama season at Sadler's Wells in which she had played Annie in Arthur Miller's ALL MY SONS with Maxine Audley, directed by Caroline Smith who became a friend, and Julia in a production of THE RIVALS in which a then unknown David Jason played Bob Acres. There had been an episode of Z CARS and some radio plays. It was a sort of Career Interruptus because of her premature departure from FIDDLER: the natural flow had somehow been diverted.

It would make our lives go easier to work together as we had at Birmingham: to be jointly committed to a project.

There was one other source of approval to be sought. Stephen and William were now both boarders at the King's School, Canterbury. Down we went, took them out to a Chinese meal and laid the situation before them. We would be less available in Leeds than in High Wycombe. Stephen was immediately enthusiastic. He was a great railway enthusiast and foresaw lengthy trips over new track. William thoughtfully gave the venture his fourteen-year-old blessing.

So I said Yes and engaged Linda Gardner as the first member of the new ensemble. And I might as well get it out of the way now and say that any success I subsequently had was 50% hers.

I set about persuading others I had worked with and who by now had a bit of a name, to join me. Derek Godfrey for one. I offered him Azdak in THE CAUCASIAN CHALK CIRCLE and Macbeth. It was a struggle. In Telly you can get whoever you like but the work is hardly worth doing. In rep the work is wonderful but the casting is hell. Long lunch followed long lunch as I tried to overcome their natural reluctance to leave London and commit for a year to Leeds. In the end I decided, dammit, I'm no longer going on my knees to anybody. I won't take a single actor who isn't clamouring to get in. That was the spirit we would need to deal with the crisis of confidence in Leeds. I put an ad in The Stage and was naturally inundated. But intensive auditioning rewarded me with a band of sixteen committed young people who included Hugh Ross, Joanna Van Gyseghem, Ian Barritt and Peter Bourke.

Ms. Gardner, at 32, was the senior member!

Drowning My Book in Leeds

*'It was a delight to enter a world created with such whole-
hearted pleasure by the company; and Hugh Ross's "Goodnight"
after the epilogue marked the end of a rich personal encounter of
author, actor and audience.'*

CHARLES LEWSEN. The Times. 27th November 1972

We opened with Brecht's CAUCASIAN CHALK CIRCLE in a
production which embraced the audience from the moment they came
in. The actors lounged on the auditorium steps chatting up the
customers. (All this was new then.) On a chord of music from Terence
Hillyer's guitar in the centre of the platform they rose as one from all
over the house and joined him on stage in Diccon Shaw's mesmerising
new music for 'Once upon a time...'

I'd dispensed with the prologue about collective farming. The play
can do without it. The moral is plain. And Brecht, if he's allowed to be,
is the most magical story-teller since Shakespeare. 'Mr. Harrison's
sense of narrative,' wrote Lewsen in The Times, 'is given impetus by a
company who commit themselves to the process of presenting the play
in more ways than adopting character or caricature. Four of them back
the action with guitar, flute and mouth organ accompaniment which is
considerably more than competent; and - cooing like pigeons or
clicking their tongues to evoke the melting of snow in spring - with
their own physical persons, the cast create a strong aural environment
for the action.'

The audience responded and took us by the hand. We were home
and dry.

Afterwards in the bar the great Alfred Bradley, doyen of northern
radio producers and midwife to so many successful dramatists, said
'How did you dare to cast your wife in such a make-or-break role as
Grusha?' I could tell him frankly. Because I knew her performance
would guarantee the success of the production. Alfred remained a

staunch fan of Linda's and cast her many times on radio.

A detailed history of the Leeds Playhouse is a different book, and preferably not written by me. I signed for one year and stayed for nearly twenty, standing by at last like a proud parent as it moved into its new multi-million pound home, the West Yorkshire Playhouse.

There came a point, about half way through my tenure, when Mr. Sharkey said you must either get out now or never. He'd advised me initially not to bother too much about Leeds. Just do productions that drew attention to themselves. But once I start paying council tax and travelling on the buses I can't think like that. I become devoted to making a go of it for whatever city I'm in. So I was a dead loss to James who wrote me off, in the friendliest way, from that moment. When, years later, I turned to him to arrange a contract for an independent production he said, 'My God! It'll be like opening Tutankhamen's tomb!'

I well knew by now I was out of place on the commercial scene, ill-at-ease in television and unlikely to break, at this late stage, into the National or the R.S.C. I had gone up the wrong ladders. (Or fallen down too many snakes?) But of the rest of the country I realised there was nowhere I would rather be than where I was. The audience was more open to adventure than at either Nottingham or Birmingham. Magnificent countryside on the doorstep. And (Déjà Vu?) a new theatre in the offing.

This was because the original Playhouse was a temporary building, housed in the shell of what was supposed to be a university sports hall. The agreement was to return the shell after ten years, in 1980. So it was always a theatre under sentence and many and varied were the proposed stays of execution before the final master-plan came to fruition and our new theatre opened its doors in 1990.

A re-building inside the disused Gaumont cinema in Cookridge Street, originally built as an Edwardian Circus, which we still used as our carpenters' workshop, was keenly supported by two active board members, Alec Baron and the architect of the existing Playhouse, Bill Houghton-Evans. I always felt this would be limiting. Unlike the original Nottingham Playhouse, it felt like a cinema.

A more imaginative scheme was dreamed up by Ian Mackintosh, 'Courtyard Theatre' freak and designer of the National's Cottesloe, to house us within the Leeds Grand Theatre complex, a corner of which when I first came to Leeds was still a Blue Movie House. Ian's idea was to put us in a small auditorium somewhere in the roof with the option of doing 'Big' productions on the main stage when the Matcham-designed Grand would otherwise have been dark. 'Don't you just long to do productions on that stage?' he asked, bright eyes gleaming enthusiastically behind his heavy specs. Well, no. Not really. But, in the days before Opera North was proposed as a solution to the Grand's problems, it was a bold and civically-minded scheme. It fell down ostensibly on grounds of cost but more immediately because neither administrator really favoured it. It would clearly leave one job where two previously existed.

Another Baron/Houghton-Evans scheme, with University approval, was to extend the original building into the car park. This appealed to Chairman Arthur Dower's cautious sense of Yorkshire housekeeping. The large sums of public money rolling into millions that the other plans envisaged brought deep guilt to his Quaker soul.

But it was the dedicated backstairs work of his successor, the long-serving Bernard Atha, City Councillor and Chairman of Leisure Services, that finally opened up the present site at Quarry Hill.

Bernard is something of a chameleon. Fly politician alternately reviled and respected on all sides but also a member of the actors' union Equity who had appeared in the film KES. Jokey public speaker with a good line in cheeky patter (He used to hint to Linda of a distant past as a hoofer on the Halls) he was on the face of it, before retirement, a lecturer in Law at Huddersfield Technical College. As a chairman he was a fixer and a reluctant democrat, cajoling and navigating his motley crew into ever more dangerous waters and yet finally bringing us through the rocks and on to dry ground at Quarry Hill. A theatre whose first sod was turned by Donald Sinden, which was 'topped out' by Albert Finney, and whose foundation stone was laid by Dame Judi Dench, should certainly bear Bernard's name somewhere. Many astounded councillors must still regard it bleakly as Atha's Conjuring Trick.

For once the design brief was originated and seen through to completion by the people who were working in the place, led by William Weston, a congenial administrator.

The Arts Council primed the pump with the final scrapings of its Housing the Arts Fund, £750,000, on condition that the design was put out to architectural competition; and with its dying gasp the deposed West Yorkshire Council (Government shake-up of councils 1986) willed us £4,000,000 on condition that we changed the name to the West Yorkshire Playhouse. This put us firmly on the road. William and I masterminded the most exhaustive brief in the history of theatre. Everybody who worked in the place had a say in it. The audience had already, over the years, declared in favour of retaining a thrust stage for our main auditorium. We needed to embellish it with full-height flying, an understage with traps and lifts, none of which existed in the old building. When we did Michael Frayn's re-written quirky farce BALMORAL poor Peter Laird (in a double role) spent much of the evening tunnelling beneath the floorboards like a pit-boy of the 1800s.

For our second auditorium I was determined to carry the day against certain backwoodsmen on the board and have a flexible space capable of seating over 300 people. I didn't want it ghetto-ised into a Studio for an inward-looking minority. Proper playwrights can only emerge if they have the chance of addressing a sizeable section of the community rather than a coterie of the chosen.

We also knew we wanted to preserve the friendly informality of the old Playhouse's minuscule public areas in our new larger domain. For example we had never had a stage door. I used to say to the actors they must come in the same door as the grown-ups. This created a casual and user-friendly atmosphere unique in a large theatre. When some superior people criticised the completed new building for reminding them of a supermarket I knew we had achieved our objective. One of the single greatest problems in increasing theatre audiences over my lifetime has been how to give people the temerity to cross the, to most of them, unfamiliar threshold.

As we judged the final top dozen, by now anonymous, competition entries over a weekend in Leeds Town Hall one design above all others was returned to again and again as fulfilling the terms of our brief in remarkable detail. When we opened the sealed envelopes Ian and Marjorie Appleton from Edinburgh, a husband and wife team and rank outsiders, had stolen a march on as distinguished a list of theatre architects and consultants as could have been assembled anywhere in

Britain. The result is the one triumphant new theatre building in Britain in my lifetime and it was a joy for me (if a bit of a marathon) to have lasted to the opening and done a production in each of the two auditoria before being translated to Artistic Director Emeritus and settling gracefully for quieter pastures, knowing I left things in Jude Kelly's brave command. We had worked sensibly together for two years and she had won my loving admiration.

It wasn't all plain sailing. The usual plots and villains put in their inevitable appearance. But I'm content to bury all that and just delight in what was achieved.

Much of my satisfaction over those years came from being able to give a bunk up to younger directors: Michael Attenborough, whose career has since climbed through the RSC to (currently) the Almeida, a dedicated 'actors' director', solidly in the service of the text; Stephen Pimlott and Nicholas Hytner, the lads from the opera, both of whom had been in the G & S Society at Cambridge with my son Stephen. There was a memorable YEOMAN OF THE GUARD there with Pimlott in the orchestra, Hytner on stage, and Stephen conducting. When Pimlott and Nick turned up in Leeds to produce for Opera North they welcomed the opportunity for crossover to the drama.

Nick's is a mint talent which I unhesitatingly backed as I did Peter Brook's. Fascinating to have crossed paths with one at both ends of my working life. Some ten years ago, in early jottings for this book, I wrote "He will have a 'commercial phase', as Peter did in the 40's and 50's. Prophecy is always risky but I believe that in the end his natural honesty and inquisitiveness will bless the theatre, as Peter's has."

Without claiming to be Nostradamus, his current re-invigoration of the National Theatre gives me the happy opportunity of telling myself "I told you so."

I have only once chosen a director from actually seeing his work. That was Ronald Eyre, when I was just about to run Birmingham. It was a production of JULIUS CAESAR for schools television and I only saw it because I was at home with flu. It was so much better than most of what was happening in adult drama that I sought him out in the mazes of Shepherd's Bush and rewarded him with his first stage production.

But you have to be careful. Seeing isn't always believing. We can all do the odd bum production and any of us is guilty of successes that owe little to our contribution. I prefer to decide during a chat over lunch. I think I know what I'm listening for.

I'd more or less given up reading reviews by this time in my career. 'Just let me know if they're good or bad,' I would ask the publicity department. But for the TWELFTH NIGHT with which we closed the old Playhouse Michael Schmidt, who was completely unknown to me except as a publisher of poetry - wrote in the Daily Telegraph (28/12/89) something I would be proud to have on the tombstone of my directing career.

"There is actors' theatre and directors' theatre; but there is also playwrights' theatre. It seems to me that Harrison has endeavoured, with considerable success, to release not his but Shakespeare's 'Twelfth Night'."

For a man who really only went into the theatre by default and because of Shakespeare I've directed an awful lot of plays. From GUYS AND DOLLS to STATEMENTS AFTER AN ARREST UNDER THE IMMORALITY ACT. From Strindberg to Stoppard: Travers to Ayckbourn: Ibsen to CHARLEY'S AUNT. Fortunately I never kept a tally. But the highlight of my year (if I hadn't written something myself) was always the Shakespeare. Arrogant as it sounds, if I really want to see a Shakespeare play, I have to direct it myself.

I knocked off MEASURE FOR MEASURE and ALL'S WELL THAT ENDS WELL, two of my closet favourites, in the Leeds years, as well as my second DREAM, TWELFTH NIGHT and JULIUS CAESAR (Togas this time just to see if it really did look, in Granville-Barker's immortal phrase, 'like a conference of headmasters'. Not really. More like animated Alma-Tadema.); my third MACBETH (with a provocatively chosen cast of 13) and third TEMPEST, now with the Amazing Grace of Paul Scofield's Prospero.

I'm not going to indulge in a nostalgic review of all those Leeds productions. But THE TEMPEST will draw several strands of my life together very nicely, as well as being neatly valedictory.

It was 1974 and Paul was doing it on the radio. I said, only slightly jokingly, why not come to Leeds and do it for real? One of the biggest names in British theatre, why should he bother to come to Leeds? But one of the wondrous things about him is that he always does what tickles his fancy rather than makes the obvious career move: like turning down the Hollywood contract in 1947 and remaining at Stratford. I truly believe he has kept faith with that one ambition, confided so many years ago in Birmingham: 'To be a good actor.' I once asked him what he looked for in a new play. 'Something that I'd like to say that the writer says better.' So if he likes a script he will do it, even if it's only ever going to be an art movie after midnight on BBC4.

In 1974 he decided he would like to do Prospero in Leeds with me.

I started to organise at the double to schedule the production for the spring before anything more tempting came along.

'Wouldn't the autumn be better programming for you?' he asked.

'Yes,' I said, 'but what will you do till then?'

'Oh, I'll do a bit of radio.'

He was going to keep himself available for six months for a fifty pound a week job in Leeds. And with no thought at all of transferring the production to London. When the managements began to badger us he said we'd wait and see. He was doing it for Leeds.

I began to send him notes of my ideas. The starting point was to be the drawings of William Blake. Blake's Job. 'When the morning stars sang together' seemed to me to catch the mood. And the drawing in the Tate - 'The portrait of a man who instructed Mr. Blake in painting and co. in his dreams.' Was this perhaps Ariel? A life in which magic is possible, acceptable, seemed to need the nutty intensity of Blake.

In the event Paul became the visual embodiment of Blake's Job.

'We are such stuff as dreams are made on...'

Even though the line has become an oft-misquoted cliché the whole play is still a kind of dream of revenge and forgiveness... as well of course as an allegory of the artist's resignation of his art. Let the scholars argue over whether that resignation is Shakespeare's or not. It's certainly Prospero's.

Under what kind of compulsion does a man give up his art? Break his staff? When he's fulfilled, naturally, and 'every third thought must be (his) grave.' That includes a comfortable acceptance of mortality. To have held the possibility of revenge in the palm of his hand - looked at it - rejected it - brings a peace in which life holds him very gently. A spectator almost. Leaving the daily task to the younger generation. Not as a cop-out but as one who has looked power in the face and found it tasteless.

Prospero's anger is in direct proportion to his innocence. A man who harmed no one - except perhaps through neglect? 'being transported and rapt in secret studies'. What a shock it must have been when they rudely broke into those studies and hustled him into a boat with his little daughter - 'me and thy crying self'. Like a rending of the temple of his existence. And soon on the island he finds himself again wrestling with the problem of evil face to face in Caliban; and again he behaves like the detached liberal he is until he finds he is up against one 'on whose nature- Nurture can never stick: on whom my pains/ Humanely taken, all, all lost, quite lost.' The admission is painful, particularly as Caliban is only twelve when he arrives and obviously teachable ('You taught me language'). Prospero the colonist put a lot of work into Caliban: a being close to the truth of nature, growing with all the rudimentary surprise of a potato among the choice berries of the isle. Much talk, in 1610, about the divine, primitive savage from writers like Montaigne (whose work the old courtier Gonzalo can quote from). To endow this primitive with language! What a triumph! But Shakespeare is more of a realist than Montaigne. Alas you cannot imprint a morality in a beast, an animal, only train it with whip and spur. And so another golden dream of the Renaissance dies in ashes. But we mustn't cry. At the end: 'This thing of darkness I acknowledge mine.' As before in Milan Prospero has reckoned without the loiny thrusty side of human nature. He doesn't understand it. 'You, my brother...' How do they do these things? And in a sense perhaps the grand revenge is an attempt to find out. He whips himself up into a high old rage, goading on the terrible dogs. 'There, Mountain, Fury...!' He allows himself to experience for a brief while what it's like and yet ...and then... 'They being penitent- The sole drift of my purpose doth extend/ Not a frown further...' The rage burns out like something simulated - like something one almost had to get drunk for - and extends not a frown further. Even to one whom 'to call brother would almost infect my mouth'. Is he almost surprised to find himself forgiving them? Surprised to find so little rancour in his heart?

And how much-of a Puritan is he? It was Caliban's attempt to violate

Miranda that put him in the dog-house. 'Till thou didst seek to violate/The honour of my child.' Nothing else material is ever brought up against him. And look at all those warnings to Ferdinand: 'Look thou be true ...the strongest oaths are straws to the fire in the blood...' What does Prospero know (In his secret heart? In the Past?) about the fire in the blood? I think he's quite serious about this. Some Prosperos play it jokey, teasing the young couple. Make it almost cosy. But it would even be quite natural if there were an element of jealousy. After all he's been Miranda's entire male society for twelve years. On the other hand 'it all goes on as (his) soul prompts it'. I find the whole push-me pull-you of his relationship with Ferdinand fascinating. And very human.

The static nature of the play, and its lack of two-dimensional conflicts, makes it imperative that Prospero ground everything in his relationship to Miranda.

'A thrid of mine own life - or that for which I live.'

'...nothing but in care of thee, of thee my dear one, thee my daughter...

'Smile not that I boast her off...'

'The like loss, as great to me as late, for I have lost my daughter.'

The isolation of their life has formed a closer bond than even the natural father-daughter one. How right Shakespeare's choice of sex is! It could so easily have been a son. To remove from Prospero all human society save one. That one a young female. A daughter. And rescue now must mean almost certain loss. He even courts this loss. 'It works...' 'So glad of this as they I cannot be, / Who are surprised withal, but my rejoicing/ At nothing can be more.'

How wry. How painfully tender. And now 'every third thought shall be (his) grave'. But not in any lugubrious sense. As a true philosopher who has been forced for twelve years to lead an unexpectedly active existence. As the man who has looked into the dark possibilities of revenge in his own heart and rejected them. Those 'third thoughts', hopefully, will go on for years yet. He's not one *foot* in the grave, just every third *thought* and he's going to get immense pleasure from thinking them. How Shakespeare himself must have looked forward to that well-earned retirement to New Place. And retiring, he would think, young enough to enjoy it. Prospero is physically fit and by the end of the play emotionally detached: an excellent state of mind and body in which to retire. And it's only every *third* thought that's going to be his grave!

It is terribly important, if the play isn't to die on its feet, to imbue Prospero with immense physical energy. He must begin the play in a high old excitement. He has a long tale to tell which he must have planned to tell her so many times and yet, but for the 'accident most strange' that brings his enemies to this shore, perhaps he might never have done so. But today's the day. No escaping it now. 'The very moment bids thee ope thine ear.../...my zenith doth depend upon/ A most auspicious star, whose influence/ If now I court not, but omit, my fortunes/ Will ever after droop...' Yes, 'There is a tide in the affairs of men...' An old Bardic belief. What urgency, what excitement there must be for him, as well as for her, in the telling. Excitement we shall get from her eyes and bearing as much as his.

Another source of overt drama is the sheer difficulty for Prospero of controlling - white wizard-wise - the magic forces he unleashes: the constant tussle for supremacy over Ariel: each time he goes into those duologues like a Wimbledon finalist.

Who or what is Ariel to him? is a question that has to be asked. 'I shall miss thee' is one of those supreme Bardic throwaways like 'I was ador'd once too.' Best, I think, to take him quite literally as a spirit found 'confined to a cloven pine'. Who would have thought, as Gonzalo says, there were 'such men/ Whose heads stood in their breasts?' Who would have thought there were..? Amerindians? Pygmies? Travellers' Tales were coming back to the port of London daily. Aboriginals living in a stone age? Incas sacrificing daily to the sun? Eventually Kangaroos? Just as likely to be an airy spirit confined in a cloven pine. That's what he found. And by his art he set it free. (White Man's Magic). Better far to take all this literally and let the audience soak up the symbolism. You can't act symbols.

'Ye elves of hills...', the speech in which he renounces his art, is of course the heart of the play. Everything else is framework for this. This is what Shakespeare burned to say. This is the poem he might have written in his Stratford garden and then decided to build a play round. Was there ever such word music as this? 'Maestoso'. (Only Caliban, in the play, is allowed to equal it with his 'Be not afear'd. The isle is full of noises...' Does he here speak with his master's voice? 'You taught me language...')

I wondered if, but for Miranda, Prospero might have been content to live out his life on the island? 'I have done nothing but in care of thee' right at the start supposes that his care for her future, her 'brave new world', has at least equal weight with his revenge fantasies.

I wondered too why Prospero has to ask Ariel to 'Make thyself like a nymph of the sea' (as if this disguise were essential to the plot) when nobody but he is going to see him. Self-indulgence? A sense of fitness? A delight in his art? I decided this had to be the answer for all the elaborations - the Harpy and so on ('Of my instruction hast thou nothing bated') - he is glorying in the final exercise of his art - one last great magical splurge, like THE TEMPEST itself, before drowning his book, and silence - 'retirement to my Milan'. He's on a last great bender exulting in every trick before the (all the more telling) renunciation.

In all Elizabethan plays I think one must (you'll know by now), to preserve their vital continuity, declare one's architectural structure from the beginning. Sean Cavanagh designed me a two-tier set. The upper rainbow level was Ariel's habitat where Prospero joined him when the afflatus was on him. Nobody else went up there except the lovers and then only for the masque, when they were mesmerised to this imaginative plane by Prospero and there saw wonders which we, the audience, could not. I still carried the dread memory of galumphing nymphs and reapers from Stratford long ago.

'The isle' Caliban tells us 'is full of noises...'

I decided to fill it with vocal sounds. Paul Todd wrote some 'Marvellous sweet music'. I always prefer to keep the performance as much as possible in the hands of the living actors and away from the dead bleep of technology. 'Painting and Carpentry are the Soule of Masque.' (As Ben Jonson somewhat surprisingly said.) Our vocalising spirits hung about the scaffolding that supported the upper level in positions that, as one critic put it, 'must be as uncomfortable for them as it is jolly for us.'

As the managements came a-begging director and leading player took a walk in the life-affirming Yorkshire countryside to decide the production's future. Striding along with his Prospero's staff, which he had typically chosen for himself in a wood near his digs in Farnley,

Paul said thoughtfully 'I think we've still got somewhere to go with it.'

So that was that. We transferred to Wyndham's under the joint management of H.M. Tennent (long post-Binkie and but a shadow of its former glory) and film director Michael Winner who put up most of the money because he was wanting Paul to make a film. We ran for almost six months, from February to the summer of 1975. The longest recorded continuous commercial run for a Shakespeare play on the West End stage. And it was still playing to packed houses when it had to make way for the prior booking of Pinter's NO MAN'S LAND.

The most perceptive review was that of the playwright Frank Marcus (THE KILLING OF SISTER GEORGE) who was doing a stint on the Sunday Telegraph. So often a practitioner can beat the critics at their own game.

'It is an astonishing fact that each generation seems to choose one particular Shakespeare play and bestow on it a special kind of representative status...

Now it appears to be the turn of THE TEMPEST (Wyndham's): its very ambiguities, the multiplicity of interpretations which it can accommodate, give it a nagging relevance. Last year John Gielgud, directed by Peter Hall, showed us the resigned artist, wrenching himself painfully from his imagination (Ariel): an imagination illustrated spectacularly in theatrical terms by means of transformations, resplendent goddesses, and the whole Jacobean bag of tricks. Gielgud's austerity was slightly at odds with all this ostentation.

The Leeds Playhouse production, now happily made available to London audiences for a limited season, goes to the opposite extreme...

Paul Scofield's Prospero anchors his love and concern in his flesh-and-blood daughter, Miranda (Nicky Guadagni), to the virtual exclusion of all others. He is most moving and conjures up moments of incomparable beauty. There may be strange sounds in the air, but they are nothing when matched against the voice of this Prospero. Miranda's joyful exclamation at the sight of so many other humans ("O brave new world, that hath such people in't!") is answered by Prospero's "'Tis new to thee." Mr. Scofield invests these four words with a smiling, benign tenderness that warms (and breaks) the heart.

This Prospero is no enslaver. Tall, bearded, and silvermaned, he bestrides the stage with the spiritual authority of John the Baptist. There is much evidence of close rapport between the actor and his director, John Harrison. As an impressionable teenager, I recall seeing them in their early days, often working under the prodigious Peter Brook.

Mr. Harrison rightly puts his trust in Mr. Scofield's imaginative powers. He has avoided distraction. The stage is two-tiered and uncluttered. A highly competent company - among whom Paul Brooke and Ronnie Stevens's Laurel and Hardy double-act and Tony Steedman's fraught Alonso demand special mention - provide a firm setting for the central gem.

Scofield leaves the clue to his interpretation to the very end. A light shines from his eyes as he utters in a rapt whisper the final words "set me free." Here is a man who, like his author, has decided that life must take precedence over art. He does so not with self-pity, but with excited hope.'

Much of the later part of my time in Leeds was overcast by Linda's brave and brilliant fourteen-year struggle against cancer. That, too, is another book. All I want to put on record here is that her last seven very active and enriching years were won against all the medical prognostications by her adoption of the philosophy of the Bristol Cancer Help Centre. By diet, by meditation, by creative visualisation, she brought us both to a realisation that we are more in control of what happens to our bodies than the medical profession, in its despair, can often dare to admit.

The upside of the experience, and there was much that was uplifting about it, was that it introduced us to a number of people in the world of alternative healing, many of whom, like the White Queen, could believe as many as six impossible things before breakfast. Without them our lives would have been much less enriched. I cannot always share their beliefs but I accept their integrity and bask in the embracing warmth of their humanity. For them Wordworth's Ode is no dog-eared anthology piece. 'A sense of something far more deeply interfused' indeed. I walk among them still, a foreigner but never an out-cast.

Raking through Linda's jumbled collection of cuttings, never pasted into an ego-tripping volume, I came across this from The Times which gave me a sudden bright vision of her. The play was ALL MY SONS at Sadlers Wells.

'...Linda Gardner with her ruffled brow, an intense forward inclination of the body, and hands that open with simple candour ...makes her changing relation to all these people utterly present and dramatic.'

And a last word on her from Michael Attenborough, who had been my trusty Associate Director from 1974 to 1978. This is from his beautiful obituary notice in The Independent (11/6/91):

'...For me as a director she possessed that precious quality of being prepared to risk anything. Her performances were both specific and startling. She would unearth what was extraordinary about her characters, while also unfailingly touching us by finding that with which we could not but identify.

She unhesitatingly gave, both to her fellow actors and to her audience, and that same generosity of spirit marked her out as a person and as a friend. She had time for everyone, and in the close-knit community of a theatre it cannot have been easy being the artistic director's wife, but she carried it off with dignity, humility and tact.

Linda Gardner had a ferocious commitment to life. It was tangible both on and off the stage. It clearly fuelled her extraordinary fourteen year battle with cancer, having been given only three months to live. Indeed, when I last saw her she looked younger and more beautiful than she had in 1974.'

Not so much a Chapter... more of a Postscript

"Go out and bring something in. Preferably your resignation."
GROUCHO MARX in A day at the Races

I had thought I might pontificate on the arts of acting and directing, the state of the theatre and so on. But it seems to me it would be a very dull reader who hadn't picked up most of what I think about this from the story so far. And a very bored reader who would be forced to sit through it all again.

I've never much fancied myself as a teacher of drama. I quite enjoy being an Elder and handing down the Tablets, but the role of confident Domini doesn't sit so happily. You can't teach chimpanzees to sing. The best you can hope to do is recognise the real thing in time and nurture it.

Back in the '60s when I was living at High Wycombe and trying to make a go of it as a writer I thought I might usefully put in a couple of days a week at the Royal Academy of Dramatic Art. Get me out of the house. Keep me in touch with the young. So I offered my services. Not for anything high profile like an end-of-term production but just to do some work with beginners. My first downy chicks, in excerpts from Ann Jellicoe's THE KNACK, included an actor I knew at once was going to make it. 'You'll be all right, John,' I said. Then I went back a year later to work with the next intake and saw him performing some Chekhov in his second year. I couldn't believe what had happened to him. Where was all that marvellous promise? I sat him down in the canteen with a cup of coffee and asked what was going wrong. He pulled a long miserable face.

'Well...' At length, in the tones of one who has been told he should ring a bell at his approach, 'They say I've got Audience Contact.' Audience Contact! And I suppose they were trying to cure him. This is a system, it seems, beloved of drama teachers. If they see confidence and talent, rip it all away. Create a gibbering wreck. So that they can spend the remainder of the overlong course trying to build it up again.

I comforted him, told him he should be so lucky, bought him another coffee and, eventually, got him taken on by my Mr. Sharkey, who knew a good thing when it was pointed out to him. His name is Jonathan Pryce.

I am very suspicious of teachers of acting.

So no pontificating.

I've just read through the whole book to this point and found one loose end. I promise in Chapter Nine to return to the architecture of the Nottingham Playhouse. Might as well get that off my chest.

Hugh Willatt first sketched it out for me. 'Peter Moro's idea is that it's a drum, you see' (Peter Moro was the architect. He seemed quite a catch. He'd had a hand in the Festival Hall).

Hugh drew a plan of this drum. A circle. And then he sliced off about a sixth of it. That's the stage. The rest is the auditorium.'

I stared at the paper.

But what on earth happens in those half-moons on either side?

'They'll be boxes' 'Boxes of what? 'The audience.'

They'll be the worst seats in the house.

And what happens to the acoustic as the sound funnels about in this enormous chimney? And the circle for some mad reason is so high as to be totally divorced from the rest of the audience. Like a tiara.

Once again a design was sacrificed to a 'concept'. How I loathe the very notion of a 'concept.' When Michael Attenborough was rather young and my associate in Leeds I decided it was his turn to do the Shakespeare. He looked at me in concern, 'How do you have a concept John?' You don't. You read the score. The text. Or examine the brief. And you react. With every professional skill you possess.

A theatre in particular has to be designed from the inside out. A drum indeed!

I experienced the building's lack of charm or any true sense of function when I had a play premiered there in 1983. A bit about that too, to show that my hat was still in the ring.

I had been reading with intense delight William Hickey's (the real one's) journals which covered voyages to India in the late eighteenth century. Most of our famous diarists are stay-at-home folk so it was quite unexpected to be transported so vividly to shipboard life. I thought at first I might write a play about him, but then I thought, no, that would be too inhibiting. I'll write about my own people and my own preoccupations and set it aboard an East Indiaman. Linda was disappointed. 'Why are you writing a costume piece?' she wanted to know. 'Why not something contemporary?' (She always thought UNACCOMPANIED CELLO was my best play.) I had no more convincing answer than that I was enjoying myself. And that there was a very good part for her.

Paul, who was working at the National Theatre, really liked this one and showed it to Michael Rudman there, who didn't. He also showed it to Lord Miles, who did. But unfortunately it was just too late in the day to get it mounted at his Mermaid Theatre which was in grave financial difficulties and about to close down. Richard Digby-Day, who had directed UNACCOMPANIED CELLO, was running the Nottingham Playhouse and wanted to stage it there so we went ahead with him. A bird in the hand, by this time in my writing career, was worth a whole aviary in the bush. Under-directed by Andrew McKinnon, polymath, man of sweet reason, and starring Kenneth Colley and Linda, SCENES FROM A VOYAGE TO THE INDIES was treated quite respectfully by the critics. John Barber in the Daily Telegraph even went so far as to think that 'in a less troubled theatre climate, this would be a certainty for the West End.' But the winds were not blowing southerly.

Paul played it on the radio, with Linda, in a skilful production by Kay Patrick in 1984 and I revived it myself at Leeds with Linda and Hugh Ross, finally proving satisfactorily to myself (if rather too late for comfort) that the author, if he knows anything about theatre, is the best man to direct his own plays. It's the next stage after completing the text, as Shakespeare and Alan Ayckbourn had nouse enough to know.

Once again I'd failed to make my fortune. Never mind. The hat was still in the ring in 1995. Still trying to come to terms with Linda's death, I wrote an even better part for her in a play called HOLIDAYS which I directed, with Jude Kelly, at the West Yorkshire Playhouse. The notices, apart from The Guardian and the Financial Times, were not particularly encouraging. Some of them seemed embarrassed at viewing what they took (due to the wrong kind of advance publicity) to be a slice of raw personal experience on stage. Hell, nobody held that against Ibsen or Strindberg!

I comforted myself with the knowledge that Nick Hytner read it and thought it 'a terrific piece' and Paul came up and approved. And Samuel French published it. For once a play of mine came into print without even posthumous aid from John Trewin.

I suppose for a time I hoped that, like the composer Janacek, I should fully unfold my creative talent in my eighth decade. After all if we only had the music he'd written before he met young Kamilla Stosslova when he was 68 he would have remained a very minor Bohemian. His late-flowering passion gave us the Sinfonietta, The Cunning Little Vixen, The 'Intimate Letters' quartet, the Glagolitic Mass...

Perhaps I should have been looking for my Kamilla?

Would Linda have minded?

I know she wouldn't.

But could I have made the effort?

I think probably not.

In the meantime adapting Melville's BILLY BUDD for Paul to do on Radio 3 and writing a play for him on Radio 4 (RE-DISCOVERING LEO with the clever Sammantha Bond) have kept the pen in the inkwell. Yes, I do still always begin in longhand. Though nowadays one has the bliss of being able to transfer to the infinitely correctable word-processor instead of banging out copy after copy on that museum-worthy typewriter Hugh Willatt presented me with on my last first night in Nottingham.

Otherwise I've turned back to poetry. Pace Rossini, my 'Sins of Old Age.' But there is no thought of publication.

Sometimes life goes in satisfying circles. A few years ago Paul Scofield and I were reminiscing about the dear old Birmingham Rep and I came out with my usual refrain, 'What a crying shame that it no longer functions as a professional theatre!' 'But it does,' he said. 'Don't you know about Neal Foster and his Birmingham Stage Company? I'm one of his patrons. Derek Jacobi's the other.' Apparently I'd completely missed the news that this Mr. Foster actor-managed a company in Station Street producing an annual Christmas show and one or two other productions a year - depending on finances, as he was completely unsubsidised. 'Joy and I saw an excellent production of 'Cat on a Hot Tin Roof.' Marvellous girl in it. Sandra Reinton.'

Soon after this I was in Stratford to see the newly knighted Jacobi in 'Macbeth' and have dinner with him afterwards in The Dirty Duck. When I reached his dressing room he said he'd made a mix-up, got himself double-booked, but he didn't think I'd mind. 'It's this chap Neal Foster who's trying to keep the old rep going.' Had I heard?

So I met Neal over dinner in The Duck, found him to be passionate about the lost legacy of Barry Jackson, and was sufficiently intrigued to take myself down to Birmingham to check out the standard in a production of 'The Glass Menagerie'. It was quite as Paul and Joy had led me to believe and a wondrous time-warp to be again in that magical building. Afterwards in the bar I said to Neal, 'I don't really feel the need to direct any more, but this is the one place that could draw me.'

Not long afterwards he invited me to do 'She Stoops to Conquer' - the choice for my previous return to the Rep in 1961 - with a clever cast including Stephen Mangan and Diana Coupland. And he's twice inveigled me since. And now I think, having come if not full circle, then at least in concentric circles, I really am ready to put up.

Summaries...conclusions... I resist them. I've always preferred beginnings to endings. The first paragraph of ANNA KARENINA. The overture to THE MARRIAGE OF FIGARO that makes you hug yourself in delighted anticipation. The opening scene between Chico and Harpo in a Marx Brothers movie when you know you've still got Groucho to come...

But I'd better run up half a flag.

In my unfinished Australian novel in 1949 I wrote, when the hero was down in the dumps and trying to cheer himself up:

'There were so many things to be thankful for: the experience of love, the plays of Shakespeare, Beethoven and sea bathing...'

And in an aborted play of 1957 I gave a character this to say:

'...if you were living in the declining Roman Empire that wouldn't excuse you from living a personal life. If you were living in the very last day of Pompeii it still mattered whether you loved or were loved, whether you believed in a God, whether you liked music...'

I stand by those.

Music continues to sustain me beyond all. I listen for at least an hour a day and mostly to chamber music. Because that's where I listen. In my chamber. I'm never quite at ease accommodating an entire symphony orchestra between the sofa and the bookshelves. But the string quartet is at home. From Haydn to Hindemith, Beethoven to Bartok, Tchaikovsky to Tippett. Even composers I don't generally enjoy I can appreciate at chamber scale (Debussy, Reger, Shostakovich). There are in fact only three composers in the history of music whose company I have to avoid. I will be bold and name them. Wagner, Richard Strauss and Mahler. Their music gives me actual physical distress. I can feel my blood pressure rising. A psychoanalyst could probably tell me what I'm refusing to admit here. Not just romanticism because in the right mood I can enjoy Berlioz and early Schönberg.

I love particularly Haydn, the Haydn of the quartets; Beethoven, the late quartets and the piano sonatas; the songs and song-cycles of Schubert and Schumann; the piano quartets and the quintets and sextets of Brahms. Ah. Hard-core German Classical you say. No. I love the Bohemians too, Dvorak and Smetana. Janacek and Martinu. Is a picture trying to emerge of a very private listener? That would be wrong. I worship the Mozart of the operas and more and more I relish Handel. I will admit that the whole Italian Grand Opera scene leaves me fairly cool. In opera I jump straight from the exhilaration of Beethoven's FIDELIO to Janacek, Martinu and Britten. I'm a great Martinu buff. Keen on all those concertante works. I like his theory of music as light. Have I not mentioned Bach? Yes: I frequently start the day with one of Bach's 48, as Stravinsky did. The difference being he could play it himself. Then there's Vivaldi, even Telemann. My God, I nearly forgot Rameau, a man who always makes me want to get up and dance. And late at night I'll go back to Palestrina, Hildegarde of Bingen and beyond.

Nothing more modern than Martinu and Britten? I can enjoy much of Ligeti, and some of his descendant minimalists like Arvo Part or Sculthorpe, but not for long. Similarly Jazz, When it starts up on the radio I think, oh yes, I like this. But within ten minutes irritation sets in. I enjoy piano jazz like Oscar Petersen's. And I still listen with nostalgic delight to that 1930's dance music with which I began.

I don't want you to think I'm a total recluse. I enjoy going to concerts and operas and putting all the sounds in perspective. But I rarely go to drama for pleasure. Too much of a busman's holiday. Though I do try to keep up with the work of my friends.

Another great enthusiasm of my life, up there with St. Cecilia and hinted at just a moment ago, has been the films of the Marx Brothers. There was a time when I would travel the country like Sir Percival after the Grail to pick up a rare showing of something obscure like ROOM SERVICE. TV retrospectives have given me the opportunity to collect them all on video now, from the rawly photographed stage-show of COCOANUTS (1929) to the pitiable shambles of LOVE HAPPY (1949). The sad thing is that I've watched them all so often I can't laugh any more. But I still get a warm glow inside. I am just so grateful that such clowns existed. On dark days at the BBC I only had to imagine them descending on Shepherd's Bush and troubles burst like bubbles. It's the great lost Marx Brothers movie: A DAY AT THE BBC.

Despite my London origins I have never become a natural townee, although the necessity of large urban conglomerations for the support of theatres has forced me to live in them. I survive on regular fixes of the countryside in all her moods and seasons - except those times when the sky is thick for days on end and I become like a fretful passenger in the underground stuck in a tunnel without explanation. I need to see something beyond a bank of low-hanging cumulus, to be able to peer out from our planet so that I can take this mystery tour on some kind of trust.

Wine I take seriously and I like the way that meals can shape a day, though I am not much more of a cook than when I was dishing Don up his fried spam and reconstituted potato. I'm wiser to a few health points now. When I started to live alone for the first time in forty-three years providing meals for myself seemed the thirteenth labour of Hercules. In my generation boys had not been expected to cook. A hand with the drying up on Sundays was the limit of our domestic obligation. And Linda, being of Bretonne descent, had been a daunting Chef. She even managed to make the Bristol Diet taste like haute cuisine. I've now got it down to a few simple dishes, a lot of steamed vegetables, and a really good wine to cover a multitude of omissions. We started to get into wine on French holidays and I like their no-fuss attitude to it. I have never, since my early and actorish Birmingham excesses, drunk to get drunk. I can get high enough on a poem or a phrase of music. The hangover is more pleasurable. But to take a glass of a long gone summer is a very special sort of communion.

In the first half of my life I preferred, in the main, the company of men to that of women. In the latter part it is the other way about. Perhaps that was what my wives had to teach me. I moved from a position of total male arrogance and ignorance (initially as a cover for my ghastly shyness) to one where the eternal feminine seems to offer so much more in the way of surprise. I suppose I've come to believe that the world, life, is based on a female principle. This is only going back to the pre-Christian beliefs in an earth goddess, a mother goddess - those extraordinarily provocative lumps of clay found in the Danube basin. In the natural world the male peacocks his way about in a strut of beauty: but the female reproduces, encloses.

This doesn't mean I have much relish for female politicians. Maggie Thatcher and Boudicca are not the first images to spring to mind when I breathe the word 'woman'. Politics doesn't seem to me to be their natural domain. It's a 'games' area, appealing to the left-dominated male brain. And neither, with rare eccentric exceptions (Sappho, Dame Ethel Smyth) have they contributed a lot to serious, as opposed to decorative, poetry and music. Yes, of course, a few lines of Emily

Brontë. The unfairly hidden talent of Fanny Mendelssohn. Certainly Emily Dickinson. Not to mention my dear friend Chrys Salt. And the burgeoning Caroline Bird (Jude Kelly's daughter), whose work I've been privileged to read since she was about eleven. History just hasn't been on their side, relegating them unfairly to the hearth. It's always dangerous - though oh so tempting - to generalize. And in fiction we see them reign equally with men. Austen with Trollope. George Eliot with Tolstoy. Woolf with Forster. Is it because they are creating habitable worlds rather than abstracts? Man creates art because he can't create men: woman is born with the art-work in her womb.

This is probably too contentious an area for the last page! And wasn't Barbara Hepworth a wondrous creator of abstracts?

I do thank my little sister for setting me off down the loving path all those years ago. And I must be grateful to Daphne for suffering the sixteen years of my extended adolescence and above all for our sons who are a great joy to me. Stephen, at this time of writing, is Artistic Administrator of the Düsseldorf Opera House and William, Head of Performing Arts at a Comprehensive in Henley-in-Arden. They both rally round in the hour of need. But more than that: they are favourite company. And now that, after a variety of false starts, they're finally married to the right women, Marta and Maggie are cherishable too. Meanwhile four grandchildren from their mistaken unions bud precociously.

I thank Linda for teaching me joy and sorrow. For leading me ultimately to an understanding of grief.

More and more it seems to me, as we hang precariously for our brief while between birth and death, that those of us still here are simply survivors.

Let me put a little favourite claret, ten years old and browning at the edges, into a large tulip-shaped glass and hang my nose over the edge...

The survivors! Especially the women...

To Chrys and Chris... to Michele and Jude and Jo... to Joyce and Mavis... to Sylvia and Karen... to Vanessa and Pat and Kellee and Kate...

INDEX